I0822066

WORTHY OF RECORD:

THE CIVIL WAR AND RECONSTRUCTION DIARIES OF COLUMBUS LAFAYETTE TURNER

WORTHY OF RECORD:

THE CIVIL WAR AND RECONSTRUCTION DIARIES OF COLUMBUS LAFAYETTE TURNER

Edited by
Kenrick N. Simpson

This first edition is limited to seven hundred and fifty copies,
of which this is number 483.

Office of Archives and History
North Carolina Department of Cultural Resources
Raleigh
2008

ISBN 978-0-86526-335-2

Printed by Edwards Brothers Inc.

CONTENTS

ILLUSTRATIONS

PREFACE

In 2003, four brothers, grandsons of Columbus Lafayette Turner, decided to donate their grandfather's Civil War diary to the North Carolina State Archives. The historical and evidentiary value of the account of a Confederate officer in Federal prison-of-war camps was immediately apparent, but there was some hesitation by the Archives in accepting the journal as a contemporaneous recording. The diary is somewhat unusual in composition, written on four different lots of paper in three distinct styles. The first eight pages were composed on lightly lined eight-by-ten-inch "Congress" writing paper with the printed letterhead of the 1870s North Carolina House of Representatives. The first and fifth pages are headed, "(Prison)," and the last page bears the signature, "Leroy." In his appraisal of the diary, private collections archivist George Stevenson Jr. recognized that these pages, as well as a separate legal-sized sheet with the heading, "Extracts from My Prison Journal," an altered version of page five and part of page six, were obviously "written later in life instead of at the same time as the prison journal." Entries in another diary kept by Turner in 1874 (not then available to Stevenson) confirmed that he drafted these introductory pages for publication in *Our Living and Our Dead*, a weekly newspaper published in New Bern by Stephen D. Pool. While in Raleigh representing Iredell County in the General Assembly, Turner met Pool, who served as clerk of the North Carolina House of Representatives during the 1873-1874 session, and promised to send him extracts from his prison journal. The pseudonym "Leroy" was suggested to Turner by the middle name of a teenaged girl he met while traveling through eastern Randolph County in January 1874. A slightly altered rendition of the first four of these eight pages was published in the May 20, 1874, issue of the New Bern newspaper.

Stevenson noted that the main body of the diary, consisting of fifty-eight pages, was composed on "standard octavo-size writing paper folded to form two leaves." The paper was from two different manufacturers: the first thirty-eight pages had an embossed watermark of "a shield divided into quarters, displaying a nag's head in two quarters and a starry ribbon in the other two"; the succeeding twenty pages bore the watermark of Union Mills. Both lots of writing paper, he concluded, had been purchased from the sutler at the Johnson's Island prison before the closing of his shop in November 1863.

This portion of the diary is composed of two "books" divided into chapters. Turner's initial imprisonment at Fort Delaware in the summer of 1862, his exchange that August, his capture at Gettysburg, and the second brief internment on Pea Patch Island in July 1863 are narrated in chapters one through six. The first five months (August-December 1863) of his lengthy incarceration at Johnson's Island are divided into a second sequence of chapters, numbered one through ten. Each chapter bears a subheading noting in key words (or "headlines") its content, a popular literary device of the day both in fictional and historical works. These fifty-eight pages were written in a smooth hand, with evidence of subsequent editing. After a careful examination of the diary, George Stevenson concluded:

> Lt. Turner's method in creating his journal seems to have been to have jotted down in a memorandum book, or on scraps of paper, key words relating to occurrences and weather, or even to write a short account of an extraordinary event, as a sort of aide mémoir. At the close of a month, when ready to write in his formal journal, Lt. Turner appears to have arranged his experiences categorically rather than chronologically within the month. He then wrote a carefully thought out, well-composed account in a well-formed and finished handwriting. The result is an unusually detailed contemporary account of most aspects of a Confederate prisoner's life in a U.S. military prison during the war. (George Stevenson, private collections archivist, North Carolina State Archives, to Donna E. Kelly, administrator, Historical Publications Section, November 29, 2004)

The final fifteen pages of the Civil War diary, covering the period from January 1 to February 9, 1864, were written on a fourth lot of paper bearing the watermark, "O & REW CO." These pages are in the rough hand as originally drafted by Turner, and the abrupt termination of the diary no doubt indicates the point of exhaustion of his supply of paper.

Walter R. Turner, one of the four grandsons of Columbus Turner who donated the diary to the State Archives and a historian with the North Carolina Transportation Museum, first suggested the publication of the Civil War journal in early 2003. (The Historical Publications Section had recently published his history of the North Carolina Department of Transportation, *Paving Tobacco Road*.) Besides doubts about the contemporaneity of the prison diary, soon laid to rest by George Stevenson's analysis, there was concern regarding the brevity of the journal, whether it could stand alone as a full-length publication. After several months of trying to locate a suitable companion piece—

several possibilities were weighed but found wanting—Walter Turner mentioned that his grandfather had also kept a diary while serving in the General Assembly in 1874. This journal not only answered the need for additional text, but also provided important clues to several unresolved issues relating to the earlier diary. For instance, the legislative diary verified Stevenson's assessment that the introductory material to the prison journal had been written at a later date than the diary itself, indicated dates on which Turner mailed extracts of the journal to the editor of *Our Living and Our Dead*, and explained the origin of the pseudonym, "Leroy."

This is not to suggest that the legislative diary has been included in this edition merely to fill out the pages: on the contrary, it has obvious historical value in its own right. In mid-January 1874, Turner began daily jottings in a three-by-six-inch pocket-sized volume, labeled by the manufacturer, "Perpetual Diary." Like so many well-intentioned diarists over the centuries, Turner steadfastly maintained the journal for about five months, though some of the entries were recorded days after the event. During a trip to the North with his brother in the summer of 1874, he noted some of the sights, their accommodations, modes of travel, and expenditures. But days went by with only the briefest of entries in the journal. Finally, after his return to Richmond in August, he gave up all pretense of keeping a diary.

Fortunately, he maintained a daily chronicle during the nearly two months he spent in Raleigh in the winter of 1874. The freshman representative from Iredell County recorded his impressions of fellow legislators, at work on the floor of the house and at play in their boardinghouse. He provides rare insights into the effort to impeach carpetbagger judges Watts and Tourgée; the bitter recriminations between the director of the state insane asylum and his critics in the legislature; caustic attacks on a Catholic priest who attempted to arrange a convention to attract immigrants to North Carolina; and the difficulties faced by the state geologist in trying to accomplish his mandated duties on a shoestring budget. Turner was by no means a dispassionate observer: he thoroughly enjoyed the discomfort of white Republicans as their African American partisans insisted upon equal rights. Turner also offers an outsider's view of postbellum Raleigh. He visited such entertainments as the capital city had to offer, including a concert at Peace Institute and an evening of song provided by the residents of the State Institute for the Deaf and Dumb and the Blind. He was a regular churchgoer who was then (and apparently for much of his life) seeking a satisfactory denomination, and therefore attended Methodist, Presbyterian, Episcopalian, and Baptist services during his time in Raleigh.

A word on the editorial method employed is here in order. Both diaries have been transcribed with a modicum of editorial intervention. Use of the otherwise omnipresent (and generally annoying) "*sic*" has been avoided in the diaries, though used sparingly in footnotes, introductory passages, and appendixes; misspellings are corrected with brackets only when the meaning might otherwise be obscured. The diarist on occasion inadvertently repeated words, usually articles or prepositions; these duplications have been silently deleted. Turner's subsequent edits to the Civil War diary are indicated with the original word struck through, as he did, except in the few instances where his corrections so obliterated the initial draft that it could not be deciphered. Occasionally, he would insert a letter, word, or phrase between the lines, either as he composed or in the process of preparing the diary for publication. These interlineations are indicated between diagonal lines at the point of insertion in the text. Superscript letters have also been brought down to the line. Turner sometimes used a form of footnoting to further explain a point, employing an asterisk to direct the reader to the exposition at the bottom of the page. His technique has been retained in this transcription. In the 1874 diary, Turner often ran out of room on the small page allotted for each day and would continue his final thought in either the left or right margin. On a few occasions he used both margins and twice resorted to crosshatching to finish the entry. This marginalia is preceded by explanatory phrases, such as "In left margin," in brackets.

This publication would not have been possible without the assistance and contribution of numerous individuals, particularly several of Columbus L. Turner's descendants. Each of the four aforementioned brothers, sons of Columbus Turner's youngest son, Reginald, provided copies of original documents, family histories, newspaper clippings, and/or photographs that were in their possession. They also contributed significantly to the funds raised to underwrite this project. They are James R. Turner of Greensboro, Wilfred Turner of New Bern, Walter R. Turner of High Point, and Terrell C. Turner of Kure Beach. A copy of their father's unpublished memoirs was deposited with the Civil War diary in the State Archives, providing intimate details of the years at Monbo Heights, where Columbus Turner operated a textile mill and raised a family on the west bank of the Catawba River in Catawba County.

James Turner shared a transcript of an unpublished family history he had written in 1997, as well as several invaluable original materials, including the minute book of Monbo Manufacturing Company, a notebook his grandfather kept at Trinity College, an 1862 letter from Columbus Turner to his father, and the text of two speeches Representative Turner delivered to the house in February 1873. He also allowed me access to the 1874 diary, which he has since graciously donated to the State Archives. Wilfred Turner sent a copy of the comprehensive family tree that he had compiled, and shared a number of family photographs and an 1863 letter from Wilfred Turner to his son at Johnson's Island. Terrell Turner found the prison journal in the family home at Kure Beach and preserved it for several years. Walter Turner conducted research in Statesville and at Duke University and prepared papers concerning his grandfather's education at Olin High School and Trinity College. He directed the family's fund-raising effort and arranged for the copying of photographs that had been donated to the Iredell Museum of Arts and Heritage. Even more important, Walter suggested several avenues of inquiry along the way, and his boundless enthusiasm and unwavering optimism fueled this project from the beginning. Another grandson, Charles S. Young of Greensboro, shared a brief sketch of Monogram School, the public school in Catawba County that Columbus Turner helped to establish, which he had prepared for the 2007 Turner family reunion. Nancy Jones of Burlington, a grand- daughter of Columbus Turner's sister, Virginia Turner Willson, furnished photographs of and genealogical information about the children of Wilfred and Dorcas Turner. A host of Turner kinsmen contributed financially to this publication, including Mary Frances Lack, Norma Young Latta, Pamela C. Lee, Elizabeth Stevens, Jason Tucker, William Tucker, Natalie Marie Turner, William Joel Turner, Richard Wilkins, William G. Wilkins, William G. Wilkins Jr., A. H. Young Jr., Catherine M. Young, Charles A. Young, Charles S. Young, Julia Dorcas Young, and Marcella Young, as well as the Anson County Writers' Club.

A number of colleagues in the parallel universes of archives and historical publications also assisted in this venture. Anyone who assays to research and write about any topic concerning eighteenth- or nineteenth-century North Carolina without the assistance of George Stevenson Jr., former private collections archivist at the State Archives, proceeds at his own peril. George has contributed to this project in countless ways, not the least of which was training this editor to be a reference archivist in the State Archives nearly thirty years ago. George retired with the year 2007 after thirty-seven years of invaluable service to the state and its citizens.

In the State Archives Search Room, archivists Earl Ijames, Kate Martin, Gwen Mays, and Ron Vestal provided their usual exceptional reference and copying services. Larry Odzak, proprietor of the microfilm reading room, was especially helpful, allowing me access to the microfilm holdings during the long months of 2007 that the Archives was closed for remodeling. I am also grateful to state archivist Dick Lankford and Debbi Blake, supervisor of the Search Room, for granting access to the Archives stacks on two occasions. Iconographic archivist Kim Cumber and her assistant, Vann Evans, identified and arranged for copying many of the illustrations included in this volume. Alan Westmoreland prepared digital copies from the negatives. My wife, Druscie Simpson, and her staff of the Information Technology Branch of the State Archives created the digital images of maps and newspapers. I am particularly appreciative of Richard Carney, who copied two maps from the Civil War atlas; Athena Jackson, who scanned the newspaper article concerning "The Murder of Mrs. Surratt"; and Lee Todd, who performed the mysterious rites of OCR upon a copy of Columbus Turner's address to the Ladies' Memorial Association of Iredell County that he had scanned, saving me countless hours of mind-numbing typing. The reference staff of the State Library of North Carolina, especially Steve Case, Cynthia Jones, Cheryl McLean, and Bonnie Spiers, as well as Joy Heitmann and Pam Toms of the Genealogical Services Section, were most helpful in patiently locating the odd volume or reel of microfilm. Theresa Golas, executive director of the Iredell Museum of Arts and Heritage, and Sandra Campbell, a member of the museum's board of directors, made a special trip to Raleigh to deliver Turner family photographs to be copied. The staff of the Iredell County Public Library, especially local history librarian Joel Reese, assisted Walter Turner in compiling information concerning Olin High School. Jack Zehmer of Richmond, Virginia, searched in vain in several Episcopal churches in the city for record of Columbus Turner's second marriage.

Several colleagues in the Historical Publications Section, especially Bill Brown, Matthew Brown, and Mike Coffey, experts all in various aspects of Civil War history, answered (or at least graciously endured) my occasional question regarding obscure sources. Documentary editor Lang Baradell proofread the transcription of the prison diary against an original copy and offered many valuable suggestions to improve the presentation. Susan Trimble performed her customary magic in typesetting the text and arranging the images. She and Bill Owens, the section's marketing specialist, designed the cover. Lisa Bailey proofread the manuscript with her usual keen eye for violations of the rules of grammar and punctuation. Donna Kelly, administrator of the section, also proofed the manuscript, coordinated funding for the publication, and ushered the volume through the production process.

Kenrick N. Simpson

Columbus Lafayette Turner (1842-1918) in middle age. Image courtesy of the Iredell Museum of Arts and Heritage, Statesville, N.C.

INTRODUCTION

Columbus Lafayette Turner was, above all else, a practical man. He was not given, neither in his life-style nor in his writings, to soaring flights of fancy, nor was he driven by relentless ambition for personal attainment. Turner was firmly rooted in the foothills of North Carolina, the product of solid English stock that first settled in this country in Maryland in the early eighteenth century. His practicality and sound business sense found profitable application in the booming southern textile industry of the late nineteenth century. Like his father, Turner became in middle age a prosperous industrialist by tapping the natural power of Piedmont waterways to develop cotton mills.

Turner was well educated for his time and place, enjoying the benefits of high school and collegiate instruction. Probably because of his educational achievements and relative affluence, and despite his youthfulness, he was elected as an officer in his company of North Carolina volunteers soon after the Civil War broke out. But his military career, most of which was spent in Federal prisoner-of-war camps, was unexceptional. He apparently demonstrated little capacity for leadership as a junior officer. As he admitted years later, others were "more ambitious for glory."[1] He suffered poor health for much of the war, twice attempted to resign his commission, and may have spent an unauthorized furlough at home.

Unlike many journals kept by soldiers during the Civil War, the diary in which Turner recorded his wartime experiences devoted less than a single page to descriptions of combat. It is completely devoid of the grand maneuvers of large armies, as it is of ruminations upon the glory of dying for one's country. His primary concern, as with prisoners of every war, was for the basic necessities of life: warm clothes against the bitter cold of a Lake Erie winter, seasoned wood for a warmth-giving fire, something new to read, paper on which to record his thoughts, and, above all else, sufficient food to sustain the semblance of good health.

At Johnson's Island, Ohio, Turner does not appear to have been an especially convivial inmate, though perhaps it would be fairer to say that his personal taste ran to a more cerebral form of entertainment than did that of the majority of his fellows. He shunned the games of baseball and the amusing presentations of the prison theatrical company enjoyed by many of the prisoners, preferring instead the mental challenges offered by the debating society and the Bible study group. He condemned the rampant gambling and mindless cursing by the prisoners as being beneath the dignity of godly men; even as an old man, he forbade the playing of cards in his home.[2] These were expressions of sincere religious convictions, yet Turner spent much of his life questioning articles of faith while seeking a denomination that could answer his spiritual needs. Still, his belief in a better world to come enabled him to accept the death of two wives and the loss of his major source of income to natural disaster. Most importantly for our purposes, Turner was an astute witness to his surroundings who recorded his observations at two key junctures of his life.

The progenitor of the Turner line in this country was Adam Turner, who arrived in Port Tobacco, Maryland, in 1728 with three sons. One of these sons, James, was born in England in 1700. James was the father of William (1737-1801), who married Rhoda Dent in 1764 and sired eleven children. William Turner was a Tory who signed the oath of allegiance after the Revolutionary War. Two of his sons, John "Jack" and Wilson, moved to western Rowan County, North Carolina, in 1797 with a number of fellow Episcopalian families, accompanied by the Reverend Hatch Dent. Soon after this congregation founded Christ Church Rowan, Rev. Hatch Dent returned to Maryland.[3]

Samuel Turner (1784-1857) was born in Maryland, the last of the eleven children of William and Rhoda Dent Turner. In 1806, he married Elizabeth Anna Dent (1785-1825), the daughter of Rev. Hatch Dent and probably a relative of Rhoda Dent. Samuel served in the War of 1812. Sometime between 1818 and 1820, he moved his family (including Wilfred, about ten) to North Carolina and eventually settled near River Hill in northern Iredell County. In May 1820, Samuel Turner "of Rowan County" bought from John Nichols 234 acres on Little Dutchman Creek and the north bank of South Yadkin River. In 1823, he bought the River Hill tract (262 acres) and house from Robert Simonton, who had purchased the property at a sheriff's sale. By 1831, Turner owned 1,011 acres between the river and the creek; his spread was known as River Hill Plantation. He was a progressive farmer, reclaiming rich bottomland by re-channeling creeks. "River Hill was a self-sustaining plantation . . . more or less a little town, so it got its own post office." He was not, however, a large-scale slaveholder. In 1850, Turner owned twenty-one slaves, only six of whom were males of prime working age; nine were children less than ten years old.[4]

Samuel Turner's first wife, the mother of Wilfred and nine other children, died on July 6, 1825. Samuel married Mary Tucker on February 2, 1826. She would deliver four children, two of whom were stillborn, and die giving birth to a fifth child on March 5, 1835. Later that year, Samuel married Clarissa Nichols, who bore him five children (one born dead), including James Martin Turner (who is mentioned in Columbus Turner's 1874 diary) in 1836. Samuel died in 1857 and was buried with his first two wives and several of his twenty children in the family burial ground surrounded by a stone wall at his old homestead, 150 yards south of his residence.[5]

Wilfred Turner (1809-1893) was the second child of Samuel and Elizabeth Anna Dent Turner. He was born February 15, 1809, in Charles County, Maryland, and received five months of rudimentary education before the family moved to North Carolina. Wilfred bought his first piece of property, seventeen acres on Dutchman Creek in northeastern Iredell County, in 1830. He was briefly employed as a clerk in a store in Statesville owned by S. R. Bell, working for his room and board. On August 16, 1832, he married Dorcas Tomlinson (1813-1900), daughter of John and Tobitha Wheat Tomlinson of the Harmony neighborhood of Iredell County. Soon after his marriage, Turner ran a store for Bell at County Line, on the South Yadkin River in Davie County just across the Iredell line. By 1838, he had saved enough money to buy the store, which he operated on his own for twelve years. Although he never bought land in Davie County, he did purchase a slave in 1841. He acquired a second tract in Iredell County, 150 acres from B. F. Boswell, in 1843. The following year, Turner was a member of the committee for common schools in District 15 of Davie County. He also served as postmaster at County Line and later at Turnersburg. Nine of Wilfred and Dorcas's twelve children, including Columbus Lafayette Turner, were born at County Line.[6]

On December 2, 1850, Wilfred Turner bought a one-third interest in the Rocky Creek Shoals factory and store in northern Iredell County for $4,684 from Notley D. Tomlin of Olin, his wife's uncle. Tomlin had been in business there since 1847 with partners Dr. Aaron D. Gage, whose plantation adjoined the mill, and James Wilson of Morganton. The plant consisted of a dam, cotton gin, flour mill, and cotton mill. Earlier in 1850, Tomlin had bought out his partners. On the same day that Turner bought an interest in the mill property, he also purchased the adjacent plantation of 515 acres from Dr. Gage. Soon thereafter, Turner moved his family from County Line. In 1852, Wilfred represented Iredell County in the state house of commons, leaving the operation of the mill to Tomlin. Four years later, he bought out his partner for $8,000 and, for many years thereafter, ran the yarn mill and store. In 1858, the

The Turner family cemetery at River Hill, the plantation of Samuel Turner, first of his line to settle in Iredell County. The Turner homeplace stands in the distance. From Iredell County American Revolution Bicentennial Commission, *Iredell County Landmarks: A Pictorial History of Iredell County* (Statesville, N.C.: Brady Printing Company, 1982), p. 77.

town and post office were officially named Turnersburg (on the suggestion of Newton Spiers, superintendent of the cotton mill), and the factory became known as Turnersburg Cotton Mill. On the eve of the Civil War, Wilfred Turner owned eleven slaves, only three of whom were males of prime working age; one was a sixty-year-old female, and four were children under the age of five.[7]

Wilfred Turner overcame his lack of formal education with a strong work ethic and sound business practices to become one of the wealthiest men in Iredell County. In addition to his term in the house of commons and his many years as postmaster, Turner served his community as a justice of the peace. Upon his death in 1893, the Statesville *Landmark* commented: "In all of his 84 years of life no breath of suspicion tainted his name. He was opposed to all forms of speculation and the profits of his business were strictly legitimate profits. So rigid was he in this matter that he would not even buy a piece of property with the idea of selling it at an advanced price." Which is not to suggest that he did not engage in the buying and selling of land on a grand scale: between 1830 and 1885,

The Turnersburg Cotton Mill, owned and operated by Wilfred Turner from 1856 until it was destroyed by fire in 1890. Even though it was a principal source of employment for the community and the source of much of his personal wealth, Wilfred felt relieved of "a great burden" when the mill burned down. From *Iredell County Landmarks: A Pictorial History of Iredell County*, p. 164.

Wilfred purchased more than 2,668 acres in Iredell County and several town lots in Olin. He also acquired at least 210 acres in the capacity of trustee of land sold under foreclosure. By 1890, he had sold 1,910½ acres in 37 separate transactions. Interestingly, 8 of these sales, involving 257 acres, were to African Americans. In 1880, Wilfred sold the one- acre lot encompassing Rocky Creek Church to the trustees of the African Methodist Zion Church; that same year, he donated the one- acre parcel on which the Turnersburg Church stood to the Methodist Episcopal Church. During his lifetime, he also gave nearly 600 acres to his children Mary, Columbus, Adeline, and Ella. After his death, his executor sold an additional 635 acres, including 72 that Wilfred held under the terms of a mortgage deed.[8]

Over the span of twenty years, Wilfred and Dorcas Turner had twelve children, all but one of whom survived infancy. As they will all appear, at least in passing, in one or both of the diaries, an introduction, in order of their birth, seems appropriate. The eldest was Mary Elizabeth "Betty," born at County Line on March 23, 1835. She married William Tyson Gaither (1826-1885) of a prominent local family in February

China Grove, the home of Wilfred and Dorcas Turner at Turnersburg, built in 1812. The house in northern Iredell County still stands and is known today as the 1812 Hitching Post, available for rent for "plantation-style" weddings and receptions. From *Iredell County Landmarks: A Pictorial History of Iredell County*, p. 44.

1853. They built a large house near Harmony on the old Wilkesboro-Statesville Road, about two miles from her parents. In 1869, Wilfred Turner bought Gaither's interest in the Eagle Mills Company on Hunting Creek, which comprised four hundred acres, mill houses, and machinery; three years later, he assigned this interest to his daughter, Gaither's wife. In 1875, Turner bought 250 acres from Gaither at $3.00 an acre; he then gave the land to his daughter in 1879. Betty Turner Gaither died at the age of ninety-four in 1929, surviving all of her siblings except the last born.[9]

A second daughter, Tobitha Olivia, was born on May 12, 1837. She attended Davenport Female College in Lenoir before the Civil War. In the summer of 1862, Tobitha married Dr. John R. Anderson, but she died of typhoid fever six weeks later. Another daughter, Julia Louisa, followed on November 1, 1838. She married Dr. Robert Henry Wyche (1823-1904) on March 31, 1868, and settled in eastern Chatham County, where he had an established medical practice. She will appear on several occasions in the diary that her brother kept while serving in the state House of Representatives. Julia Wyche died in 1878 on the eve of her fortieth birthday, survived by three young daughters, who were thereafter raised in Turnersburg by her parents.[10]

Wilfred must have begun to wonder if anyone would carry on the family name when a fourth pregnancy resulted in still another daughter on August 7, 1840. Sarah Elizabeth "Sallie" Turner was destined for a lonely, unhappy life, far removed from her close-knit family. On December 22, 1859, she married Newton A. Holman, a timberman from Davie County who soon after the Civil War moved to western Tennessee where, according to family tradition, Sallie suffered from loneliness and depression. After the death of her husband in 1901, she spent her last years in the state mental hospital at Morganton, where she died on January 20, 1916.[11]

Wilfred Turner was finally blessed with a son on February 25, 1842, with the birth of Columbus Lafayette, the author of these diaries. The next two children were also boys: William Graham, who died before his second birthday in 1845; and John Augustus, born May 3, 1845. Like his older brother, "Gus" Turner would serve the Confederacy and spend time as a Federal prisoner of war. At Mocksville on June 20, 1863, he enlisted for the duration of the war under Capt. Baxter Clegg Clement in Company M of the Seventh Confederate Cavalry. He was wounded and captured at Suffolk, Virginia, on March 5, 1864, when he "rode so near the enemy and, refusing to surrender, was shot from his horse."

Wilfred (1809-1893) and Dorcas Tomlinson Turner (1813-1900), parents of Columbus Lafayette Turner and his eleven siblings. Images courtesy of Nancy Jones, Burlington, N.C.

Two of the eight sisters of Columbus Turner. Tobitha Turner Anderson (*left*) died of typhoid fever six weeks after her wedding in 1862. Sallie Turner Holman (*right*) spent her last years in the state mental hospital at Morganton after a lonely marriage in an isolated section of the mountains of western Tennessee. Images courtesy of Nancy Jones, Burlington, N.C.

After a brief confinement at Fortress Monroe, Turner was transferred to Point Lookout, Maryland, where he died of consumption on February 13, 1865, and was buried in the prison graveyard.[12]

Another sequence of four daughters followed the run of three boys, beginning with the birth of Adeline Dorcas in January 1847. She married Laz. T. Stimpson, son of another prominent northern Iredell County family, on November 20, 1873. Her father gave her 150 acres on Rocky Creek in 1884 and, with her husband, a half-interest in the Turnersburg Mill and Cotton Factory and its 35-acre tract in 1890.[13]

Columbus's favorite sister, Laura Catherine, was born June 17, 1848. She died of typhoid fever on August 5, 1863, much lamented by her eldest brother (then confined at Johnson's Island), who considered her "the flower of the family." The tenth Turner child, Virginia "Jennie" Ann, followed on October 18, 1851. Two days after her twenty-third birthday in 1874, she married the Reverend James D. Willson, the third Turner daughter to be wed in the space of eleven months. Willson had been raised in the Turner household after being orphaned at the age of ten. He served as a musician in the Forty-second North Carolina Regiment from February 1864 to the end of the war. Willson became a

Addie Turner Stimpson (*left*) married into another prominent Iredell County family and, with her husband, inherited a portion of her father's homeplace and mill operation. Jennie Turner Willson (*right*) married a Methodist minister who, after being orphaned, was raised in the household of Wilfred and Dorcas Turner. Images courtesy of Nancy Jones, Burlington, N.C.

Methodist minister in 1871 and for fifteen years preached throughout the Western North Carolina Methodist Conference before settling in Statesville, where he edited the *Statesville Christian Advocate*. Jennie died tragically in 1925 when her clothing caught fire while she was burning trash in her yard.[14]

The last of the eight Turner daughters was christened Emily "Emma" Ella upon her birth in 1853. Her marriage to Marshall Knox Steele, a dry goods merchant in Olin, on January 19, 1874, is recorded in the diary kept by her elder brother while he served in the General Assembly. Her father presented her with 53½ acres in 1875, 60 acres in 1881, and, with her husband, a half-interest in the Turnersburg mill in 1890. Wilfred Turner gave power of attorney to Steele in 1884. Two years before his death, Wilfred sold 85 acres of the homeplace to two of his sons-in-law, M. K. Steele and L. T. Stimpson. Emma Steele died in 1924.[15]

The last born of the twelve offspring of Wilfred and Dorcas Turner was perhaps the most accomplished and certainly the best known. Wilfred Dent Turner (1855-1933) earned a bachelor's degree from Trinity College, then read law under Judge Robert F. Armfield in Statesville. Turner put out his shingle there in 1877, entered into partnership with Armfield, and practiced law in the Iredell County seat for the next fifty-six years. He followed his father and eldest brother to the General Assembly, serving four terms in the state senate. Turner was selected as running mate to Charles B. Aycock in the gubernatorial election of 1900, in which the Democrats drove the Fusionists from office. As lieutenant governor, he presided over the impeachment proceedings in the senate against Chief Justice David M. Furches. Turner served on the boards of trustees of Trinity College (and Duke University) and the North Carolina College for Women. At the time of his death in 1933, he was president of the Iredell County Bar Association. A biographer characterized Wilfred Dent Turner as "conservative, solid, and sound," a description that would fit his older brother just as comfortably.[16]

The author of these diaries, Columbus Lafayette Turner, known as "Lum," attended field schools in northern Iredell County before entering Olin High School, four miles northwest of Turnersburg. There he received instruction from Methodist ministers Baxter Clegg and Samuel Lander (who later founded Williamston Female College in South Carolina, renamed Lander College in his honor in 1904), and Prof. A. Haywood Merritt. The school at Olin was established as New Institute Academy in 1850 by Clegg and Brantley York, another Methodist preacher and educator. York had previously organized schools throughout western North Carolina, including Union Institute in Randolph County. When he moved to Iredell County in 1849, York was "prevailed upon by the people around Nesbit and Turner's tanyard to start an academy." He served as agent for the school, sending students

Columbus Turner's younger brother, business partner, and traveling companion, Wilfred Dent Turner (1855-1933), lieutenant governor of North Carolina from 1901 to 1905. Image courtesy of the Iredell Museum of Arts and Heritage, Statesville, N.C.

from his several short-term schools, while Clegg came over from Mocksville to run the academy. With dreams of developing the school into a college, York arranged a loan of $10,000 to build a three-story brick schoolhouse and chapel. Brothers Osborne and John F. Foard borrowed the money from Moses Holmes of Salisbury, with a number of prominent citizens, including Lawson Nesbit and Wilfred Turner, standing as security. Soon after the academy was chartered by the state legislature in 1855, Clegg renamed it to honor Stephen Olin, an early Methodist educator and the first president of Randolph-Macon College in Virginia. The school building, nestled in a ten-acre grove, included eight recitation rooms, two large classrooms, and a "society hall," with a detached chapel that would accommodate twelve hundred people. The school operated in some fashion until 1880 but never did acquire the status of a Methodist college.[17]

Olin High School was open to girls and boys and included female teachers on the faculty. In 1858, Lum Turner's last year at the school, the sixty-member student body included forty-five males and fifteen females, among them his older sister, Sallie. Tuition ranged from $50 to $55 per session. Students lived in boardinghouses in the community. Columbus and his uncle, Alfred Turner, who was only two years his elder, roomed with Mr. and Mrs. Jack Anderson. Little is known about Turner's academic course work, but Henry A. Chambers recalled that he and Lum were members of the Ciceronian Society, a debating club that met weekly in Philomathian Hall.[18]

In August 1859, Lum Turner enrolled at Trinity College, located in Randolph County six miles south of High Point and approximately sixty-five miles from Turnersburg. The institution had been founded in 1839, when a one-room academy, Brown's Schoolhouse, was formally organized by the Union Institute Society, a group of Methodists and Quakers in northern Randolph County. The society was led by Brantley York, the Methodist minister and principal of the schoolhouse, who subsequently helped to organize Olin High School. In 1841, the legislature chartered the school as Union Institute Academy. A decade later, the academy was re-chartered as Normal College, a state-supported institution charged with the training of teachers for the public schools. In 1856, the North Carolina Methodist Episcopal Church South selected Normal College, rather than Olin High School, to be its affiliated institution of higher learning in the state. The name of the school was changed to Trinity College in the year that Turner arrived.[19]

At Trinity College, Turner boarded for at least part of his two years with William Trigg Gannaway, professor of Latin, Greek, and natural philosophy. Annual expenses at that time were approximately $163: $50 for tuition; $105 for room and board; $5 for "society" expenses; and $3 for janitorial fees. During his first semester, Turner studied Greek and Latin grammar, geometry, and geography. He compiled a list of subjects he wrote about as a student: during his freshman year, these included truth, passions, infidelity, intemperance, the truth of prophecy, the immortality of the soul, Henry Clay, David Fanning, and the red man of the forest; as a sophomore, he tackled friendship, the value of time, genteel carriage, the temptations of a city life, the choice of a wife, the advantages of female society, and complaisance after marriage. He also maintained a list of books "perused" at Trinity, which included biographies of the Marquis de Lafayette (by Pasley), George Washington (Mason Locke "Parson" Weems), Francis Marion (William Gilmore Simms), and Oliver Cromwell (Joel Tyler Headley); sketches of the Revolutionary War in North Carolina (E. W. Caruthers); a two-volume history of the War of 1812; Kirwin's *Sketches*; and *The Evidence of Prophecy*, by Alexander Keith.[20]

In June 1861, Turner was one of eight speakers during the annual four-day commencement service at Trinity College. He represented the sophomore class with a declamation on the topic, "The Southern Confederacy." Before the end of that school year, approximately 40 of the 215-member student body at Trinity had volunteered for military service, "and the remainder planned to follow their example or talked of not returning to school the next year." In a notebook Turner kept at college, in which he recorded his expenses as well as the above-mentioned lists of subjects studied, books read, and papers written, there is an undated note, apparently scribbled as he prepared to leave school while his classmates celebrated the opportunity to fight some Yankees: "Home. Now whilst I set thinking of home and feel gladened [*sic*] because the day for my depart is almost here pistols afiring around me and listening every moment for the tolling of the bell. . . ."[21]

On July 16, 1861, nineteen-year-old Columbus Turner enlisted at "Youngs" in a company of volunteers being raised by Robert V. Cowan, a graduate of Olin High School who had attended the U.S. Military Academy at West Point until the outbreak of sectional hostilities compelled him to resign. Captain Cowan took his recruits into camp at Graham and taught them the rudiments of drill. At the fairgrounds in

Members of the Trinity Guard assemble in 1861 in front of the new classroom building on the Randolph County campus. Columbus Turner was one of many Trinity students who volunteered for service in the Confederate armed forces during the initial rush to arms. Image courtesy of Duke University Archives, Durham, N.C.

Raleigh on October 31, the company was organized into state service for the duration of the war as Company D, Thirty-third Regiment North Carolina Troops. Turner was mustered in as third corporal of the company. From Camp Mangum on New Year's Day, he wrote home, the only letter that survives from his four years of service:

> Some time past I have been on the sick list. It is a noted uncommon thing to see companies of not more than a dozen go out at dress parade and today there were not in all one hundred men. There are not more than 170 fit for duty. As soon as the health of the regiment will allow we stand ready to go anywhere we may be directed. I want to go someplace where we can see learn and do something. Here there is nothing but the monotony of camp life everywhere. It is the same thing all the time.

When the regiment was transferred to Confederate service on January 9, 1862, Cowan's unit was re-designated Company A, an honor customarily awarded to the best-organized and disciplined company of the ten that normally composed a regiment of infantry. Soon thereafter, the Thirty-third, commanded by Col. Lawrence O'Bryan Branch, moved from Raleigh to New Bern.[22]

Victorious Union troops surge over the Confederate works before New Bern on March 14, 1862, in this panoramic view from *Leslie's Illustrated Newspaper*, April 5, 1862.

Turner was absent with leave from January 21 to February 6, 1862, suffering from a severe attack of "typhoid pneumonia and was near the borderland for some time." His father came to New Bern to take him home. Turner returned to his unit, then camped at the fairgrounds near New Bern, in time to participate in its trial by fire. Still weak from his long illness, Turner was ordered by Captain Cowan to stay behind when Company A went out on picket duty during the "dark and drizzly night" of March 13, "and thus escaped a very unpleasant experience." As Turner recalled in his account of the Battle of New Bern in *Our Living and Our Dead* in 1874, he slept soundly in a deserted tent belonging to the Twenty-sixth North Carolina and awoke "greatly refreshed." He hurried out to join his command, posted in reserve behind the Twenty-sixth and Thirty-fifth North Carolina regiments and a battalion of militia. Soon after the rattle of musketry erupted along the line, Col. Clark M. Avery (who had succeeded Branch as colonel when the latter was promoted to brigadier general) was directed to hurry the regiment into a gap in the lines at a brickyard by the tracks of the Atlantic and North Carolina Railroad from which the militia had been driven. Company A was sent in advance of four other companies of the Thirty-third under the command of Maj. William Gaston Lewis to the right of the railroad.

Image courtesy of the North Carolina State Archives, Raleigh, N.C.

As minié balls whizzed around them, they pressed forward through a ravine and an abatis of trees to take position on cleared high ground beside the tracks, "where a ditch had been dug and the dirt thrown on the wrong side, thereby affording a great deal less protection." With assistance from elements of the Twenty-sixth North Carolina, the Thirty-third restored the broken line but came under heavy fire from fresh Federal regiments of Brig. Gen. Jesse Reno's brigade in the low ground at their front, which "kept the air vocal with minié balls." Lewis's infantry "repulsed the enemy time and again, and twice charged them with detachments of companies, and each time made them flee." Even after the Thirty-fifth North Carolina on its left had fallen back, exposing its flank to envelopment, the Thirty-third held its ground until the regiment was "well nigh surrounded." Colonel Avery never received General Branch's orders for a general retreat. Corporal Turner and at least thirteen privates in his company were among the 144 officers and soldiers of the regiment captured in their first fight. Thirty-two of their fellows were killed and twenty-eight wounded, including ten dead and eight wounded in Company A.[23]

The captured Confederates were first placed in the old brick kiln, "where the sharp points of numerous brickbats became their easy chairs and downy couches." Colonel Avery was "beset by a yankee woman, who was apparently half attired in male and half in female garb, who urged him to allow her to cut off one of his brass buttons." A field hospital was established by the Federals in a nearby log hut, and surgeons commenced the amputation of shattered arms and legs. Turner obtained permission to lead a detail of prisoners to bring in the Confederate wounded in order to give them "the best attention circumstances would allow, answering their calls for water and changing their position." He recognized a former schoolmate, Lewis Brock Tysor of the Twenty-sixth, who was badly wounded through the thigh and died three days later.[24] Several days after the battle, the Confederate prisoners of war were loaded aboard an old transport, the *Albany*, anchored in the middle of the Neuse River.

THE CIVIL WAR PRISON JOURNAL OF COLUMBUS LAFAYETTE TURNER

[EDITOR'S NOTE: *The "first sketch of first article," referring either to this introduction to his Civil War prison journal or his account of the Battle of New Bern* (see Appendix A), *was prepared by Turner on March 19, 1874, after he had returned home from serving in the lower house of the North Carolina General Assembly. The introduction to the diary was written on eight pages of official stationery, with "House of Representatives, Raleigh, N. C., 187_" printed at the top of the first and fifth pages. He was preparing the diary for publication in* Our Living and Our Dead, *keeping a promise to Stephen D. Pool, editor of the weekly newspaper, who also served as clerk of the House of Representatives during the 1873-1874 session. An edited and somewhat altered version of the first two paragraphs was published in the May 20, 1874, issue of* Our Living and Our Dead *under the heading, "Extracts from the Prison Journal of a Confederate"* (see Appendix B). *Turner signed this section, "Leroy," a nom de plume suggested by the middle name of a young female acquaintance from Randolph County. Turner may have referred to the original journal entries recording these events when he noted in his diary on March 19: "Some lady took off part of it and would not return it."*]

(PRISON)

In the middle of Neuse River the "Albany" lay anchored about one month.[1] All the room on it was well occupied by prisoners. It was a steam transport old rickety and ungainly in appearance. When on deck we barely had elbow room. When night came on we had to go below, into the dark foetid gloom of the hold of the vessel—and sleep on broad shelves, one above the other, beneath the water. The isle or passage was very narrow—the air close, and the whole place ~~rather~~ damp and offensive. Here for the first time I observed some of that pestiferous tribe of insects, which were afterwards so universally known in both armies. One or two of the advanced scouts had no sooner attacked me, that I was seized with a feeling of loathing and disgust, and very imprudently as it afterwards proved to be—drew off a good shirt almost an only shirt and threw it overboard.

From this time forward it became necessary to keep up a ceaseless warfare, to mantain freedom from their depridations. Some of the men actually surrendered. It would seem that they could not do otherwise being without change of raiment. When they washed their underclothes, they were compelled by the force of circumstances to wear none until they were dryed. There was not much room for sitting down or for any

Nineteen-year-old Columbus Lafayette Turner posed for this picture soon after his enlistment in Capt. Robert V. Cowan's company of volunteers on July 16, 1861. Image courtesy of Wilfred Turner, New Bern, N.C.

other purpose, and nothing to sit upon but the deck. There was not room sufficient for issuing rations, especially the soup which was served in wash tubs. Beneath the hatch way in a narrow gangway down in the hold of the vessel, a tub was set and a horse bucket was filled with the soup near a big boiler and let down by means of a rope—emptied and drawn up again and the same process repeated. This was not the worst for we had neither spoon cup or anything else to eat it with or from. Went without my soup rather than push & crowd around such a bowl or tureen and in common with some take my hands or a stick to it. Here was a picture that beat "Harper" or Leslie.[2] Some of the men would have eagerly dipped it up with their hands, but it was generally too hot. Many inventions were sought out to convey to their mouths. Wooden spoons became numerous, or would have been so if sufficent /raw/ material could have been found to make them from. All around the tub pale lines of soup could be seen where it had dreaned back from spoons sticks and fingers. I took seeing for my share and was vividly reminded of times gone by when a pan of doe was thrown to or set down for /a large flock of/ chickens. Happened to be able to start 15cts with which I bought a pint cup, and thereafter came in for my share. This cup was useful to more than one, and was sometimes the fortunate receiver of coffee. Fat meat and hard bread were also used. Some might think our food did not taste good, but it did. We could relish the meat very well without cooking.

The /Grease/ meat when /the meat was/ cooked would drop like water from a dish rag. It is much better to live on crackers and fat meat /and use only fingers/ than on the richest soup, and bread and have no spoon. If I were a school boy again I would write a composition on "The Spoon" and not fail to urge its importance by an allusion to Gen Butlers great propensity for that article.[3] His superabundant supply would be referred to, and our excessive scarcity put in contrast therewith. School boy days are gone and the contemplation of them forms a pleasent contrast to monotonous experience on the "Albany." I can almost imagine myself writing an essay on the aforesaid subject and saying "The spoon how useful it is—how convenient it is—the for[k] is too—but it wont hold liquids, or small grains of any thing. The spoon will and any of those things you can carry to your mouth without any trouble." Some people have been so unfortunate as to be without forks but worse still some have been without spoons, for a sharp stick can be used for a fork.

[EDITOR'S NOTE: *The published version concluded:* "It is now time to weigh anchor, both for a voyage to Governor's Island in New York harbor, and for closing this extract. The former will be speedily disposed of in the next—bringing us by a near cut to Fort Delaware, concerning which, much may justly be said." *Turner noted in his diary on May 7, 1874, that he had "prepared and sent 2d Article to 'Our Living & Our Dead' " from Richmond. Some time after sending Pool the extract of the above paragraphs, Turner prepared a first and second draft of another article for* Our Living and Our Dead. *No further entries from "Leroy" have been found in subsequent issues of the newspaper, which continued to publish Confederate diaries and reminiscences until March 1876. I have been unable to locate copies of the issues of June 25 and July 1, 1874; perhaps Turner's second journal extract appeared in one of those numbers. The complete version of the second article below is written on the same official house stationery as the unpublished version of the first extract, above, so it presumably was likewise the initial draft.*][4]

(PRISON)

It was with pleasure that we saw the anchor weighed to begin a trip somewhere. To remain stationery on an old vessel in the middle of a river for a month is very trying to ones spirits. Every object had been so often seen that it would have been a great relief to fall asleep and continue to slumber until prison life should end. After anchoring at Hatteras Inlet for the night, where a wild waste of water & sand bars, with high rolling billows were presented to the view, we passed out to sea.[5] The steamer seemed to be in a regular swing—prow low, stern high—stern low prow high. It creaked and rolled. Many of the prisoners became very sick and crawled about on deck and to the sides of the vessel like lizzards. The salty dampness of the sea—the press on board—our gloomy dingy state rooms, and in fact all things connected with the voyage were highly enjoyed, ironically speaking.

As we came in view of the Narrows,[6] our countenances brightened, as we beheld the grand panorama, of high cliffs, fine structures—beautiful gardens and yards, and passing vessels of all descriptions. We passed Fort Lafayette and on into the harbor of New York city near the battery where all was bustle life and animation.[7] We were not here long before we were landed on Governors Island and safely ensconced within thick walls of Castle William which is near the beach, and open to the howling winds or scorching sun.[8]

We occupied the casemates, and slept upon the flo[o]r with such blankets as we had until pallets of straw wer[e] furnished. The soup was good—but the quantity to each rather small. This was made at F Columbus on the highest ground of the Island and a much more desirable place than the old Castle.[9] It appeared so from our stand point on account of its beautiful trees and landscapes by which it was surrounded. A detail of prisoners under guard went out to the fort to bring down the soup in large cans. When they came within the open court of the Castle a general rush was made, with cups. No system was observed in distributing. They the prisoners would crowd and press around, heave and set—some would rush between the legs of others—some would mount the pile of human beings crowding around like a herd of hogs about a slop trough and over the[i]r heads walk down into the cans to fill cups. This is another picture I would like to sketch if I ~~had~~ could.

The soup and other rations were wholesome. Clothing was scarce. To cover the nudity of some the Yankees did furnish a few garments.

Here were prisoners from Roanoke Island and Fort Pulaski, who upon the whole seemed to be better off than the Newbern prisoners.[10]

Some of the Germans among the latter would sometimes discourse about music to us. It was soothing to listen at them. ~~Those~~ Some of the Irish would occasionall[y] have a fight. Sometimes were on the outside near the walls just within the guard lines. These were all the matters of interest, except the passing of vessels, and the preaching on one occasion by some Episcopalian Clergymen. Here we all got a view of the Great Eastern—the great Leviathan of the deep. The tug boats and other vessels compared with it lik[e] horseflys to the horse which th[e]y annoy.[11]

Having remained here about   we were embarked on the steamer Baltic and sailed for Fort Delaware, which place will receive more notice in the next extract than any other place has.

Leroy[12]

This modern-day aerial view of Fort Delaware on Pea Patch Island vividly illustrates the watery solitude of the Federal prisoner-of-war camp in the middle of the Delaware River. Image courtesy of Library of Congress, Prints and Photographs Division, Washington, D.C.

CHAPTER I

Fort Delaware & Pea Island
The fort, The Island—its name, condition &c. The barracks &c.

Fort Delaware is a large stronghold of the United States situated on Pea Island near the mouth of the Delaware river and fourty miles below Philadelphia.[13] The Island is near the middle of the river, and surrounded by a high embankment of dirt to prevent tide water from overflowing it. It contains about fourty acres and takes its name from the circumstance of a vessel loaded with peas having been wrecked there, before the wall or embankment was built, the peas having been scattered over the place and grown up. The island is low and marshy, and intersected by ditches and moats. There are very few trees, the most of which are immediately on the bank, and all ~~of which~~ are small. Whenever there comes a heavy rain, the Island becomes one vast mud hole, and does not soon dry off. The mud is of a peculiar kind, slimey and full of stench. The water is filthy, sickly, and brackish. Rain water is mostly used, and is by far the best that can be had, although it is kept in large tanks, where it often stagnates. A few dwellings are on the island, which are occupied by the officers in charge, together with their families[.] The fort is a massive structure of stone, and occupies about two acres of ground. The walls are about thirty feet high, filled with portholes, and has three tiers of large guns. The whole is surrounded by a moat. The place is now used for the confinement of Confederate prisoners. Besides the officers who were confined in the fort, the prisoners were at first kept in tents pitched on the low, marshy grounds: but a large portion of the island is now covered with barracks, sufficient for the confinement of more than seven thousand prisoners. The barracks are frame houses, all of which are joined together, forming rectangles, and each of which is about two hundred yards long, twenty two feet wide, and twelve feet in hight, from floor to joists. On each side are three tiers of bunks, which are six feet wide and have for their length that of the entire house. The dimensions of the main rectangle of barracks is about 200 by 300 yards★, and the inner ground is intersected by three other frame works or barracks. There are a few openings for doors and windows every few hundred

★It is perhaps smaller. I must guess not having measured

feet. Beyond the main moat and just over the water's edge ~~are~~ is the ~~open ways~~ out house several hundred feet long, an open box-like concern supported on posts. Every point of these barracks and every portion of the island is well guarded, rendering it impossible to escape. If a man were to escape the vigilance of the guard, he could not get off the Island, as the river on both sides is too wide for the best swimmer, and there is no chance of getting a boat to cross in. Every thing about the island is very disagreeable, except the barracks which are in a degree comfortable, and by far better than any thing else that a prisoner of war can expect.

CHAPTER II

*Fort Delaware

July 1862

My first visit. Our accommodations. The officers and men. Our sufferings. The rations. The water. Our quarters on a rainy day.

We arrived at this place about the 11th July 1862 on the steamship "~~The~~ Baltic" from Governor's Island, in the harbor of New York City. There were about twelve hundred prisoners on board, 100 captured at Newbern N.C. 250 at Ft. Pulaski, Geo. and 500 at Hanover C.H. in Va. and the remainder at various places.[14] We were landed on the island in row boats, and then marched to that portion of the island where there were neither barracks nor tents, counted and then ordered to give up every /thing/ we had in the shape of a weapon, together with balls caps and powder. Large pocket knives were taken as well as dirks and pistols. A strong guard was put around us, and we were left on an open morass or meadow, without shelter beneath a hot July sun. In a few days tents were given us, which we pitched upon the same ground, which was surrounded by ditches to drain ~~the ground~~ it, and a portion of which was overflowed when the tides were up. It was a damp dreary, sunny, uncomfortable place. The tents were without flooring and many prisoners without blankets. We had to shift for ourselves, as best we could. The next day a few crackers or "ironclads" as we called them, were issued to us, together with fat raw meat. About two thousand other prisoners were already here and quartered in barracks—stored away like fodder in a barn loft. The weather was intensely warm. The island is without shade trees. The prisoners were so crowded and dirty, with ~~but~~ so few priviledges and accommodations, tha~~n~~t vermin existed by thousands. All manner of filth was within the bounds of the guard lines. The consequence was that in some places the ground was sprinkled with creeping maggots, as thick as ants about an ant-hill. The Yankee officers and men were dutchmen, scraped together from the foreign refuse of the city of Philadelphia. A dutch major was in command.[15] All were a set of real "hard cases"—mean and careless and such as I lately heard them termed, "sour crouted, bench legged, tub-eating dutchmen," cowardly

*For the sake of convenience we will designate the whole Island Ft. Delaware, which it is commonly called.

and unworthy of the priviledge of guarding brave men. Shortly after landing on the island two men were sent to the guard house, for asking a few questions. Threats and blustering were common. The prisoners however were not to be terrified or scared. They were 'rebels' and manifested themselves as such. Working details were frequently made from the prisoners, to draw lumber /& dirt/ on a cart, to where carpenters were building the new barracks. Some of the prisoners refused to work, and would not be scared into it, and were consequently put in close confinement. Working I always avoided, and a Yankee has never yet caused me to do any thing of the kind. I may say that all the prisoners not only suffered from hunger and thirst, but from sickness, heat, scarcity of room and want generally. Diarrhoea and dysentary were the most common. A large majority were afflicted by these diseases. Chills and fevers were common. There were a few cases of smallpox.

Some of the men who were afflicted with the diarrhoea were so reduced that they were barely able to carry themselves a few paces, others could not do so much, and many died[.] It was a very common thing to see a cart-load of plain coffins, sometimes empty going to the hospital, and sometimes with the corpses piled one box on top of another. All the prisoners at first robust and healthy, became thin, weak, sickly and suffering for something relishable to eat[.] Every man suffered and craved for something /good/ to eat. The water and rations were so bad that the prisoners eagerly devoured all the vinager that they could obtain and then desired more. A small sutler shop or tent was near with a few edibles, but few of the prisoners had current money. Expressions of the following kind could often be heard, viz:—"I wish I had something good to eat," "I would like to have some vegitables," "I can't eat the rations we get," "I am so sick, my appetite is not sufficient for the rations we have," "I feel mighty bad," "I hope we will soon get out of this d-----d place," "I hate the Yankees more and more every day," "I will fight them harder," "I wish they would make haste with the exchange," and "I hope we will soon be in Dixie." Many complained, but others bore all with seeming content or sullen indifference. In addition to the severe warmth of the weather, sickness, the openness and lowness of the island, bad water and rations, we had but few clothes, little soap, no tubs, nothing /to/ read but a few bibles, nothing to write upon, and nothing to see or hear, but ourselves and what passed among ourselves. Horrible monotony was our constant companion. Virmin were numerous, a constant plague, and we were crowded together[.]

Twice only, each day we were marched around to the barracks which were near the fortress, and where there was a large room filled with long tables, on which were placed our bad rations and around which we stood. For each man was placed on the table a tough sour piece of black light bread, or four saltless /flinty/ crackers, which we called 'ironclads,' a piece of fat salt pork or bacon, or else a piece of beef which was sometimes fetid, and for breakfast a tin cup of bad tasted black water, made out of some queer stuff called coffee, and for dinner a cup of soup, or the water in which the beef was boiled. Sometimes but not often we would get pea soup. These two meals were served each day, one about 10 A.M., the other about 4 P.M. The tables were so close together that our backs might rub together as we stood and eat. We marched from our tents, around a pond of water across the main moat, through a filthy offensive gangway, passed through by the cook room full of what would be to others, than soldiers, a very disagreeable smell, besides the scent of that which was cooking coming up amidst the steam from a half dozen large boilers, like water tanks. From thence we passed through the interior grounds of the barracks where the other prisoners were, many of whom crowded around to see us pass, looking miserable and dirty. We were marched to the farther end of the dining room, where we entered through a narrow door, and after a considerable time of crowding pushing sweating and moving up and in by degrees, we found ourselves around the tables. Men stood as thick as /growing/ wheat. Many were ready to return as soon as they entered.

Flies were very numerous and the soup was generally well peppered with them. Sometimes there would be no less than a dozzen in one cup. After we got through we marched out at another door, and went back to our tents as we came, to loll about on the ground and in the sun, and boar away the time as best we could, until the next meal. Our own men did the cooking, there being a number of them ~~as~~ for that purpose, under the superintendance of a Yankee steward. A whole beef or hog might be boiled up together in any one of the boilers. The meat was thrown on a platform chopped up with an ax and then pitched into the boilers. The bread was baked elsewhere, and bad enough to blast the reputation of the most filthy bakeries in our largest cities.

The water was impure unhealthy warm and offensive. The most of the time w~~h~~e had to drink the river water dipped up near the bank, and when the tides were up it was brackish. All the cooking was done with the river water. A few times we got a drink of water which was brought on vessels from Brandywine creek, warm, but purer and much better.[16]

The Yankees used ice. When a barrel of water was brought to the prisoners they would push around it, scuffel heave and set, until all was gone. A set of drunkards would not be more determined around a whiskey barrel.

On a rainy day all the ground around our quarters and wherever else we were allowed to tramp became one vast mud and splashy hole. All the ground was soft and watery. As an old woman would say in either rainy or clear weather "it was awful." Pea Island /or Ft. Delaware/ is indeed the <u>Inferno</u> of the United States.

CHAPTER III

Fort Delaware

The ice house. Its shade. Prisoners reposing. Scuffles for pieces of ice. The wounded. The sick. Selfishness. Washing. Sleeping. Pastimes. News papers. Expected exchange. My time, how spent. Sickness, thirst, and hunger. The oath.

Upon a little artificial kno~~w~~ll which rose from the level like a potato hill was an ice house, surrounded by small willow trees. The ice kept in this house was for the use of the Yankee garrison, and under no circumstance were the prisoners allowed to have any. No water that could be had there, was fit for use without ice in it; yet the prisoners had to drink it all the time without any thing. The water was warm, filthy, and nauseous; and consequently ice was craved as much as any thing else. Even without ice the Yankees had better water than the prisoners. The shade about this knoll was a great luxury to the prisoners; but not sufficient for the accommodation of all. Every day, at all times, when the sun was shining, every foot of this hillock, was covered with prisoners. It was mostly disagreeably crowded. Some had their blankets, and would stretch out at full length, and their remain during the day. Others were lying ~~are~~ or sitting whichever was convenient. They were like a large flock of sheep, taking shelter from the burning rays of the sun beneath the spreading branches of a small cluster of trees, far out in an open field. There they reposed, almost mute craving cold water or dainties, with far less contentment, and about the same human enjoyment, and I may say with less cleanliness than a flock of sheep. There was nothing else to cheer, not even power of speach.

Every day one of the Yankees would come to the place with a wheel barrow to get ice. As he would throw it out a number would be standing around to gather up the crumbs. He was not allowed to give any to the prisoners but sometimes he would be kind enough to let a piece fall, as if by accident, and then they would struggle after it, like so many avaricious boys after a silver coin. Whoever got it would be selfish enough to appropriate to his own use. It was invaluable. He would put it in water and then satiate his long thirst.

The wounded, most of whom~~e~~ were taken at the Battle of Seven Pines, June 1st/62, and were convalescing, were confined opposite us, in tents, pitched likewise in the sun.[17] They had the advantage of only one large apple tree for shade under which most of them reclined during the day. There were about 100. Many were cripples, and such as had been severely wounded. Some with one leg, others with one arm[.] The sick were very numerous, many of whom~~e~~ remained in their tents, and the worst were taken to the hospital. There were two hospitals, both disagreeably situated on the level in the sun. Some days there would be an average of 4, 5, and more deaths. The patients would linger and die, suffering much for delicasies. Some died of despondency and extreme weakness. Hundreds were thin and emaciated from the effects of diarrhoea and dysentery, which were common to nearly all the prisoners, in consequence of bad diet, bad water and I may say bad every thing.

So needful were all, that when any one obtained any advantage over the rest in clothing, edibles, or any other comforts, he unscrupulously applied all to himself. Selfishness was so common, that the smallest favors were not expected. Every one depended upon himself. The general mottos seemed to be, ["]<u>To let alone and be let alone</u>," "<u>Every man for himself and God for us all</u>." However there were some, who, if they could stealthily take any thing, would do so. Whatever a man had he kept securely by him, or else it was taken. Self was the great motive power all the time.

Around on the low muddy banks of the ditches and moats many of the men were collected each day washing the dirty ragged clothes, without tubs or wash boards. Some would have to go naked until they could wash their clothes and dry them, or else let them dry on their backs. The water in the main moat passed through from the river, by the prisoner's tents, and thence around the fort and back into the river. All manner of filth would collect in it; and the water was muddy and offensive: yet it was as good as we had for any purpose. The only shade was the clump of willows refered to above; ~~as~~ but they were not on the same ground with the tents.

Sleeping was the greatest comfort; yet it was not that pleasant refreshing slumber which all have experienced at home in a good bed, with clean quilts and other surroundings. On dirty boards with a few dusty blankets in the low moist ground, beneath the pavilion through which the heat of the sun would stream if in day time, the prisoner would recline to ease away the wearisome hours. Sleep was a friend[.]

Pastimes were in great demand, but were scarce. All reading matter that could be obtained was very acceptable. An occasional newspaper, besides a few bibles and testaments was all. A few played cards, others whittled, and wallowed about, whilst many slept. Sleeping however was not so easy to come at as may be immagined. There was nothing tempting any more than to pass the hours which weighed so heavily. The expected exchange was our greatest cheer. Every paper was eagerly sought after to see what was said about it. Negotiations were in progress, and the great fear of all was that the commissioners might not agree, or if they did agree that even then something would turn up to prevent the exchange; so little confidence had we in the Yankee Government. Before leaving for City Point we were removed to the new barracks part of which had been finished. There we remained about one week.[18]

My time was spent in a very cheerless way. I had no way to pass off agreeably, the hours which weighed heavily. There was nothing of any kind that I could obtain to read, except a testament. My last resource was my thoughts, which brought very little comfort. Had comforts of no kind, but bore all complacently and with seeming content. Had three companions with me in the same tent, who were ~~of~~ a very little comfort, but were good fellows. The association did not suit me. Here for the first time I began to get sick. The food and water were so sorry that diarrhoea and dizziness was the consequence. Sometimes I would have to leave off going to meals, because of temporary blindness and virtigo. Often my appetite was too weak for either the water or the food.

This is a very uncommon thing in a stout healthy person like myself. All the previous confinement and privations I had endured without the least sickness. Here it was necessary to use vinager in the water or the essence of Jamaica Ginger provided it could be obtained.[19] Something to prevent as much as possible the bad taste and smell, which was enough to turn the appetite. Acids were necessary to health and strength. A pair of boots that I purchased in New York and intended to carry home I had to sell. Was always craving a cool drink of water, and something fit to eat, but endured all, as one who accepted privations for his lot. Depended upon myself. Asked nothing and expected nothing.★

About three hundred of the thirty five hundred prisoners took the oath of allegiance to the U.S. Government. These we looked upon as the cowardly off scouring of our army. We felt that the tares were thus gathered from among the wheat. They were seperated from the other prisoners, and always kept out of the way, for fear of their former comrades who were true men. They looked as if they felt themselves disgraced. They were not fit to be respected by brave and true men on either side.

★My thoughts were occupied much of the time in meditating an escape, which seemed impossible. I could not have travelled much because of sickness. but still hoped.

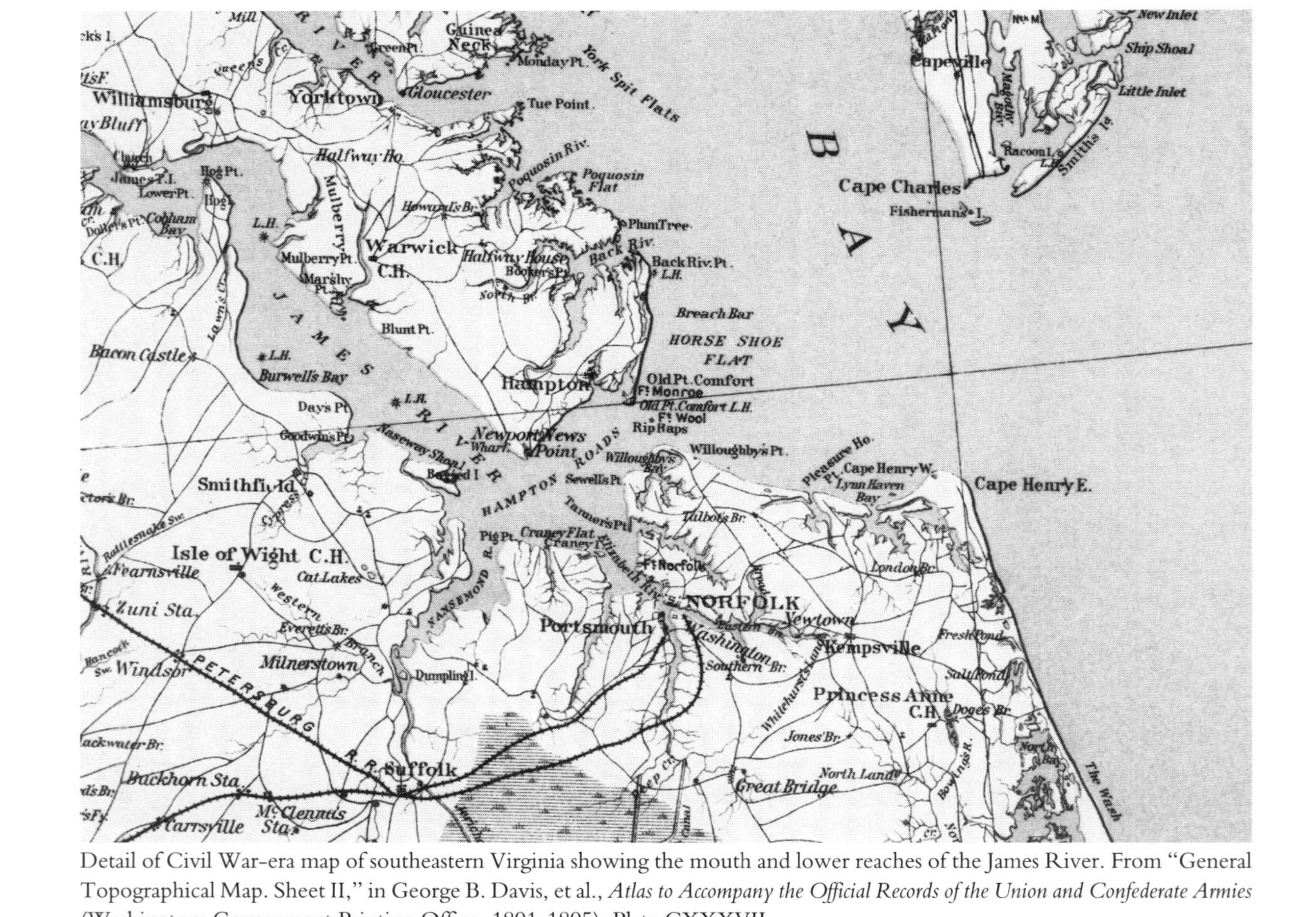

Detail of Civil War-era map of southeastern Virginia showing the mouth and lower reaches of the James River. From "General Topographical Map. Sheet II," in George B. Davis, et al., *Atlas to Accompany the Official Records of the Union and Confederate Armies* (Washington: Government Printing Office, 1891-1895), Plate CXXXVII.

CHAPTER IV

The Exchange

July 31st/62

Ships at the landing. Leave our quarters with much gladness. Embark on the steam ships 'Eagle' and 'Merrimac.' The press on board, heat &c. Arrival and stay at Old Point Comfort. Proceed up the James River. Anchor at City Point. Fight at Malvern Hill. Are landed at Aikin's or Verina. Gladness.

For several days previous to our leaving the island the masts of vessels could be seen at the landing, which gave us fresh hope of soon leaving that accursed place. We had already seen in the papers that a cartel of exchange had been agreed upon, and tra/n/sportation ordered for the prisoners, and ships about the landing assured us that it was so.[20] Before we left our quarters all were told to come out who did not want to go back to Dixie; but very few responded. Such as did were hooted at and scowled upon, and made to look like puppies just whipped for sucking eggs. Those who had taken the 'Oath' looked like criminals, and were unable to meet the glances of their former comrades. They could not even answer their taunts. They felt bad and looked as they /felt./ We leave our quarters amidst much scrambling and in a hurry to quit the place so much detested. We march out, but it is a long time before we are all crowded on board the ships. We were towed out to the ships on canal boats, crowded together as thick as we could stand. Was placed on board the Merrimac a very large steam ship, with hull encased in iron. About 1600 or more were put on this one ship. We were thicker than bees in a beehive. Was among the first who came on board and consequently had to go down into the hole of the vessel where there was neither light nor air, and there remain until all were aboard.

It was the last day of July and the weather was very warm. The heat in this part of the vessel was oppressive and the atmosphere suffocating, all rendered doubly so, by the numbers who were breathing the same air, and continually pouring in, blocking up the narrow gang ways and shutting out light and air. Every pore of the skin seemed to have been sudenly opened, and the sweat was oozing through copiously. After all were aboard, with some difficulty and much hurry lest we should be completely shut in from air, we got on deck, and gladly breathed fresh air once more, and there every man that could remained. The ship was crowded worse than any chicken coop, except the portions where the Yankees occupied. All could not lay down nor set down, nor move with any ease from place to place. They passed the night like hogs. Many of the /able/ sick were on board and occupied the bunks. They suffered much from heat and want. A few carckers were scattered among us for provision. We were so crowded that it was difficult to ration us. The press was so great that passing and repassing had to stop. The gangways could not be kept clear. About midnight the vessel got under weigh and when morning came we were near the mouth of the bay, where we swept around Cape Henlopen, and passed out to sea. The two ships were always in sight of each other, but part of the time out of view of land. When night came the beacon on Cape Henry could be seen. The width of Chesapeak Bay was the distance to Old Point Comfort. We anchored at Fortress Monroe before midnight. The comfortless journey was endured with patience and hope of exchange.

Aug. 2d/62

When morning came the prisoners were more than anxious for the journey to be resumed. They were all the time fearful that something would turn up, which would cause them to be taken back to Purgatory.★ The view of Old Point, Willoughby's and Sewells Points, and the Rip-Raps in the midst of the water, and a number of vessels in the harbor, were ~~of~~ some relief to them in their crowded confinement, since they had so long been shut out from the view of every thing.[21] About 10 A.M. we were on vessels of lighter draft preparatory to going up James River viz. The State of Mane Catskill, Kennebec and some others; the former of which my crowd was on. Rations of hard bread and coffee were issued to us during the day. The meat was so fat and greasy that it might be wrung like a dish rag. So eager were the most of them to get their rations that issuing was any thing else but pleasant. They would crowd and press and jam together and push forward. Part would 'flank' and others would storm out to mind the 'flankers,' "Dont let them flank you there" "Look there he'll flank you" &c. Some flankers would get a cup of coffee drink it up and commence flanking again, and so on. Some did not get any. The narrow gangways of the vessel rendered it still more disagreeable.

★Fort Delaware or Pea Island

Aug 3d. After remaining in the Road the greater part of the day, to our great satisfaction the vessels were ordered to proceed up James River, taking care not to neglect flying a 'flag of truce' on the way.[22] Near Newport News the vessels came to anchor and there we remained during the night.

Aug 4th. Proceeded on up the River. The scenery on either side was beautiful and refreshing. The morning was clear and pleasant. As the day advanced it became very warm, and the heat on the vessels in their crowded condition was oppressive. In the lower parts of the ships it was suffocating. Some of the prisoners died from hea~~d~~t and suffocation—two on the State of Mane and several on the other~~s~~ ships. We came to anchor at City Point about noon and thus the prisoners felt themselves wearied with impatience. They were still apprehensive that they would be taken back from whence they came. It was bandied from vessel to vessel that we had to go back to Ft. Delaware, and this was very annoying to some. During a portion of the day the distant roar of artillery could be heard. We afterwards learned that it was a fight at Malvern Hill, where a considerable number of the enemy advanced against our advance guard, and took the Hill. They were driven from it the day following without a fight.[23] The hot day wore away heavily. Every man was wet with sweat. Some were overcome and fainted. Some whiled away the time looking over their clothes for virmin. This was an old and common sight.

Aug 5th/62. This was the best day of all. We weighed anchor and proceed up the River to Verina or Aikins Landing.[24] Our pickets could be seen. The banks near farm houses were lined with darkies, waiving hands and hankerchiefs, with many grotesque demonstrations. To our great delight we were landed on Dixie soil.

Cpl. Columbus L. Turner was among the first group of prisoners of war exchanged under the auspices of the Dix-Hill cartel. He rejoined his regiment and brigade, which during his nearly five months of imprisonment had been assigned to A. P. Hill's division of Thomas J. Jackson's command, near Gordonsville, Virginia. Whether he arrived in time to participate in the Battle of Cedar Mountain on August 9, in which the Thirty-third N.C. lost six killed and thirty wounded, is uncertain, but he was present for company muster two days later. Nor is there specific record of his service in the ensuing campaign, which included the Battle of Second Manassas, where Branch's brigade was engaged in severe fighting for two days; the engagement at Ox Hill, in which the brigade advanced in the midst of a blinding rainstorm; the brief investment of Harpers Ferry, after which Hill's division accepted the Federal surrender; and the Battle of Antietam, where the division arrived in the nick of time to secure the Confederate right flank after a forced march from Harpers Ferry, and in which General Branch was killed. The losses of the Thirty-third during the campaign from Second Manassas to Antietam were relatively light, with five killed and thirty-three wounded. On October 6, Corporal Turner was promoted to third (or junior second) lieutenant of Company A.

At the Battle of Fredericksburg on December 13, Branch's former brigade, then commanded by Brig. Gen. James H. Lane, was posted near the center of Jackson's line, which comprised the right of the Confederate position. The Federal assault found and exploited a gap in A. P. Hill's front between Lane's right and the left of James J. Archer's brigade, the unhappy result of marshy terrain. Despite stout resistance, Lane's North Carolinians were driven back but, reinforced, eventually regained their original position. As Turner later recalled the battle: "When a single file of our command stood in the open on the railroad at Fredericksburg to receive the on-slaught of double columns of the enemy, and when looking them in the eye at the track on the other side, we were ordered to fall back to reserves in the woods. With rapid speed we did so." The regiment suffered nine killed and thirty-two wounded during the battle. Afterwards, Lee's army settled into winter quarters.

At some point during the winter, Lieutenant Turner went home. His compiled service record indicates that he tried to resign his commission on January 15, 1863, but there is no further documentation to indicate what became of the request. The company muster roll for January-February 1863 reported him "absent without leave." We do not know his reasons for leaving the army or for attempting to resign (though his subsequent effort in early June is likely suggestive), nor precisely why or when he returned. He noted in his diary in July the sale of a gold watch that his father had given him in April, perhaps as a parting memento upon his return to the army. The records do not indicate whether or not he was back with the regiment in time to participate in the Battle of Chancellorsville in early May, during which skirmishers from the Eighteenth North Carolina, another of Lane's regiments, fired the fatal volley that mortally wounded Stonewall Jackson.

While Lee's army nursed its wounds, reorganized its command structure, and prepared for the next move after Chancellorsville, Columbus L. Turner was still attempting to extricate himself from an undesirable situation. On June 5, he again sought to resign his commission in a note addressed to the captain commanding the company:

> I do respectfully take this opportunity of tendering my resignation . . . provided permission be granted me to report in Raleigh N.C. or some other place in that state. My reasons for so doing will be apparent from the

Capt. Joseph H. Saunders of Company A, Thirty-third North Carolina Regiment, the company officer who approved Lieutenant Turner's resignation because of a low opinion of his subordinate's competency and efficiency. From Walter Clark, ed., *Histories of the Several Regiments and Battalions from North Carolina in the Great War, 1861-'65* (Goldsboro: Nash Brothers, 1901), 2: facing page 537.

> following, which I hope will be sufficient to insure [?] its acceptance. First, In consequence of my father's feeble health I design taking upon myself the management of a cotton factory and other business, where I am very much needed or some one else. Second, I wish to dissolve my connexion with this company as I am somewhat disagreeably associated, believing I can do as good service elsewhere in some other.

The precise nature of this disagreeable association is unclear. Capt. Joseph H. Saunders had succeeded Robert V. Cowan in command of the company when Cowan was promoted to the field and staff of the Thirty-third N.C. in April 1862. After Chancellorsville, Saunders was also promoted to major. Capt. Henry Hyer Baker of Halifax County succeeded him in command of Company A, effective May 13, though apparently the transfer of authority had not been accomplished as of June 5. It was Saunders who approved Turner's request that day, cryptically noting: "As I do not deem him as efficient or competent neither does he avail himself of opportunity to improve."

As Lieutenant Turner's resignation slowly made its way up the chain of command to army headquarters, he was sick with an unspecified illness and admitted to General Hospital No. 4 in Richmond on June 11, under the care of Dr. James P. Reed, surgeon-in-charge of the hospital for commissioned officers. While Turner was in the hospital, General Lane returned his request to his company commander to inquire as to which regiment Turner would like to be reassigned. Captain Baker informed Lane that the lieutenant was absent sick, "with no probability of his returning soon." Turner was released from the hospital on June 18, but according to a later entry in his diary, he did not leave Richmond until June 22. By then, his regiment had broken camp near Fredericksburg and started the northward march towards the Potomac. Finally, on June 29, Turner's resignation reached the field desk of Maj. Gen. William Dorsey Pender, who led Hill's former division after the latter's promotion to corps command. Pender routinely approved the request, "as this officer is represented [by Saunders] as being very inefficient & would no doubt be better in the ranks." The resignation was approved later that day in the field office of General Lee, with the notation that Turner was still absent sick in Richmond. The order of approval stated that his name was to be given to the Confederate enrolling officer in Iredell County. However, events of the ensuing four days dictated a different course for Columbus L. Turner, who for the second time in sixteen months, returned from sick leave just in time to be taken prisoner.[25]

CHAPTER V

Diary

July 3d 1863. The advance upon the enemy was made in two complete lines across an open field, from a distance of half mile. The enemy were behind a stone wall fence, crags and other breastworks. The cliffs were posted with sharpshooters. The whole crest of the hills bristled with artillery. For two hours three hundred cannon had been letting fly their pent up wrath, when the order for an advance was given. Amidst the scream of shells and whizzing of grape and canister we steadily advanced. Soon the rattle of musketry extended along the whole lines and men fell right and left like autumnal leaves. The position of the enemy was carried in some places, but the enemy sent forward reinforcements in time to save the day. In the confusion which prevailed, [I] became a prisoner. In my company Capt H. H. Baker and Lieut. Cowan, T. A., were killed, also as reported Or. Sergt. R. W. Shields, and Priv. Bowers who died afterwards.[26] Others were seriously wounded. The field of Gettysburg was fatal to many of our best officers and soldiers. Maj. Gen. Trimble who was in command of our Div. was wounded and taken on this part of the field.[27] Lieuts. Cooper,* Watson, Caldwell and Gibson of the 33rd N.C. were also killed.[28] The greater portion of the Yankee army were scattered to the winds—the straglers were innumerable. All were preparing to give up the field. We, the prisoners, were marched about three miles to the rear and closely guarded.

July 4th 1863, Saturday.—About 23 hundred had already been collected in the lot where we were guarded. At midnight all were arroused to be hurried off to the rail-road 22 miles distant, without provision. We were guarded hither by the 2d. Penn. Cav.[29] In front and rear was a squadron of Cavalry and a line of guards on each side, all mounted. We marched till about day light before halting to rest. The day opened warm and we suffered much from thirst and fatigue. Every possible chance we would get water. Some of the citizens brought water to the road. The heat was so oppressive, the march so tiresome, and sweating so free, that we suffered /much/ for water. We passed through Little Town, and arrived at Westminister Md. about noon, marched through the town, crowded with wagons and Federal soldiers—their

*severely wounded, but now well

sick and wounded.[30] Slurs were cast at us and as readily returned. We were confined in a lot South-east of the town. The sun shone with great warmth, but was soon overclouded and it rained hard the bal~~l~~ance of the evening. All were drenched to the skin. None ~~scarcely~~ had a change of clothes and besides that every blanket was wringing wet. Raw fat meat and crackers with some sugar and coffee were issued to us during the evening. Many had no way of carrying rations. In the rain the coffee and sugar became a mess and we were rationed with difficulty. About sun-down we were marched back through town to the depot, and remained during the night in a lot. The people were not allowed to give us any thing. They were pushed away both men and women.

Sunday

July 5th A train of about twenty five box cars took us to Baltimore. All along the way the ladies showed signs of sympathy. They would have aided us with necessaries but were not allowed. Several were arrested. Some were affraid to speak to us or show any sign of sympathy. The poor were enthusiastic in their demonstrations. At Baltimore the 51st. Mass. Regt. and a squadron of cavalry guarded us to Ft. McHenry.[31] The distance from the depot through the city to the fort was five miles. We passed through in the early part of the night. The walks were lined and crowded and the rebels filled the city with yells. The guards were very strict with the populace. Several arrests were made as we passed through. At no time could I find a chance to escape.

July 6th. The officers were seperated from the men. Rations were issued to us for two meals. We were crowded together in the barracks. The Yankees told us many lies about their successes. They enrolled our names and counted us over and over again and again. After getting a few pieces of hard bread and fat meat we were embarked on the Steamer Kennebec near the mouth of the Patapsco river about 6 o'clock in the evening. The vessel was much crowded. About three hundred officers were on board, besides a number of men.

Tuesday July 7th. Far down the Chesapeak Bay and still on our way to that hated place, Purgatory, Ft. Delaware. I made some effort to get up an attempt to capture the vessel and run it to the Virginia shore, but felt that influence was liking and then some were opposed to it and others talked as if willing but would do nothing towards conserting a plan. The danger was preferable to Ft. Delaware.

Wednesday July 8th. 1863. Out at sea. A heavy rain fell. Entered the mouth of Delaware Bay the same morning. Arrived at the fort early in the evening. I felt very bad at the idea of paying that place a second visit almost on the anniversary of my former visit. At the landing we first heard of the fall of Vicksburg which we in no wise believed, knowing the Yankees to be such monstrous liars, and tremendous boasters.[32] We were landed and marched to the new barracks, where all were searched, for any thing that they might choose to call contraband. Sword belts and spurs as well as pistols were taken, whenever found, except in a few cases. Here money of all kinds was often taken, In some cases it was taken to be returned again. From some both Federal and Confederate money was taken, whilst from others none was taken. The officers of the line were all confined together in one portion of the barracks, and the field and staff were confined in the fort. The bunks were about 100 yards long, on these we took up lodgings. A passage between from one end to the other. We eat one meal that day served in the dining room, which was filled with long tables like work benches, around which we stood and eat hard bread and some beef. This place had any thing else, but a pleasant smell. The floor was like the bottom of a floored pig-pen. Fetid mud, with which the whole yard abounded was brought in on the feet of so many men, that it was pasted all over the floor. The tables were the length of the whole room, and so close together that the backs of those at different tables might rub together.

CHAPTER VI

Fort Delaware

July 1863

The prisoners generally. Disagreeableness of the place. Sickness.
Cruelty of the Yankees. Gambling, speculating and traiding.
Necessities, inconvenencies &c.
Diary

There were about five thousand prisoners at this place, most of whom were taken at Gettysburg and many of the rest in the west.[33] They were tolerably well clad, but had only one suit, either of outer or under clothes. Meals were furnished to them twice a day, which were served with great crowding and much patience and waiting in co[n]sequence of the great numbers thrown together. No one can well know what it is to live in such a place without experiencing it. The cook room was indeed a filthy looking place, and all the water used was filthy and impure also. The whole ground that the prisoners had use of was nearly all the time ankle deep in mud and sloppy water, because of the lowness of the ground which would not soon dry off after a little rain. There was nothing to cheer the sight but the ugliness of the place,—the space which we occupied—and our own dirty phisiognomies, which were so common, that they were very irksome, and annoying and depressing to ones spirits. If some private corner could have been found where there was scarcely any person to be seen, it would have been by far the most agreeable. Men were so numerous and nothing else but men, to which kind of animals we had been so long accostoned, that the sight was rather tiresome than pleasing. The foremost maxim of all was "Every man for himself and God for us all.["] "O tempores! O Mores!"[34]

The hospitals were filled with the sick. It seemed as if some fearful epidemic was raging. Ten deaths in a day were common. Fever, diarrhoia and dysentary were the most prevolent. Besides those at hospitals the majority of the remainder were afflicted with disordered bowels. Water, rations and every thing else seemed to induce sickness. The battle of life and death was constantly raging. On this sickly island hundreds of our Southern braves have become victims to disease far from home, country, and sympathizing friends. Numerous mounds of earth will long testify to the bleaching bones of Southerners, lying beneath on the shores of the

Delaware, as well as those of the Rappahannock.[35] Here is the grave of the patriot who yielded up his life in his country's cause as well as there. Here he lies unwept, except by a very few, unsung and unknown, far from the place of his childhood. His greatest joy was a good conscience. He suffered on the march, endured privations of every kind, and depression of spirits, and many toils and mishaps. Here he lies to wake no more to the sound of battle. Death, the last battle, has been fought. Melancholy, longings, cravings and blunted prospects hasten the deaths of some. Whatever be the fate of a soldier he ought to submit to it, and content himself as far as practicable. The path that he travels leads through many and various uncirtainties. He should endure all without surprise or disappointment. Many would be better off if it were their disposition.

Meanness and cruelty characterize the Yankee soldiers at this place and at once stamp~~s~~ them as base & cowardly minions of a cruel government. Cruelty to defenseless prisoners is a cirtain mark of cowardice. The Yankee soldiers in the field treat prisoners with a great deal more kindliness than those who are garrisoned in the rear, and are never in danger of battle. Brave men always treat their prisoners better. A man ~~that~~ who will unnecessarily strike one than has his hands tied, is the man to run or keep at a respectful distance when he is loose. It was common for the sentinels to strike with their guns any of the prisoners and not only to strike but to shoot among them, both killing and wounding and that too when it was not necessary. One man was killed whilst quietly reposing in his bunk,—the shot being intended for another.

Gambling perhaps never was more extensively and continually followed than at this place. A whole quarter of an acre of ground was covered with crowds of men playing and betting at chuckaluck, keno, faro and various games at cards, from sunup until sundown. The chucking of the dice of more than half dozen different banks could be heard at the same time during the whole day.[36] 'Confed' seemed to be superabundant. $1000 and more were often won or lost. Five cents in greenbacks or one dollar in Confederate was the lowest bet. The greenbacks were worth 20 & 25 times as much as the Confederate. A good chew of tobacco was considered to be worth /about/ 25 cts in Confederates.

Scores /of/ speculated on a small scale. Those that had a few greenbacks would buy from the sutler a few cakes or a little cheese or butter and bread and some molasses and sell to those that had the Confederate for abott thirty times what they gave. These petty

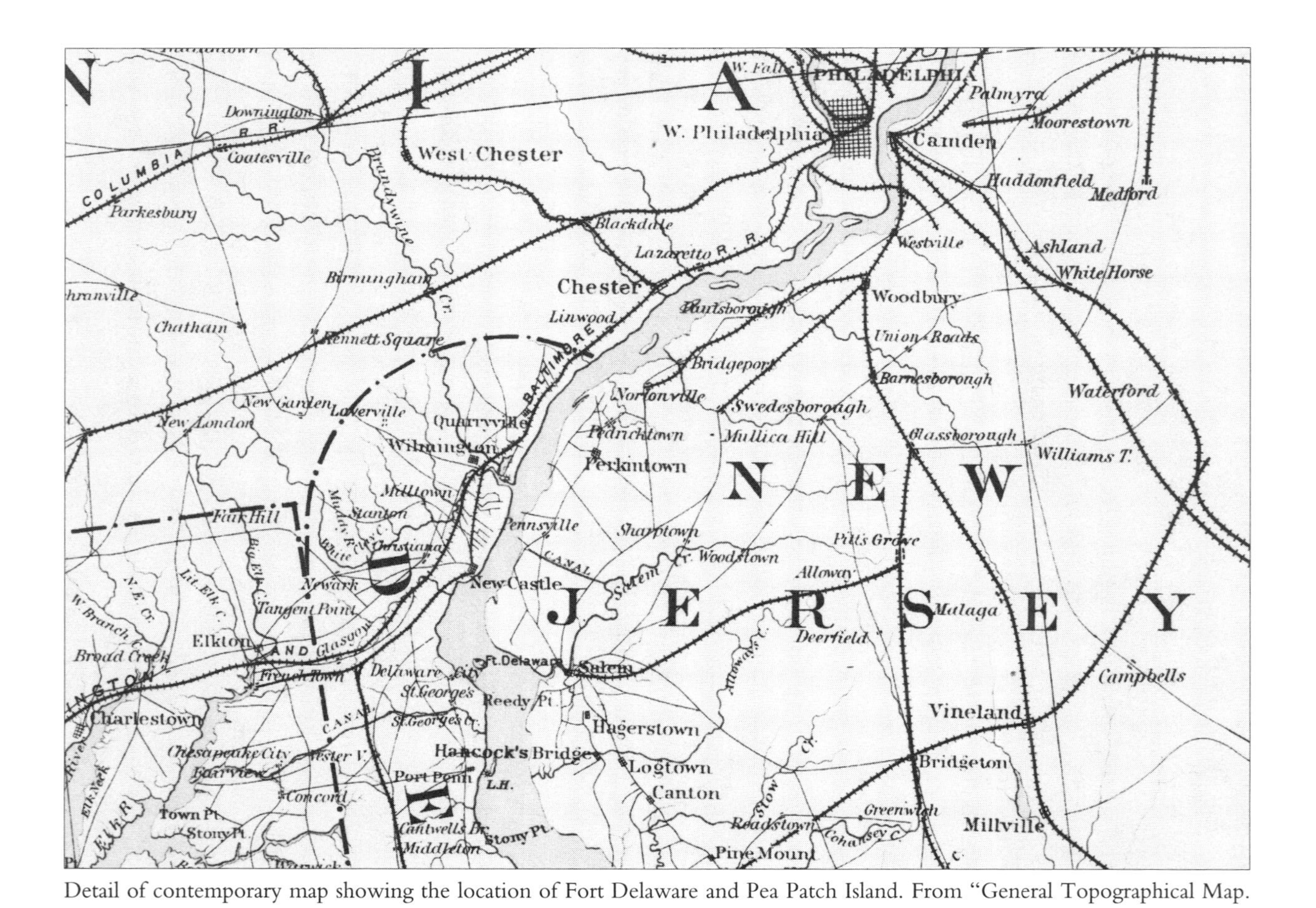

Detail of contemporary map showing the location of Fort Delaware and Pea Patch Island. From "General Topographical Map. Sheet I," in Davis, *Atlas to Accompany the Official Records*, Plate CXXXVI.

speculators could be seen sitting all over the muddy yard all day long, or as long as the sutler shop was open, selling a few hands full of provision or tobacco, and then returning to the sutlers and buying again; and in this way some kept themselves busy all the time. Many had no money of any kind and were as a matter of course in such a place reduced to great straits. The ill, scanty fare of the Yankees was all they could get. The necessities and inconveniences of these five thousand men huddled together were greater than most persons can imagine. Dirty and without change of raiment pennyless, half sick hungry and without cool water, crowded and without any thing to read, they had to suffer the oppression of endless monotony from day to day. Such was my condition among the rest, that after a long time and much hesitation, I sold a gold watch for fourty dollars, which had been given me by my father in April; and for which reason I prized it very much and intended to keep it, but necessity at last prevailed. Hoping we would soon be exchanged I began to sell some of the money for Confederate with the prospect of buying another for the same in Richmond, but on the 16th of July we signed a parole of honour to go to Johnson's Island and left that purgatory on the 18th.[37]

Saturday July 18th. 1863

We left the prison barracks with willingness and the assurance that Johnson's Island would be better than Pea Island or Ft. Delaware; for we could not believe that there was a worse place in the United States, if as bad. About four hundred of us, all officers, were embarked on the steamer 'Daniel Webster.' We proceeded up the Delaware river, and were delighted with a view of the fine scenery on either side, although under adverse circumstances. We had a very interresting view of Delaware City and especially the city of Wilmington, with its towering steaples and dwellings situate on rising ground and extending from the shore far back towards the interior. ~~Havre de grace~~ Newcastle in Maryland is a neat village situated immediately on the Southern bank ~~and~~ which was burned by the British in the War of 1812, and of which we had a nice view.[38] The smiling home steads that came under our view ~~would~~ rekindle/d/ in me a desire to see the peaceful times gone by, and to enjoy the pleasures of home,—free from wandering and molestations. Finally came a view of the forts, wharves, & suburbs of Philadelphia on the South side and Camden in New Jersey on the opposite side of the river. Cars on the Pennsylvania Central R.R. were run down to the landing, on which we took passage to Pittsburgh Penn. We passed through Swaney Street Phila. The people crowded around the cars with whom we had considerable amusement, and than whom I never saw a more homely and motley-looking mixed crowd. Some ladies told us that a great many of our wounded passed through there and were well cared for. Some were around the cars selling cakes & such like to all that would buy. Any papers that the citizens ~~would~~ g~~i~~ave us were ordered to be returned by the Yankee guard. Some wanted a rebel button or ring or any /small/ thing that was rebel. We crossed the Schuylkill river near the water works on a turning bridge, very high and long. We traveled all night and in the morning were at Harrisburg the capital of the state. The people through the state had just commenced cutting wheat.—crops good. Corn was three and four feet high. Sunday July 19th. The day was cloudy with sprinkles of rain in the morning. Passed over the Susquehannah river on a bridge 5 or 600 yards long—river shallow and rocky—a canal along the bank. The country is very hilly and broken. Every now and then we passed a town, mostly of a sombre appearance. People seemed to be clever, but the guard was the reverse and would act harshly towards the citizens. Passed through four or five tunnels in the mountains and arrived at Pittsburg about sundown where the people pressed thick and tight around the cars. Changed cars—traveled all night, and Monday July 20th. were at Lyons Ohio. During the day passed three or four trains loaded with cattle. Changed cars again at Mansfield O. and arrived at Sandusky City about sundown.

CHAPTER I

Johnson's Island
Aug. 1863

Its situation and condition. United States military prison, or Bastile

Johnson's Island is situated in the south western portion of Lake Erie, three miles from Sandusky City, Ohio. It contains three hundred acres and was purchased by the owner, whose name it bears, about ten years ago for seven thousand dollars. It contains a great deal of wood land, and produces grapes in great abundance, which have ample time to ripen and can be had a greater portion of the year than else where, in these northern regions, because the constant breezes from the lake, as it is supposed prevents frost. The vines are planted in hills about eight feet apart and cultivated like corn. The timber is principally, ash, burch, lynn, elm, and box———[39]

The United States rented fourty acres since the breaking out of the war for five hundred dollars, and afterwards built prisons for the confinement of Confederate soldiers and other prisoners. Four/teen/ acres are enclosed by palings ten or twelve feet high, within which are thirteen prison houses or blocks including a hospital. Four feet from the top of the enclosure is a platform four feet wide which is constantly patroled by sentinels, eighteen in number, who watch the movements of the prisoners and allow none to approach nearer than within thirty feet of the palings, the line of stakes being that distance from the enclosure. The prison houses are two stories high and placed in two straight rows facing each other. Eeach building is about one hundred feet long and well supplied with bunks. About fourty paces in rear of the blocks, ~~as they are termed are the prisons~~ 15 by ten feet, ~~ten~~ thirteen in number, beneath which are sinks. About fifty paces further to the rear and nearer the lake, are two pumps, which bring water from the lake. In the south eastern corner are the cells. At the north eastern and also the south western corner is a blockhouse, containing a twelve pound howitzer, in position, loaded and manned by six soldiers. A larger sutler shop is on the inside. On the outside are other houses, for the garrison, stores &c. The place is garrisoned by four hundred soldiers, Commanded by Major Pierson.[40] The whole cost the government $40,000.

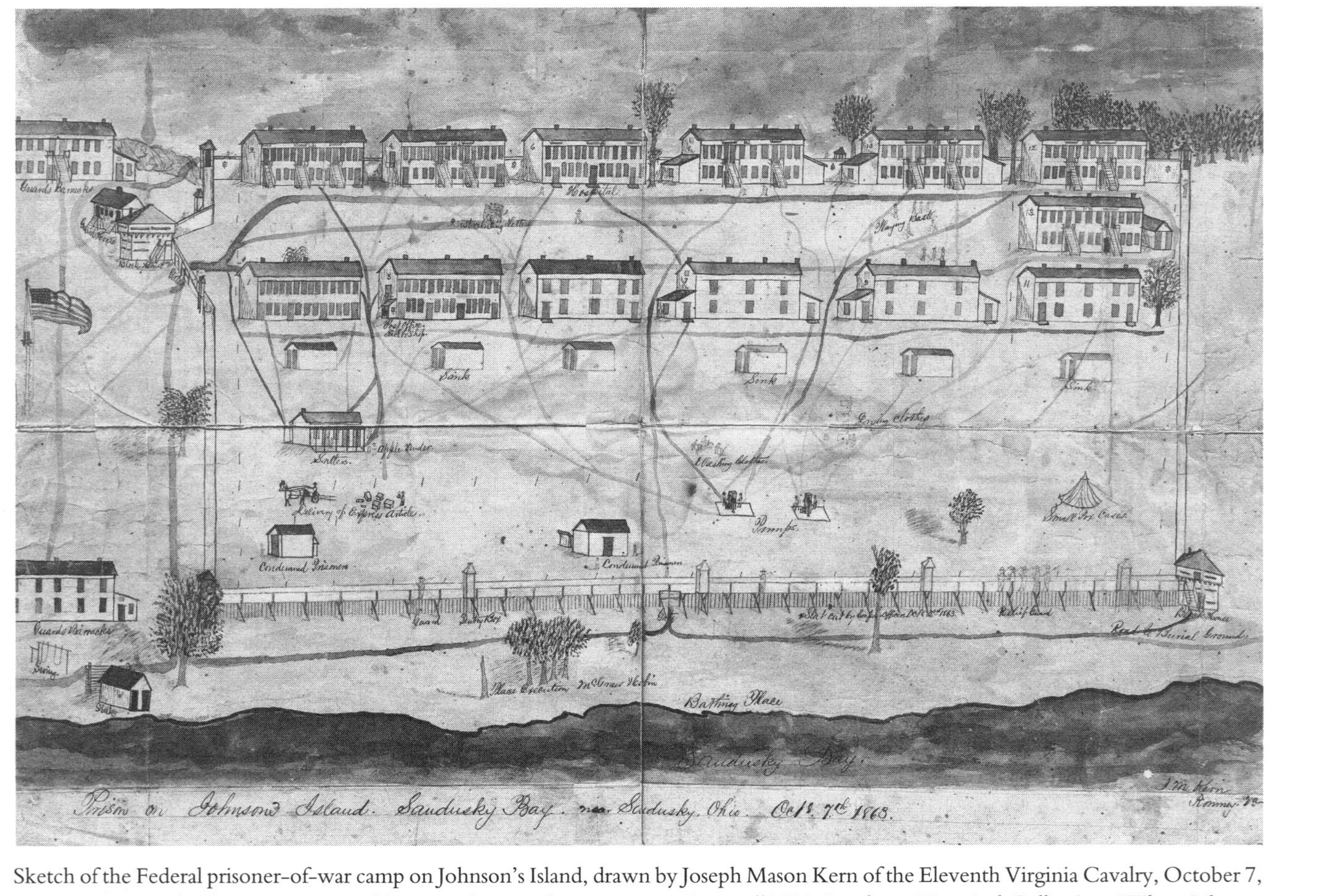

Sketch of the Federal prisoner-of-war camp on Johnson's Island, drawn by Joseph Mason Kern of the Eleventh Virginia Cavalry, October 7, 1863. From Scrapbook, 1861-1865, Folder 2, in the Joseph Mason Kern Papers #2526, Southern Historical Collection, Wilson Library, University of North Carolina at Chapel Hill.

CHAPTER II

My arrival here. Disposition of the prisoners—number and accommodations. Settling down for a stay of considerable duration. Rules and regulations. Contrasted with Pea Island.

Four hundred and thirty officers left Fort Delaware on the 18th July/63. and arrived here on the 20th, myself among the number. We left Sandusky City on the little steamer Island Queen, before dark and embarked at the wharf on Johnson's Island, about 8 o'clock.[41] The night was dark and dismal and before we were assigned to our quarters were sprinkled with rain. The officers counted us three or four times to make sure that the exact number were there, and then we were marched off by eighties to our quarters each eighty constituting a mess and occupying one half of a block. We were marched from the outside to the enclosure of the prison grounds, beneath the platform on which the sentinels walk, a little gate was opened and we were soon on the inside, safe and without any chance of escape, within the confines of this military 'Bastile.' The night being dark and drizzly I could not tell what sort of place it was, but it seemed to be any thing else but a pleasant abiding place. The first thing that called our attention on entering was the prisoners already domiciled, calling out from the windows, to know where we were from. "What regiments—any Georgians, North Carolinians, or such a Miss/is/sippi regiment or Virginia" as the case might be. My mess were soon safely ensconced in block No. 5. where every one was hurrying about to get the most convenient bunk, and looking around to see what there might /be/ that he /could/ gather hold of, to make himself more ~~convenient~~ accommodated. A number were soon in the cook room, where there were tin plates and cups, knives and forks, a few cooking utensils and two cook stoves, all for the use collectively of a mess of eighty men; but each man saw fit to take a plate, a cup, a knife, and a fork as long as they held out, so that he might not be wanting in any thing in his individual mess. Self first and last and always with soldiers prisoners especially.

A few loaves of bread and a few boxes containing meat sugar and coffee and salt and soap were set in to us which occas~~s~~ioned such a Bable of co[n]fusion and impacience, that it seemed to be impossible to get the rations distributed equally. Every one was anxious to get his share, and consequently the press was so great, that nothing towards a distribution could be affected. Every man then took as he could get to it, and the consequence was that some did not get any. Finally the lights were put out and all were composed to sleep as if reconciled to their fate, and to my great pleasure I awoke the next morning, to find myself in a better place than I had immagined.

The next thing to be done was to organize the mess, so that the distribution of rations, the cooking and policing might be ~~done~~ accomplished with some regularity. Accordingly several persons were chosen to superintend the whole affair, called Steward, Commissary, and Orderly Sergeant, the latter of which kept the lists of names and made all the details, whilst the former attended to the cooking and the arrangement of meals, and the other received the rations. Three cooks were employed and a detail of three made from the mess each day to set the tables, clear them and keep the room clean. Eight tables were arranged in a row against the wall, each one for the use of ten men, for some of which there were benches. On the opposite side of the room are the bunks of eighteen men, and those of the remainder /of the men/ are up stairs.

There are about 160 officers in our block (No. 5), 80 of which occupy one end of the building and are called Mess 1, whilst ours, Mess 2, occupy the other. This block★ has five rooms, ~~besides the cook rooms which are at the ends,~~ two of which are cook rooms, one at each end about 12 feet by the bredth of the house, whilst the intervening space constitutes one large room about 70 feet long which with the /three/ rooms up stairs would make six.

The space allowed to the prisoners is marked off by stakes and no one is allowed to go between them and the palings. The roll is called once each day after breakfast. All are expected to be in their quarters after retreat. After Taps no lights or fires are allowed. If the lights are not extinguished at the signal, which is 9½ o'clock P.M. the sentinels are expected to fire at them. Rations of bread and meat are halled in to us each day—★★coffee and sugar every weak. ~~Each day~~ /for dinner/ we get rice, homony or peas. The slop is halled out in a box cart made for the purpose. The sick are kept in a seperate block, called the hospital, and every thing is better than at Pea Island, or Fort Delaware, which is doubtless the worst place for prisoners, among all the Bastiles in the United States. That place is sickly, low marshy and comfortless. The water is bad and the rations are bad, and in fact every thing else, except the quarters, which of themselves will do very well when not too much crowded. Johnson's Island is more healthy; is a nicer situation and the rations and water★★★ are good.

★Each building is called a block.

★★Kind of composition—a mixture.

★★★The water is warm but clean.

CHAPTER III

Johnson's Island

A day in and out. Breakfast. The mail and express. Employment. Dinner. Faro-banks. Games at cards. Supper. Playing and exercise.

Suffice it to say that one day is just like another, when there is no change in the weather; and therefore the discription of one will answer for a majority. From sunup until breakfast, which is about two hours after, the prisoners are rising and going to and from the pump, with towels, cups or pans and soap to wash. Each day, from sunup till late in the evening, a number of men are scattered all around the pumps with wash-tubs and boards, washing ironing and drying clothes. Nearly all of the latter are privates, who wash both for themselves and officers—for five cents a piece in 'greenbacks' or fifty cents in Confederate money. About five hundred of the prisoners are non-commissioned officers and privates, the remainder (1000) are officers. When breakfast is announced, all hurry to their plases carrying their rations of bread with them, to eat with a cup of coffee, or rather substitute, and beef or hog's meat. These the regular cooks prepare, but many cook little extras for themselves, such as hashing the beef with onions and bread, and making puddings, of bread, butter, eggs and sugar or molasses: the ingredients of which they buy from the sutler, excepting the bread and beef.

Shortly after breakfast is done with, the drum is beat or bugle sounded for roll-call; when each mess forms in line to the front of their quarters and the Yankee corporals call the rolls and count. Next a two horse wagon is driven round loaded with loaves of light bread.

when each mess receives the number due it for one day's rations. Each loaf is divided into four parts and one of the parts serves for one man three meals. For some the bread is just enough—for others more than sufficient and for still others quite insufficient.

Then the prisoners can be seen scattered around, setting in the doors on the steps and on sticks of wood, whilst others are standing or walking, or lazing in their bunks;—some with various kinds of pamphlets, such as novels and monthly magazines, and others with newspapers reading. A few may be seen with books, or their bibles and testaments. Soon express packages and papers are brought in, when their is a large collection opposite the gate,—many expecting packages, others wanting to see, and some buying papers. Already there is a large crowd about the sutlers shop patiently waiting for it to be opened. When it is opened five or six clerks are kept constantly busy until the shop is closed at noon.* Various little things are bought from five cents to ten dollars and more. Those that sell the vegitables have the most to do, as they are constantly in demand, and small quantities are always wanting. Other clerks sell sugar molasses tobacco &c, whilst one and two are always employed with the dry goods. About this time the mail comes in, and a little room at the end of one of the blocks, is crowded around until the letters can be distributed. The prisoners are variously employed ~~until~~ in reading, writing, loafing, talking, playing at cards and draft, gambling, cooking, baking pies and selling them, making & vending ice cream and lemonade, washing, cleaning, shaving, eating and buying, walking and sleeping, working on rings, watch chanes and canes, looking when there is any thing to see, and longing, ~~wishing~~ wondering hoping and yawning when there is'nt, playing at foot ball, musing and laughing, singing and hallooing, jumping and wrestling, swearing, smoking, chewing, spitting, whitling, fidgting, and finally resting on their couches in profound slumber, dreaming of the loved ones at home far away, and refreshing themselves for the morrow.

For dinner we have a piece of light bread (called by some 'moonshine' others 'hornets-nest', or fox-fire,)—but rather tough in the main to be called either), which may be called good, hog's meat or beef and some peas or rice or corn. Beef is always preferable to bacon. The latter does not suit the appetite of a prisoner. Those ~~who~~ that have money current here, can have vegitables and some other little extras to eat. Every thing that is boiled remains fresh and the salt is put on the victuals as they are eaten.

Several faro banks have been instituted, which are kept up regularly. Around the table where the betting is going on, there is constantly a crowd; some betting others looking on. Cards are shuffled and put in a small box, which just fits the deck, having one side out, so as to show what card is up. In two strait rows on the table are other cards, on which the betting takes place, when the cards are slipt from the box by two, and the card that appears uppermost & shows who is the winner and who the loser. Some /have/ loset as high as a $1000 /or more/, whilst others /have/ gain/ed/ as much. Occasionally a bank is broken and sometimes an individual.

*It is opened again in the evening and closed before supper.

Games at cards are very common. Some men are playing almost from sunup till sundown. Here is a set of men playing 'seven up,' there another playing euchre yonder still another set playing 'whist' or some other game known by a different name. Some bet, while others play for amusement or a pastime. Some spread a blanket on the flour [floor] and gather around, shuffle a deck of cards, break them, deal off a cirtain number to each man, turn up one card to show which is trump and proceed to play with all the pleasure immaginable, and so on from one game into another, and one hour into another. Some gather around a table or a bench or any where else convenient for a game. Games at draft or 'checkers,' chess and domino are very common. The two former are exicuted on a board or plank, having sixty four little squares, every other ~~line~~ of which is black, and are arranged in the form of a square, with twenty four /small/ blocks, for /draft,/ twelve white, and twelve black, and these are opposed to each other in the game, and for chess the blocks are very different and of various shapes and values. Domino is exicuted with a number of small rectangles marked with different numbers of dies or spots on each end of the rectangles, and are placed together on a table in a line, all corresponding numbers being set against each other. Some play at 'chuckaluck,' which is almost always carryed on by betting. Dies are cast, or small square blocks on which are dots from one to six, and so much is bet on either number.

Supper is ready about six o'clock. We then have bread and substitute coffee with sugar. The coffee is brought to us ground, or what has the appearance of being ground coffee. It is perhaps ground peas which have been parched and mixed with a little coffee. It takes an unusual amount of sugar to sweeten it;—but notwithstanding, it does very well. When supper is over, some of the prisoners walk backwards and forwards the length of our prison~~ers~~ grounds for the sake of exercise, whilst others for the same purpose play at ball, and a greater number look on, laugh and halloo.[42] Others are scattered about reclining on the ground, setting on sticks of wood hanging about the steps and doors, and standing here and there, talking, reading, smoking, chewing, and whitling. Finally the Yankee band plays an air—the flag goes down, playing ceases and the prisoners gather about their respective quarters, and when dark begins to set in, they go to their respective rooms.

CHAPTER IV

A night in and out. Lights. Bunks. Conversation. Cards. Scripture reading. Taps, lights out, "turning in," random talk & sleep.

The night sets in with the prisoners near their places of rendesvou. The prisoners on the first floor are scattered here and there around the dining tables, a few striding over the floor and others on their bunks. From the second floor the platform of the steps is crowded, with those who are interested in discussing the situation and other topics.

Here and there on some of the different bunks pieces of candles are lighted, and by their light, laying at full length some are engaged in reading the Bible, a few others in reading something else. Some are walking over the floor,—some sitting in and standing about the windows, some playing cards, and some now and then looking out upon the lake. In some of the prisons, some are gambling or playing at any of the different kinds of games. One fourth of a candle is issued to each man every week, and some burn them by join[in]g together and using the same light, thus making them last longer, whilst others burn them, seperate and alone.

The bunks are seven feet long by four wide, surrounded by plank six inches broad, and bottomed by three or four large plank. Three bunks are in a tier, one above the other three feet apart. A shelf is at the end of each. One man occupies a bunk, and has a tick of straw, with one blanket furnished by U.S.

The conversation is commonly on the news of the day exchange of prisoners, retaliation, letters, and prospects. Some are here and there talking of different and various things. Some prominade and talk philosophically or learnedly;—like the Peripetetics of ancient times.[43] Some talk of battles, pleasures past and gone, and home. Some are rapt in their own thoughts, and say not a word. Cards remain ever and anon a sufficient amusement and pastime for some, whilst others read the scriptures and then retire. Nine o'clock is soon at hand, when the band is heard to play, and half hour after the taps are beaten or bugle sounded, when all the lights except those in the hospital go out. If the lights or some of them are not extinguished at the signal, the sentinels are expected to fire at them. A majority now retire, besides those who have already gone to bed. A few still walk over the floor, or sit by the windows and look out upon the lake. A few are asleep, whilst others laugh and talk, cast slurs at each other through sport, speak of the merits of the different armies, (there being representatives from each) speak sportively of the different states, hush and go to sleep. By the time the sentinels cry out "11 o'clock & all is well" the prisoners are rapt in slumber and repose. The lonely tramp of a prisoner may be heard now and then during the night, and sometimes the discharge /report/ of a sentinels gun. At the end of every half hour, each one of the sentry crys out the number of his post, the hour, and "All is well." Scarcely any other sounds interrupt the silence of the night. Thus it is, until Aurora rolling up from the expansive waters of Lake Erie, ushers in another day, and all wake into activity, restlessness and anxiety.

CHAPTER V

Aug. 1863
Johnson's Island

<u>The hospital—rooms—bunks and patients. Provisions, cooks and nurses. Physicians. Ministers, preaching, and prayer-meetings. Attendance.</u>

The building is one hundred feet by twenty five, and two stories high, and sets opposite, Block No. 5. It is divided into nine rooms, five of which are below and the remainder above. A passage through the house is in the middle, and on either side is a large room for patients: a like division is up stairs. At one end is a smaller room for the cookery and at the other end are two small rooms, for offices and medecine. Up stairs at each end is a room used by the nurses and some other prisoners. These rooms may also be used for other purposes. In the whole building are thirty-six windows, five feet by three. The dimensions of the hospital are about the same with /the/ prisonhouses. The bunks are all seperate, made of plank nailed and fitted to four large upright pieces of lumber, and bottomed with the same (plank or slits). Each bunk has a tick of straw and a few coverings mostly blankets. At present (Aug 27th/63) there are not more than twenty patients in the hospital, whilst there are a few elsewhere in the barracks. Now and then one dies; but the deaths are not very numerous, in comparison with the deaths at some other prisons. The place may be called healthy. When a prisoner dies he is placed in a plain coffin and burried outside the walls. The number who have died here will be recorded in another place as soon as ascertained. The provisions given to the patients are about the same as those issued to the prisoners, except that occasionally they get butter milk and some vegitables. Those who are sickest are favored mostly with the latter, whenever any get such things. There are several cooks and five or six nurses all of whom are prisoners and remain at the hospital all the time.

The Yankee surgeon visits the hospital ~~every day~~ now and then and is assisted by some of our own doctors. He has a regular steward, who also is a prisoner of war.[44] Several of our own ministers who are prisoners have their quarters there and often attend on the sick. There are some other preachers among us, besides bretheren who are instant in public prayer. Services are held every Sunday, morning and evening. Sometimes two sermons are going off at the same time—one on one portion of the prison grounds and another on another—sometimes indoors, mostly outdoors this warm weather. In the morning about 9 o'clock in the shade of Block No. 5, a large congregation of prisoners assemble, and seat themselves on benches stools sticks of wood, the steps and elsewhere, whilst many stand, and listen attentively to a sermon; A him of praise is next sung, either sitting or standing, a prayer offered, and finally the music of that musical song called the Doxology wells up from a hundred manly voices, and the Benediction is pronounced.[45] In the evening the same congregations come together in the shade of block No. 4. Morning and evening services are held at block No. 13. Each night prayer is helled in some of the buildings. Some of the ministers, as they should speak boldly against faro banks and gamblers /& profanity/, but still gambling goes on, and profaning God's name.

CHAPTER VI

Johnson's Island
Aug. 1863

Sutler's shop. Grade, goods, and prices. Post office and Taylor's Shop. Express. Packages. What is allowed and what is not. Barber & shoe shops. The making of rings &c. Baking and selling of pies. Sale of ice, ice cream & lemonade.

The sutler's shop is the most important object to those who have current money, and it is even frequented by those who have not. Every day nearly the whole time that it is open, it is crowded with customers. In the mornings there is great press, and before it is open a large number are waiting. The shop is about thirty feet long, with a narrow portico on each side, and the trading is done partly on the inside, mostly through the windows and a small high counter at one end, just inside. The shop is kept by several men, one of whom is a large black-headed, dark~~ed~~ skin[n]ed, pussy, black eyed looking man, who within himself seems to feel an importance, which no other can behold. The other has a better turn for business and is more polite and accommodating. Three or four others are employed as clerks. They buy the most of their dry goods in New York and sell them here at two or three prices. They monopolize the whole trade of the prison and can sell as they choose. Notwithstanding this, the shop is a great advantage to the prisoners, and the goods are much cheaper than they can buy them in the South. If any one wants any little thing that they have not got, they will get it for him in Sandusky City, and then charge from 25 to 75 percent on what it cost there. S. C. is in view about three miles distant, and is regularly communicated with by boat. My Bible which cost 60 cts there, cost $1.00 here.

The sutlers keep ready made clothing, from boots and shoes to hats, pens, ink, paper, novels, combs, soap, brushes and such like. Also some inferior wines, syrups, cigars, tobacco, cheese, crackers, eggs, butter, and a small variety of vegitables. A neat pair of boots when the prisoners were allowed to buy them could be obtained for $5.00 or shoes for $3.50.—finer could be obtained for greater prices. A neat sack coat, made of heavy goods can be obtained for $12.00, cassimere pants for 8 & 10 dollars. Some have clothes made to order, through the sutler. A nice grey cassimere Confederate coat can be had for $25.00, pants for $10.00.

The best tobacco they have sells at 75 cts per plug (inferior) Molasses 30 cts per qrt. Sugar 20 cts per lb. cheese 25 cts, butter 30 cts, eggs 20 cts, per Doz. Melons from 25 to 60 cts (small), vegitables different prices, from 5 cts up for different amounts. Greenbacks are used almost altogether, besides the sutlers tickets or checks, which are given in change, and call for 5, 10, 25 & 50 cts, and are as acceptable as the greenbacks, as long as we are in confinement at this place, and which may be redeemed at any time or when we leave. About the same can be bought for greenbacks, that can be bought for specie. Some time since an order was issued by Burnside or some other impudent commander, that prisoners would be allowed only one suit of out clothes and a change of under garments, and no more boots would be allowed them, even though sent by friends.[46] Many of the prisoners however are well clad having several excellent suits and more than one change of under clothes besides boots of a fine quality, purchased here or sent by friends.

The post office is a small room which protrudes out from the end of block No. 7, and is used as a ta~~y~~ilors shop by several of the prisoners, who are ta~~y~~ilors by trade. The letters are deposited in a box, and sent out each day by one of the tailors, who acts as P. M. and receives and distributes the mail which comes in about 10 A.M.; when an eager crowd are pressing about the office, and only disperse when the last name is called. Only short letters are allowed to be sent, postage 3 cts.[47] A prisoner may send a letter to any part of the United States, and through the lines to the Confederate States, by Flag of Truce at City Point. A great deal of uncertainty is connected with the transportation and sending and receiving of prisoners letters. Many however receive letters, not only from the United States but from the Confederate States. Most of the letters I trow[48] are from the U.S. as flags of truce are not regular. Money from 5 to 50 dollars is sent to prisoners by friends relatives & acquaintances, and some firms in New York and elsewhere, mostly Baltimore. The commander of the post receives the money, turns it over to the sutler, and gets the receipt of the prisoner, who gets goods or checks from the sutler. Many prisoners write to many places throughout the North—Some receive answers and some do not. The tailors are constantly employed in making and mending clothes. They have made several fine suits of Confederate uniform lately. A fine frock tail coat, pants and waistcoat costs about $40.00.

The express goods come in nearly every morning, and are distributed at the gate, between it and the line of stakes, where they are closely examined, if they have not already been so examined. Boxes, valises and packages are all opened, whilst the prisoners crowd forward to receive, to ascertain and to look on, remaining just outside the line of stakes. Sometimes a suit of clothes, and especially a pair of boots are reserved. Under clothing books and little things are always handed over to the prisoner for whom intended, and sometimes out clothes. Articles reserved they say are sent back from whence they came or held subject to the prisoners order. A prisoner who gets a box of such articles is indeed fortunate, and far better off than very many of his fellow prisoners. A box of books, pamphlets magazines and news-papers is an invaluable acquisition, in such a place as this, where many expedients are resorted to for the purpose of killing time, whether to advantage or not. Money is sometimes received by express sent from New York, Philadelphia or Baltimore or elsewhere. Some prisoners write to firms with which they have done business, or to some member of a firm with whom they are acquainted, and ofttimes receive money or something else.[49] Some have written to sympathizers and to secessionists in Baltimore, both ladies and gentlemen; the latter of which are always very apt to send money or packages if allowed. Some ladies in Baltimore supplied with money such prisoners as they had an opportunity, evincing great liberality, when there.

Many of the men are intent upon making a few dimes, and seem determined to have a few greenbacks. Here and yonder you may see signs to the following effect;—"Barber Shop Block 1 Room 6." "Boots and shoes mended" "Pies for sale" "Cakes & beer" "Milk custards and pies." I concluded to try the barber shop. The barber was an awkward rough looking fellow with an impediment in his speach and very unskilled in the use of his dull razor the only one he had, which pulled like "blaazes." 5 cts in green backs or $1.00 in Co[n]federate was his price, but finding that his operations were not popular with me allowed me to go without paying any thing, inviting and perhaps expecting me to call again, which invitation I have taken care not to accede to.

Some are employed /in/ making rings and watch chanes of gutta percha some of which are very neat.[50] Most of the rings are set with /pieces of/ shell, which contrast very well with the gutta percha and many of which would please a fine lady. Square pieces of gutta percha are nicely fitted together, and set with pretty pieces of shell of different shapes and terminated with a piece cut out for a type, all of which answers very well for an odd watch chain. Gen Archer paid $12.00 in greenbacks for one.[51] The sale of pies is mostly carried on by the cooks; Some have beer and cakes of an inferior kind to dispose of, Pies 10 cts, cakes 5 cts, and beer 5 cts per bottle. Some go around pedling their pies. Some buy from the cooks and then pedle.

Nearly every day a little qcart of ice is halled around and sold out to the prisoners, and sometimes milk. The consequence is that some of the prisoners are enabled to make ice cream. They obtain freezers and such other things as they want from the sutler. Some make it, and others take it around and sell it out at ten cents per glass. Others make lemonade and sell it at 10 cts per glass. Our prison is a microcosm of itself. Trade goes on in here as well as elsewhere, and although workshops are not as common are as /in/ many places in the outside world, still their are loungers and loafers who are as numerous as in most places, all having their predominant passions.

CHAPTER VII

Heat. Weather. /insects/ Bathing. Cooking. Washing. Cleaning and sweaping

During the latter part of July and more than half of the present month, the warmth of the weather was severe. The least covering at night was oppressive, and at mid ~~night~~ day /in the sun/ the heat was little less than indurable. In New York and some other Northern cities deaths by sunstroke were common. The prisoners did not stir about much, but remained either in the buildings or reposed in their shaddow. There is no other shade inside the enclosure, except the shade of the houses. A few days ago there was a heavy hail storm, with rain, and ever since the weather has been cool. The nights are so cool that it requires all the covering we have. If it be so cool now what may we expect in winter? Aug. 28th/63/ Johnson's Island

I notice that the variety of insects on the island ~~are~~ is not very numerous. There are fewer flies than at any place I ever was at. This scarcity of flies is a great advantage. A person can eat his meals without being constantly annoyed, and occasionally swallowing one of the pest, and he can do almost any thing else with less annoyance. Furthermore his victuals approach nearer that cleanliness to which he has been used to at home. Crickets and grasshoppers, go in part to make up for the deficiency in flies. They are very numerous and may be found all through the houses as well as out doors. Many are brought in on the bed clothes when they have been laying out sunning and sometimes tickle a fellow no little. All other insects are scarce. Mice and rats are the only quadrupeds within the bounds of our prison. Fowls of the air are scarce, if there be any at all. There is one kind of parasitical insect that I should have mentioned above, and they are lice—body lice. They live in the clothes and are supported and hatched by the warmth of the body. They are not as numerous here as in many other places where soldiers stay and prisoners /are/ kept. The prisoners wash often and change their clothes frequently, and not being very crowded, can keep pretty well rid of them. However there are some who will be lousey in spite of every advantage they have of keeping themselves clean; and the consequence is that many of their /cleaner/ neighbors will occasionally have some of the abominable virmin, in spite of them.

Once every four days many of the prisoners are permitted to go into the lake to bathe, about 100 at a time. The lake is about 25 paces from the lower gate through which they are marched, well guarded, and all strip, and eagerly rush into the water. They can wade several hundred yards into the water, on firm bottom. Some swim, and others duck themselves and soap and wash. They look like a number of strange beings, come up from the deep waters of the lake, to play and revel in the shallow. Women passing by on boats view the strange and to them unusual scene with a fixed attention of wonder interest and pleasure.

The cooking is done in rooms for the purpose in the ends of the blocks. There are stoves, large boilers, and a few other things for the purpose. There are regular cooks, but scores cook for themselves, the little "snacks and nicknacks" which they buy and prepare. Some are around the stove preparing hash, pudding or potatoes, and others something else, whilst the cooks are preparing the regular ration and the whole presents the appearance of a bee hive. The regular cooks wash all the plates cups knives and forks, of each of which there are about eighty to a mess. The mess is subdivided and the /regular/ rations of the whole are chooked together. A detail of men set and clean of[f] the tables, sweep out the room and scour the knives & forks. Regular details sweep the others rooms about three times a day. Sometimes we scour and that is whenever we choose; sun our bed clothes now and then and have our clothes washed whenever they need it.

CHAPTER VIII

Johnson's Island
Aug. 1863

My situation and condition. How I employ my time. Aug. 28th. Bad news. Aug. 29th

When we first came here, I had only one suit of clothes, an oil-cloth and blanket; and this suit I had been wearing ever since I was taken prisoner, without change. I had $30.00 in greenbacks, and one of the first things to be done was to get some clothes. I bought a change of underclothes and a pair of shoes, borrowed a tub, filled it with water, washed myself clean and dressed, and then felt as if it were one of the best things I had ever done. How thankful every one ought to feel who enjoys the priviledge or constant opportunity of washing himself and dressing in clean clothes whenever he chooses. The soldier endures long marches through heat and dust and cold, sleeps and rests upon the ground, and fights hard battles, in one suit of clothes. If he has more than one suit, he cannot change whenever he wants to, and whenever he does change, he has not got time or opportunity every time to wash. So washing and putting on clean garments was as good to me, as a glass of wine is to a wearied and broken down man. I felt as if I had added another cubit to my measure, and naturally resolved to wash and change every now and then. My bunk is in room no. 5, up stairs and mid-way of one end of the room /and next to the floor/. Above me sleeps Lieut Col Morris of 37th N.C. Regt—on my right is Lt. Coggin of N.C. and on my left Lieut Asbury of Miss.[52] On the right and left is a space of four feet between us, or the bunks. I have a shallow tick of straw, two blankets and an oil cloth and these I make very serviceable both day and night. I rise in the morning about the time breakfast is announced, sometimes a little before, when I take pan soap and towel, go to the ~~well~~ pump and wash, if not I eat and then wash. I next double one end of my bed tick under, roll up my blankets, place them at the head, and cover all with my oil cloth. This prop is to support my laziness during the day, whilst I am reading. I answer to my name at roll call, take my bible, read a chapter or two, and then take up a novel or magazine fall back upon my couch and read, often, from one hour to another. I then raise up, set on the side of my bunk like a frog /on the bank of a creek/ ready to plunge into the water, muse a little while, get up and walk across the floor a few times, look out at the windows, cast my eyes toward the horizon over the lake, and then, sometimes take up Brown's grammar, stretch myself on my pallet again, and carefully read a few pages, or go down into the yard look about a little, or go the Sutlers shop, come back again, turn and twist and wallow until to my satisfaction dinner is announced.[53] Sometimes in addition to my rations of bread and meat and corn or rice, I have some vegitables or part in a pudding made of bread, butter, eggs and sugar. Might have such things all the time, but it takes greenbacks, and they are a great object here. When I finish dinner I return to my reading, or write a little, or do a little of something else, and chew my tobacco and wallow on my bunk, and bestride the floor, and think of "vanity of vanities" how "all is vanity and vexation of spirits."[54] Many pass their time at games of cards, draft, chess and domino; but in these I take no interest. I have never yet learned to play cards. Sometimes I think I will learn for the sake of knowing how; but I have never more than learned the names of the different cards. I have oftener been disgusted with the sight of cards, and those playing, than that of any thing else. It is almost as offensive, as the sight of blue coats. The phrase,—"Diamonds is trumps," "High, low, Jack and the game," "High to your low," "The deuce," "I can beat you" "The two best in three," are so common and of such frequent occurence, that I had about as leave here the old and worn out begin~~n~~ning of a letter,—"I now take my pen in hand to write you a few lines, to let you know that I am well, and hope when these few lines reach you, they will find you enjoying the same blessing."

Had I the money I should have such books as I want. Such as I have had, have been almost altogether fiction. Scotts Waverely Novels are the best that most of us have had. I have read Waverely, Castle Dangerous, The Surgeons Daughter, and the A/n/tiquary, written by Scott, and The Actress: or Under the Spell, Jacob Faithful, and a few magazines. I now write and read grammar a little; but am anxious for more reading material.[55]

After supper, I read or write a little, or look at some of the men playing ball, who have many spectators, and afford the greater amount of amusement. Night comes on when I walk about the room, talk, chew or smoke, arrange my pallet, turn about a few times, strip and go to bed.

After I retire, which is mostly at 9½ or 10 O'clock, I l~~ay~~ie wakeful for a long time. Often the lonely sound of "All is well" comes to my hearing on the mid-night air, from the sentry, before I am buried in slumber. My thoughts wander back to the "distant long ago"; when, in all the simplicity of joyous childhood, I reveled with a bevy of school boys and girls, beneath the spreading branches of the towering oaks, at the old field school house, where we met to learn the first rudiments of education, where we sported and played without a care, and without thinking of what the future had in store for us. I think of the many days misspent, and of many opportunities neglected, which might have been improved: I think of my many errors, which, alas! can never be corrected. How the days of my childhood were the happiest, and how devoid of pleasure and happiness the remainder of my life has been. Not a single day, can I recall that I would like to live over again just in the same way. Few and far between have been my joys and pleasures, and few do I expect in the future. But hope, that sweet messenger of consolation, keeps me borne up with something like contentment. My motto still is "Dum spiro spero."[56] As I l~~ay~~ie upon my couch, or as I prominade, or sit at the window looking out upon the darkness or upon the pale silvery light of the moon,

"When mortals sleep, when spectres rise,
And none are wakeful but the dead;
No shapeless vision my path pursues;
No sheeted ghost my couch annoys.
Visions more sad, my fancy views
Visions of long departed joys."[57]

In immagination, I also wander into the unfathomed future; but my air castles are less in number and magnitude than they were years ago. However I can see the clouds of war swept away, and from among the the heaps of our slain on an hundred battle fields, and the waste and desolation of our country, the Goddess of Peace and Independance arrise, shedding her benign influence ~~of~~ over myriads now afflicted, and bringing back joy and plenty to the grief and poverty stricken and sending back to their homes the citizen soldiers, who have gone forth to battle in their country's cause. I can hear the rejoicings and congratulations of fathers, mothers, sisters and friends ringing throughout the length and breadth of the land. I can see smiles of joy chasing each other over the countenances of sisters and friends; and tears of gratitude and thanksgiving rolling down the cheeks of fond mothers. There can be heard the welcome, "Well done thou good and faithful servant" of thy country,"—"The war is over, victory is won, Peace has come at last," enter into the joys of home and quietude. But all over the land there will be a great and lasting grief for those who have fallen. There will be thousands of sorrowing mothers, desolate widows and orphan children; but all will hail the reign of Peace, and view with pride and rejoicing the glory and greatness of our Confederacy, and the time when our commerce shall be upon every sea, and ride into every port, and there shall be prosperity throughout the country.

The 28th day of August was very cold for the time of year. /One/ Would not be comfortable unless he was by a fire, or well wrapt up. Some went to bed to keep warm. Those who had overcoats done very well. Most of the rooms are without any place to keep fire. Late in the evening of this day the P. M. brought me a letter, the first that I have received since I left Richmond, Va. on the 22d June.[58] It was from home. A number gathered around eager to know in what way it came through the lines, as very few letters had been received from the South. I opened and read when to my great sorrow, I learned that sister Laura died on the 5th inst. of Typhoid Pneumonia. She was fourteen years old, lovely and modest, industrious and intelligent, and the flower of the family. Death cirtainly delights in a shinning mark. I had not seen her since the winter of 1862, and was more desirous of seeing her than any of the other children. But she is gone, and no more will my earthly eyes behold her. I was hoping to see her as a ~~woman~~ lady, having but few equals in beauty, loveliness and intelligence combined. She was affectionate, and worthy of a brother's love and highest regards. By proper cultivation and encouragement, I saw that she could be /made/ not only one of the most accomplished young ladies; but one of the most amiable and confiding of sisters. I shall ever cheerish her memory, with the fond hope of joining her around the celestial throne, with our sister Tabitha, who went before in September of last year, and our little brother William who died years ago. Three are in heaven nine are on earth and the parents.[59] [*In left margin*] The 29th was equally as cold as the 28th. 30th warmer. 31st pleasant.

CHAPTER IX

Sep. 1st 1863
Johnson's Island

Observance of Sabbath. Prayer Meetings. Profanity. Observance of fast day Aug. 21st. Bible Classes. Debates. Concerts.

All respect the Sabbath. Those who do not leave off their swearing, leave off their gambling and card playing. A few when they read, read nothing else but the Bible; others read Bible and novels, and any thing else. A regular sermon comes off in the morning at 9 o'clock, in the shade of Block No. 5. and in the evening at 3 o'clock, in the shade of No 4. There are also services both morning and evening at Block No. 13. The sermons are all well attended and well listened to. There are five or six ministers among the prisoners, some of whom speak very well.

Prayer meetings are held every night before retiring in some parts of the prison. A hymn is sung, and then a chapter is read and another hymn sung, followed by prayer when they are dismissed. The voices of worshippers, card-players and gamblers mix together. The voice of prayer rises from among a confusion of noises. Here is a company engaged in prayer or sacred song, there another in the same room around the card table. However no great or intended disturbance takes place.

Profanity is a very common thing among many of the prisoners, and perhaps a greater proportion of profane swearers is among the field and staff. The North Carolina officers so far as my observation goes, are more refined in this respect, than officers from any other state. Virginians and Tennesseeans, also do less swearing. Drinking and swearing is very common among the Alabama/h/ians. Some of the officers obtain whiskey through the sutlers, and occasionally a tipsy man can be seen. Most bottles sell for $1.25. A squad of Alabama/h/ians frequently gathered in a corner near my bunk and done their carousing. The leader was one who slept just opposite. He and a comrade moved out, to the satisfaction of many of us. Two others of the same school, in a few days, to our regret, took their places but being rather unpopular it was not long before they also left the room. No officers from Alabamah are in our room at present. All the others are North Carolinians Georgians Mississippians and Tennesseans. 22 in number. Some men when they talk, precede nearly every sentence with the name of God, or "damn it" or "I'll be damned." All such is indeed very ugly and unrefined—useless, unnecessary to the sense of familiar talk, and wicked. Some glory in it. They think it is 'smart.' Some think it gives an attractive prominence to their language, and makes them respected and admired. It is contemptable.

The 21st of August having been set apart by the President of the Confederate States, as a day of fasting and prayer, the prisoners united in observing the day. Some of the messes had only one meal prepared for the whole /day/,—an early supper. Nearly all did without one meal, some /few/ having a great propensity for eating did not fast. Large congregations attended the preaching, morning and evening. Prayers were freely offered up for our common country, our armies and those in authority.[60]

There are several Bible classes, taught by some of the ministers. They are well attended, and meet every other day. Rev. Mr. Sherrill who delights in having any thing of this kind to do, is very well informed in scripture, and seems to be a hard student of the Bible. I belong to one of his classes numbering about 20. I thought I should not like him for an instructor in scripture; but I find him so explicit in giving instruction, that I shall attend regularly.[61]

A debating society has been organized at Block No. 11. called ~~called~~ "The Island Prison Debating Society,"—which convenes every other day /and which I have joined/. The officers of the society are President, Vice President, Secretary, Critic and two Curators who select questions and make the appointments. The appointments are for each meeting, two on the Affirmative of the question, and two on the Negative, two readers to read select pieces, and two orators, or declaimers. After the appointees on the question have spoken, others are at liberty to speak. The debates are well attended, and take place in the largest room of the block, where the congregation set about on the tables, benches, bunks, and stand up. "Was the banishment of Vallandigham conducive to the interests of the Southern Confederacy," has been discussed and decided in the affirmative; also "Will the establishment of an empire in Mexico be conducive to the permanent interests of the Confederate States," has been mooted and decided in the affirmative. The next question for next meeting is "Should the African slave trade be reopened after the South /has/ established her independence"; will be discussed the evening Sep 2nd 1863.[62]

Concerts are becoming common. Two have already been held in Block. No. 5. attended by large audiences. Admittance fee 10 cts in greenbacks, for the relief of hospital or our sick as stated on the hand-bills. The performers are four of the prisoners, who black themselves for the purpose of imitating the negro. They call themselves the Island Minstrels, play and sing comic songs, and converse with the negro brogue and jargon. The crowd evince their pleasure by loud applause and bursts of laughter. Many show their curiosity, and display their want of good breeding, by crowding around the house listening and peeping through the windows where ever they can find an opening not covered by the blinds instead of paying and going in, if they are disposed to ~~go~~ see and hear. If they cannot get in honorably, for the want of greenbacks, their self respect should keep them away. I have never been desirous to behold the entertainment, and hence have not seen it. I prefer the debates. The concert comes off on Monday and Friday evenings.[63]

ISLAND MINSTRELS!

Manager and Proprietor,............Mr. CHAS. L. STOUT.
Acting Stage Manager,............Mr. E. H. WALTER.
Musical Director,............Mr. W. H. HARRISS.
Treasurer,............Mr. J. C. WARD.

The Manager having had forty years experience in his peculiar line of business, is proud to announce to the friends of the *Institution* and citizens of Johnson's Island, that after unparalleled exertions he has succeeded in procuring the first order of talent from Fort Delaware, Alton, Camp Chase, and the Penitentiarys of Columbus Ohio, and Alleghany City, Pa. He is now prepared to present to the public the greatest array of talent ever before witnessed, in the United States. He has succeeded in procuring for one night only, the services of the

FOR THE BENEFIT OF

CHARLIE STOUT!

BILLY LOYD has volunteered his services for this occasion.

ALSO, THE FOLLOWING STARS:

MR. D. L. DUNHAM, the inimitable Bones,
MR. T. F. MITCHEL, the renowned Guitarist,
MR. J. C. WARD, the exquisite Flutist,
MR. WM. H. HARRISS, the modern Paganini,
MR. Ole Bull LIVINGSTONE,
MR. Paul Julien HANRAHAN,
MR. Joe Sweeney CRONIN,
MR Triangular DECKER,
MR. CHARLES L. STOUT,

Feeling that he would not be able to do justice to his own merits, respectfully invites the Public to come and see what he can do with the Tamborine.

Monday Afternoon, October 26th, 1863.

PROGRAMME.

PART FIRST.

OPENING OVERTURE,............Full Band.
" CHORUS,............"
A LITTLE MORE CIDER,............Dunham.
TILDA HORN,............Ward.
YELLOW ROSE OF TEXAS,............Mitchell.
KATIE DEAR,............Livingstone.
VIRGINIA,............Walter.
SILVER SHINING MOON,............Stout.
CLAP YOUR HANDS FOR DIXIE,............Company.

PART SECOND.

THE OFFICERS FUNERAL, (Trio,)............Harriss, Dunham & Mitchell.
PICAYUNE BTTLER IS COMING,............Company.
OUR GLORIOUS CONSTITUTION, (Lecture.)............Stout.

Concluding with the

CHECK APRON BALL!

DINAH BLOSSOM,............Miss F. Metts.
BOB RIDLEY,............BOYD,
CHARLES AGUSTUS,............Dunham.

ADMISSION 25 CENTS.

Reserved Seats,............50 Cents.
Private Boxes,............$5,00.
Children,............12½ Cts.
Niggers,............Free.

Playbill drawn by Joseph Mason Kern for a concert to be given by the Island Minstrels on October 26, 1863. From Scrapbook, 1861-1865, Folder 2, in the Joseph Mason Kern Papers #2526, Southern Historical Collection, Wilson Library, University of North Carolina at Chapel Hill.

CHAPTER X

Oct. 1863.
Johnson's Island

The Vallandigham Election. Escape of three prisoners. Theatre. The tunnel. Closing of the sutler shop. Stopping of the Express. The Babtizing. Messing. Wood &c. Weather. Room 4. Block 8.

The day having arrived for the election of Governor of the State of Ohio the prisoners concluded they would have a mimic election; accordingly they assembled in the middle of the prison grounds, some hurrahing for Brough and Abolitionism and others for Vallandigham, Freedom the Union and Constitution. Speakers for the different candidates were called upon and listened to amidst hurrahs, bullyings and pretended fights. The polls were opened and such as wished to vote for Val were driven away unless they said they had plenty of money. All passed off pleasantly with all the accompaniments of an exciting election mimicked. The crowded pressed together and waved to and fro with laughter, curiosity and excitement until the Yankees considering such demonstrations dangerous to their welfare ordered them to disperse.[64]

One dark wet night three of the prisoners from Block 5, bundled up and crawled down a small ditch leading straight to the pailings, and sawed their way through with an old case knife knotched into a saw. The sentinel was just above their heads, but they passed out unobserved. Unfortunately just as they were turning the corner of the outer wall, the officer of the day met them, and the alarm was given. They were taken before the commanding officer who complimented them for their success, and sent them back to prison. The Rebel Thespians, as they call themselves, had a little play which they acted much to the amusement of the crowd, called "A Hole in the Fence" from the above circumstance. The theatre is growing with as much rapidity as could be expected in such a place. They have scenery and act various kinds of plays. Admittance Fee 25 cts. Genls. Colonels and all classes are interrested in their performances. The curious crowd bolt in like a thunder storm to behold the entertainment. Have never been myself. Curiosity does not lead me far.[65]

Beneath Block 1 which is near the wall a number of prisoners had been engaged for a long time in cutting a tunnel about two feet below the surface, and larg[e] enough for a man to crawl through. It was about thirty feet long. One dark wet night it was completed and a number made their escape through it and many more would but a large awkward fellow got hung in the hole at the farther end and could neither go back nor forward nor be drawn out. His head was just at the outer end, and their he lay pressed on all sides by mud and water, for three or four hours chilled through, and was compelled to call upon the Yankees for assistance thus discovering the secret. All were retaken, being unable to get off the Island. The whole /of/ block No 1 had to give their parole not to dig another hole and thus a song goes they have.[66]

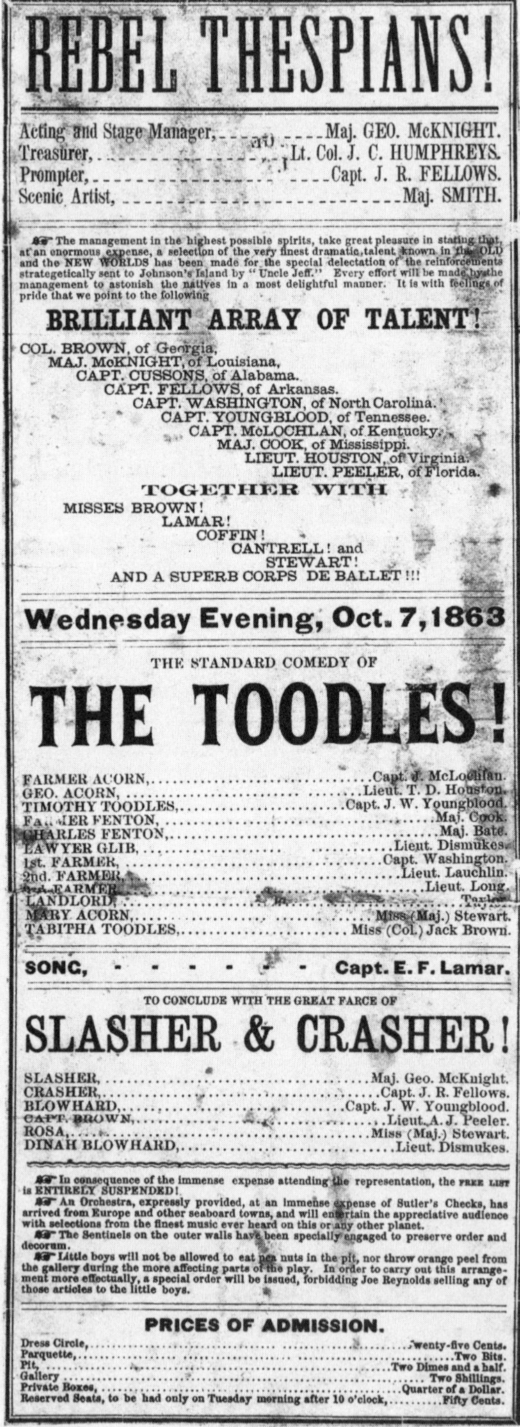

REBEL THESPIANS!

Acting and Stage Manager, ---------- Maj. GEO. McKNIGHT.
Treasurer, ---------- Lt. Col. J. C. HUMPHREYS.
Prompter, ---------- Capt. J. R. FELLOWS.
Scenic Artist, ---------- Maj. SMITH.

☞ The management in the highest possible spirits, take great pleasure in stating that, at an enormous expense, a selection of the very finest dramatic talent known in the OLD and the NEW WORLDS has been made for the special delectation of the reinforcements strategetically sent to Johnson's Island by "Uncle Jeff." Every effort will be made by the management to astonish the natives in a most delightful manner. It is with feelings of pride that we point to the following

BRILLIANT ARRAY OF TALENT!

COL. BROWN, of Georgia,
MAJ. McKNIGHT, of Louisiana,
CAPT. CUSSONS, of Alabama.
CAPT. FELLOWS, of Arkansas.
CAPT. WASHINGTON, of North Carolina.
CAPT. YOUNGBLOOD, of Tennessee.
CAPT. McLOCHLAN, of Kentucky.
MAJ. COOK, of Mississippi.
LIEUT. HOUSTON, of Virginia.
LIEUT. PEELER, of Florida.

TOGETHER WITH

MISSES BROWN!
LAMAR!
COFFIN!
CANTRELL! and
STEWART!
AND A SUPERB CORPS DE BALLET!!!

Wednesday Evening, Oct. 7, 1863

THE STANDARD COMEDY OF

THE TOODLES!

FARMER ACORN, ... Capt. J. McLochlan.
GEO. ACORN, ... Lieut. T. D. Houston.
TIMOTHY TOODLES, ... Capt. J. W. Youngblood.
FA[illegible]MER FENTON, ... Maj. Cook.
CHARLES FENTON, ... Maj. Bate.
LAWYER GLIB, ... Lieut. Dismukes.
1st. FARMER, ... Capt. Washington.
2nd. FARMER, ... Lieut. Lauchlin.
[illegible] FARMER, ... Lieut. Long.
LANDLORD, ... Taylor.
MARY ACORN, ... Miss (Maj.) Stewart.
TABITHA TOODLES, ... Miss (Col.) Jack Brown.

SONG, - - - - - - Capt. E. F. Lamar.

TO CONCLUDE WITH THE GREAT FARCE OF

SLASHER & CRASHER!

SLASHER, ... Maj. Geo. McKnight.
CRASHER, ... Capt. J. R. Fellows.
BLOWHARD, ... Capt. J. W. Youngblood.
CAPT. BROWN, ... Lieut. A. J. Peeler.
ROSA, ... Miss (Maj.) Stewart.
DINAH BLOWHARD, ... Lieut. Dismukes.

☞ In consequence of the immense expense attending the representation, the FREE LIST is ENTIRELY SUSPENDED!

☞ An Orchestra, expressly provided, at an immense expense of Sutler's Checks, has arrived from Europe and other seaboard towns, and will entertain the appreciative audience with selections from the finest music ever heard on this or any other planet.

☞ The Sentinels on the outer walls have been specially engaged to preserve order and decorum.

☞ Little boys will not be allowed to eat pea nuts in the pit, nor throw orange peel from the gallery during the more affecting parts of the play. In order to carry out this arrangement more effectually, a special order will be issued, forbidding Joe Reynolds selling any of those articles to the little boys.

PRICES OF ADMISSION.

Dress Circle, ... Twenty-five Cents.
Parquette, ... Two Bits.
Pit, ... Two Dimes and a half.
Gallery .... Two Shillings.
Private Boxes, ... Quarter of a Dollar.
Reserved Seats, to be had only on Tuesday morning after 10 o'clock, ... Fifty Cents.

Kern's playbill for performances by the Rebel Thespians of *The Toodles* and *Slasher and Crasher*, October 7, 1863. From Scrapbook, 1861-1865, Folder 2, in the Joseph Mason Kern Papers #2526, Southern Historical Collection, Wilson Library, University of North Carolina at Chapel Hill.

November/63.

Those that had plenty of greenbacks lived high until the sutler shop was closed, which happened on a sudden. For some then unknown cause, the sutler received orders to close, who immediately redeamed all of his checks (or Sutler's chips so called) with what goods he had on hand. There was a general rush from all quarters of the prison to make sure of getting the worth of the checks. The men crowded and pressed and pushed with eager impatience about the shop to buy something perhaps the last. They were so eager that they partly tore down the shop, and others carried off the pieces. The closing of the shop was especially a severe blow to the tobacco users. Within a few days thirty of forty tobacco chewers could be found in one place and among them only one or two that had any and they very little. It was a precious thing and every one felt the necessity of keeping close what he might accidentally have. The legion of beggars were dangerous to all tobacco that made its appearance. The shop I suppose was closed in order to deprive us of a sutler, because they, the Yankees thought their prisoners in Richmond were not allowed such. The sutler was not allowed to redeam but one dollar with greenbacks to any one man. All other moneys belonging to the prisoners were kept close in the hands of Lieut Col. Pierson the Yankee commander. The express was also stopped and all packages sent to prisoners were stored away. News papers and everything else from the outsid[e] were forbidden the prisoners, but smuggling was common.[67]

The love of money is the ruling passion among the Yankees and consequently if any one had money he could have any small thing smuggled in. Comparatively few had money on the inside, as the Col. commanding kept it secure from use, acting as if he were a guardian over children. They are doubtless fearful of their own soldiers being bribed, and well they may be, for all of them are avaricious. The above state of things has been /Dec./ altering and some of the Yankees /now/ bring in goods occasionally and sell higher than the sutler, who sold at an uncommon percent. The Express is given out except boots and overcoats notwithstanding it is winter /those are retained/. Breeches are sometimes withheld. Today the Yanks will act one way and to-morrow another.

Some have manifested considerable interest with respect to the salvation of their souls. Some profess to have found hope. One has been received by the Babtist brethern in confinement. He was babtized in Lake Erie one cold Sunday last month. Fourty were paroled to go out to the Lake.

The messing in Block 5, Mess 2 was carried on till lately in a manner pell-mell helter-skelter. About the time for a meal all became impatient and surrounded their respective tables before the meal was ready, and every one seemed to be fearful he would not get his share and would not give the detail time to place the victuals on the tables. As soon as the detail came from the kitchen with soup or beans for any table, they would be surrounded and pressed by the eager crowd, some holding out their cups or plates, and others charging. Nothing could be done with system. Every man distrusted all others besides himself.

Before their last arrangement every /man/ took his cup (there are 128 men in the whole mess which is subdivided) and pressed into the cookroom, pushed up around the large boiler in which were the soup beans and beef and ram[m]ed his cup in. A dozen would be dipping at a time and 15 or 20 pressing hard and impatiently in the rear. Occasionally a man would /be/ scaulded in the melee, but he would never retire from the contest until he had obtained his soup. Before the sutler closed[,] the kitchen, which is about 10 ft by 20, would be crowded by thirty or forty men, all cooking and preparing their meals. At the tables, knives fork~~e~~s plates or cups would be missing. There was sure to be a deficiency somewhere. After while every man took his own from the kitchen, besides rations as long as they ~~would~~ h~~o~~eld out, and consequently some were minus every thing. Next a meeting was held, a steward elected, and rations &c returned which made much improvement. But it is still too bad. I am glad that I left and joined Mess 1, Block 8. Set a pan full of corn doe in the middle of a yard where there are about two hundred chickens and the manner in which they would gather around, and put in their bills, will be a good deal like the men with cups around a pot of soup. The bread is a great object. The majority of the prisoners are about as jealous of their individual shares as they would be of pretty wives. Loaves of light bread a little over a foot long and about four inches thick, one to four men for a day, are issued. The rations are frequently short. They seem to grow less every month.

December 1863

Every man desires more to eat than he gets. Bread meat, peas and all are easily eat up at tow meals per day. Many of those who are able have bought private stoves and are glad to be free from the general messes. Wood and clothing are now great objects. As soon as a load of wood is brought in each mess takes their wood into the house, and as soon as saws can be obtained saw it there. The Yankees bring the saws in each day, and if one is missing at night, which is often the case, they deprive of us of all, until it is produced. They are fearful they would be used in getting out of this 'bullpen.' A great many of the prisoners are very illy clad. Some who have friends in the North have received suits of clothes from them, but the Yankees will not every time give out all that is sent. My clothing for this cold weather in this cold climate consists in one good pair of pants, a small thin waist coat, a jacket and a change of underclothes. About the middle of this month a considerable snow was on the ground and on the 17th Sandusky Bay was frozen over—ice about a foot thick. The prison grounds when not frozen are about 6 in deep in mud all over. My Room Block 8 has fifty men in it. My bunk is in a dark corner. Incoveniences of all kinds exist. For our benefit we have bible class twice per weak at night and debates as often. Prayers each night. Morality of the Room good comparitively.

Johnson's Island
Ohio 1864
Diary.
Book 2d
January. (~~WE~~)

Friday 1st

Clear and unusually cold. Difficult to keep warm within doors. ~~Lake~~ Bay frozen over during the night. All pressed close around the stove. When night came on five prisoners prepared to make their escape. Wropt close and in triple suits succeeded.

Saturday 2d

Weather colder Thermometer 20° below 0. At night we had a debate on the subject,—"Has civilization (the progress of) kept pace with the age." On the Affir. That side gained it. Men from every block prepared to make their escape, such as had plenty of clothes. Detected by the Yankees, after one succeeded by knocking down a sentinel on the outer line.

Sunday 3d

One of the five who first escaped taken at a citizens house on the shore nearly frozen to death. Feet and hands nearly ruined, face cracked open. Another retaken. Preaching in the evening. Bible class in the room on the tenth chapter of Mat., at night.

Monday 4th

Miscellaneous reading—Bible, Essay on "The Antidote of heaven to the curse of labor" &c.

Tuesday 5th

Snow on the ground four or five in. deep. Rumors of exchange of prisoners. All still hoping and fearing Read in Shakspeare "The Merry Wives of Windsor." Constantly anxious for systematic study—want the necessary books—and more light. Crowded, cold and some one all the time in the light, or shoving against you.

Wednesday 6th

More rumors of e[x]change. An ephemeral hope and joyful noise. Some are in doubt about being exchanged even if we leave here, thinking that they intend to take us to another prison, to retaliate as there papers say with bad treatment. A debate on the question—"Which has the greater influence on men the Love of Women, or the Love of Money." took place at night.

Thirsday 7th

More excitement as to exchange. Conflicting rumors. Some prepare to leave—others speak of what they will do when they get to Richmond. Too fast.

Friday 8th

Great excitement agai[n]st one who writes an application to take the oath of allegiance, but loses it and it is picked up in prison. His fellow prisoners buffet him, kick him taunt him, and drive him out under the insufficient protection of the Yankees. At night heard preach~~ed~~ one of the most ridiculous of Hard Shell Babtist. Doctrine extreme.[68]

Saturday 9th

Very cold. At night an interresting debate on the subject,—"After the Southern Confederacy establishes her independence, should foreign immigration be prohibited" took place. The feeling of the house is very much against its toleration—very few are in favor of it. My position, as chosen on the question was the Negative. After the Society adjourned conversation waxed warm on the subject all over the room, and lasted long.

Sunday 10th

Cold and clear. A Shameful altercation of words took place among a number of the room about wood and a private stove. Attended preaching at block 10 Sermon preached by Col. Lewis of Mo (Meth) From Zech. XIV. 7. "And at evening time there shall be light."—Applied it to the present time, and spoke of the final success of our arms. Also as applied to individuals. The discourse was able and well delivered.[69] An address was then made by Capt. Allen (Babt), on our condition, &c, encouraging all to stand fast, and deport themselves like men battling for freedom, and to disregard the threats of retaliation by the Yankees, in placing us under the brute Butler; and to trust in Christ. He then extended an invitation to all those who wished to join the church to come forward, whereon seven came forward and made their profession, &c.[70] Three joined the Methodist—two the Presbyterian church, and two remained undecided;—but received their cirtificates of recommedation, to whatever church they might decide on.—the others to their respective churches.

Monday 11th

Monotonous with common rumors, or the usual 'Grape' (grapevine). Preaching at night by Col. Caudle of Kentucky (Old Bap) from Isa. LV He preached a free grace offering to all, which is contrary to the doctrine of his church, but which is the sounder for that. He seemed to reprobate their d[o]ctrine of election and reprobation, and declared if he thought such to be the case he would never again take the pulpit, which was sensible, however he clings to their sing-song method of delivery, which spoils. He said he could not tell by his learning where his text was, still he reads tolerably well.[71]

Tuesday 12th

No prisoners removed yet. Plenty of 'Grape.' Reading scattering—in Bible, Magazines &c—books scarce. Hair cut. My mess had supper today. It consisted of pudding made of light bread and sugar and a little butter. All gathered around and eat like chickens out of a doe trough. Present of a knit jacket by Lt. Harris.[72]

Wednesday 13th

Weather moderate. No amusement until night when a debate took place, which was duller than usual.

Thirsday 14th

Harpers Magazine of /52 to read. Change in mess arrangement—Some unpleasantness. Pan of hash. S. A little rain.

Friday 15th

Snow on the ground ~~of~~ a few inches deep. Monotony monotony Monotony.

Saturday 16th

Read one of Shakespeare's plays entitled "As you like it." Debate at night on the question, "Should the Southern Confederacy after she establishes her independance repudiate her present issues of money" (paper) Decided in the negative. Some are very much in favor of it. The most are opposed to it. In the Neg.

Sunday 17th

Attended preaching Sermon by an old Methodist minister, on a text in Revelation. Two officers asked an interest in the prayers of the church. Episcopal service in the evening. The minister I understand does not associate with those of other denominations. A bad principle.

My reason and better judgement has constatly taught me that, if possible, I should flee from the wrath to come. I have long observed a beauty in holiness and the importance of serving that God, to whom all adoration honor and praise is due. Every hightoned principle, whether of the righteous or of the wicked, is derived from or is a portion of Christianity. Christianity exerts a great influence upon the wicked whether they accept it, or not. Many wicked although they revel and swear, yet they will not steal or lie. A man in this civilized and enlightened country cannot be what is termed a gentleman unless he have some Christian principles. A man, it matters not how wicked he be, if he be honorable has to rest~~ed~~ his honor upon some maxim of Christianity. If we find a man that regards none of the maxims or principles of religion, we behold what even the world would term a brute. He is no better than filthy swine. He is unprincipled, without honor and not to be trusted. He has no integrity of character. A dog is more than his equal.

How much greater then and more substantial must be the character of the Christian. How noble, how excellent must be religion? Even among a band of robbers there must be justice in the division of plunder or they cannot thrive together in their despicable, shameful way of life. How much more then should it be desired than riches, "yea, than much fine gold"![73] I have often desired it, and been "almost persuaded to be a Christian," but conflicting doctrines, false pride and timidity, have stoutly opposed it. Many passages /of Scripture/ discouraged me. They seemed to indicate the cirtainty of election for ordination and predestination, of some, to the exclusion of the remainder, from life eternal. It seemed that those who were to be saved were elected from all eternity whilst others were reprobated. I could never fully believe this doctrine. Again it seemed that God was the author of repentance, and yet the sinner himself is warned to repent. How could he repent unless God saw fit that he should. The spirit must "draw him." His reason may tell him that it would be well for him to repent, but how can he, unless God cause him to feel a sense of his guilt,—how can he have Godly sorrow? The following dream /which took place/ on Sunday night will show. /Explained it to myself during my sleep, mind becoming active and reproducing former impressions/ In my dream I saw two men. One held between his fingers a nail, and said to the other can you light this, and he said, no,—Then he took a lamp with a wick and said, "Can you light this?," and he /said/ yes—which having lighted the first said, Behold "fruits meet for repentance," and the smoke went up from the wick as if the fire were burning oil, and he said, "This represents /(The following blotches occur because of a change of views, but the analogy corresponds to my present belief—Faith before repentance)/ a sense of the guiltiness of sin." Then the first said to the other, "Are there any persons in your church who have foul breath?" and he said "yes"—and he then said that, that represented the guiltiness of sin, whereon I awaked fixed it in my memory, and set about the explanation, which came up very naturally. The nail represented faithlessness, because of which no one will act. The wick oil represented true faith, upon which ~~the Holy Ghost~~ a man will act and do as commanded by the word of God. Thus showing that the sinner must come to Christ in true earnest faith, "believing that he is, and that he is a rewarder of them that diligently seek him" when the influence of the ~~Holy Ghost~~ word of God will be felt about his heart, working in him repentance toward God—a Godly sorrow. God I now fully believe is the author of repentance /through his own Word/. The foul breath represents the guiltiness of sin, which will no longer reign in the heart after the purification and sanctification of the ~~Holy Ghost~~ Word. Any one who has sound and clean teath, and is free from all filthiness will not have foul breath. The above analogy Sprung up in my mind during my sleep. I had thought a good deal about the subject referred to. I had never made any such similitude during my wakefulness, furthermore I had never believed in dreams. May I make good use of this information which indicates Faith before repentance. Faith first repentance next.[74]

Monday 18th

Snow on the ground a few in. deep. It fell during the day and the night following—Monotony.

Tuesday 19th

Snow falling, and drifting, so much that it was difficult to tell whether it was really snowing or not. After dinner it ceased, when several hundred had a regular snow balling, which afforded amusement for all.

Wednesday 20th

Miscellaneous reading. Constantly in want of books. for the lack of which, I can have no system. If I had Rollin's works or Allison's or Macauly's History I could read to much advantage, notwithstanding the noise, and crowded state of the room.[75] The whole room floor dampened during the day, with melted snow. Several companies were organized during the day for the purpose of fighting a regular battle with snow. It was fought with great energy on both sides, and with considerable excitement. /colors flying/ Quite amusing to spectators.

Thirsday 21st

After breakfast, when we eat about all we had, commenced the day's work by stitching or sewing—don't know how I may end it,—like I always do perhaps. Oh! for a little more system and solitude. How I long for some quiet literary retreat. I am indeed tired of seeing so many men. Turn your eyes yonder,—there is a man's face.—so with any other direction. However I am very much enured to these things. Can make out in any crowd. Want tobacco but can't get it. Must inure myself to doing without.

Friday 22d

Read the History of the Life of Queen Elizabeth, 16th Cen[76]

Saturday 23d

Weather comparatively warm. Snow fast melting Debate at night on the question, "Which is the preferable form of government a limited monarchy or a republic?" The discussion was animating. Affir. gained it. On Aff. A great majority oppose a monarchy.

Sunday 24th

Very muddy. Col. Lewis of Mo preached and excellent sermon from the text "It is finished" Capt Allen of Va. at night, preached from the parable of the Merchantman seeking goodly pearls.[77]

Monday 25th

Spent the day mostly in cleaning up, ironing blankets, clothes &c.

Remainder of the month spent in the usual way Monotony, and hindrances at literary employment. Weather mostly pleasant—more so, than expected for this Northern clime. One more little snow, sufficient to cover the ground. Rations not enough—appetite always calling for more

Tuesday February 9th

Four hundred officers were called out from the prison in alphabetical order, A, B, & C's to be sent away. The day was cold. It is thought they were sent to ~~City~~ Point Lookout in Md. More are expected to follow.[78]

Columbus L. Turner's diary ends abruptly at this point. In all likelihood, his supply of paper was exhausted, and he was unable to acquire more from the sutler. We know very little about his last thirteen months at Johnson's Island. He was

one of the 216 officers from North Carolina in the prison that signed a letter to Gov. Zebulon B. Vance on March 30, 1864, praising him for "the distinguished ability and lofty patriotism which have characterized your administration," and for the resolute spirit expressed in his recent campaign speech at Wilkesboro. They urged Vance to hold fast against the Southern peace advocates, as "war may cover the land with sorrow and mourning, but peace on the terms of submission would cover it with the blackness of the shadow of death."[79]

One other document reflects his last year in prison. On February 14, 1865, William Mason, a "Christian Preacher," addressed a note to "any Congregation of the Faithful Bretheren in Christ": "Be it known that our well beloved Bro Columbus: L. Turner, was duly immersed and received into the Christian Fellowship of the Bretheren. (prisoners of war) on Johnson's Island O, June 18th 1864. and that as a faithful and accepted Brother is respectfully commended to the Love and kind Regard of any Christian Congregation with whom his membership may fall."[80]

Turner finally left Johnson's Island on March 21, 1865. He was first transferred to Point Lookout, Maryland, where his younger brother Gus had died five weeks earlier. He may have visited and noted the location of the freshly dug grave. On April 28, Turner was sent for the third time to Fort Delaware. On June 12, he took the oath of allegiance and began the long journey home.[81]

Sometime after his return to Turnersburg, he added the following account to the prison diary:

A Mischivous Shot

About 10 o'clock on the night of the 31st of July/64, a sentinel on the outer wall, from some insufficient cause, took aim at a crowded room of Block 5 and fired, the ball entering the room through a studding 3 or 4 in. thick, piercing through the right arm of Lt. Dillard of Va fracturing the bone, and lodging in the left shoulder of Lt. Inmon of N.C. who was asleep at the time.[82] The sentinel claimed that there was a light in the room; but there was none. If he thought there was, he must have been deceived by the reflection of the light of the lamp on his post, against the window panes. He may have expected some reward by such a shameful act. The wounded were taken to the hospital, and after they recovered, the Commandant of the post allowed them as a small recompense for their misfortune, to take choice of certain unoccupied small rooms in better blocks, and select their own roommates.[83] Lieut. Inmon selected room 8½ of Block 1, with the following officers Capt. H. J. Hawkins of

Cowan, Franklin Co. Tenn, 1st Tenn Inft, Capt John Moore, Moores Creek, Hanover Co. N.C. 18. N.C. Inft, Capt A. A. Moffitt of Laurinburg, Richmond Co. N.C., 18th N.C. I. Capt J. B. Williams 20th N.C. I. J. M. Kendrick Lieut 23rd N.C. I. Erasmus, Gaston Co. N.C. J. E. Devaughn, Lt. 2d Ga. Cav. Jonesboro Ga. & C. L. Turner Lt. Co. 'A' 33d N.C. Troops. Turnersburg N.C.[84]

Candor	Liberality
Firmness	Mercy
Courage	Prudence
Honesty	Justice
Gentleness	Benevolence

Turnersburg, Iredell County
N Carolina

INTERLUDE:
FROM JOHNSON'S ISLAND PRISON TO THE NORTH CAROLINA STATE HOUSE, 1865-1873

After nearly two years of confinement in Federal prisoner-of-war camps, twenty-three-year-old Columbus Lafayette Turner returned home to Iredell County in June 1865, where he found that "the young girls and pine trees seemed to have outgrown everything else." According to family tradition, he immediately returned to the North with his father to retrieve the body of his brother, John Augustus Turner, from the prison graveyard at Point Lookout, Maryland. Gus was reinterred in the Mount Bethel United Methodist Church cemetery, where his brother William and sisters Tobitha and Laura were buried. The family home and factory at Turnersburg had survived the incursion of Federal troops through Iredell County in the closing days of the war. In April 1865, Maj. Gen. George Stoneman's cavalry burned the nearby Eagle Mills, but according to Wilfred Dent Turner (who was ten at the time), his father "heard they were coming and sent to Statesville and got

The cemetery at Mount Bethel United Methodist Church near Turnersburg in which Wilfred and Dorcas Turner and eight of their children are buried. From *Iredell County Landmarks: A Pictorial History of Iredell County*, p. 78.

the militia headed by Col. S. A. Sharp, and stationed them on a hill above the Factory, and built breast works out of cotton bales, with space to see between. With local guns they faced the bridge over Rocky Creek. The breast works were finished and the men remained there several days but Stoneman did not come."[1]

Exposure to the elements while in service, and particularly during the two winters spent in drafty quarters on Lake Erie, would adversely affect Turner's health for the rest of his life. As he noted in his diary after a business trip to Statesville in 1874, "I take cold in the head very easily. Have to observe the greatest regularity and uniformity. Service in the army and suffering in prison, started this trouble."[2]

An unpublished memoir written by his son Reginald suggests that Lum Turner tried to resume his education at Trinity College in the fall of 1865, but found that "he could not study and soon he gave it up." He returned to Turnersburg and took up teaching, just "to be doing something." He most likely taught in a one-room field schoolhouse in the neighborhood, though perhaps it was at Olin High School, five miles northwest of Turnersburg. He had attended the school as a teenager in the late fifties, and his father was on the board of trustees. In the back pages of the notebook in which he noted expenditures, books read, and subjects written upon during his days at Trinity College before the war, Turner recorded lists of students and grades, accounts of pupils' fees, subjects taught, and a daily class schedule. The first roster of students is dated August 2, 1865, and includes the surnames Allred, Bailey, Begarly, Lazenby, Love, Ward, Whitaker, and Wilson. He also taught his four younger siblings: Addie Dorcas, 18; Virginia Ann "Jennie," 13; Emma Ella, 12; and Wilfred Dent, 10. The school day began at 8:00 A.M. and concluded at 5:30 P.M., with morning and afternoon recesses and a two-hour "playtime" at midday. Turner instructed his charges in geography, arithmetic, algebra, grammar, spelling, writing, and reading. After twelve weeks of teaching, he had earned $35.64 from thirteen pupils, excluding his brother and sisters.[3]

In 1866, he "merchandised" in his father's mill-village store. He formally went into business with Wilfred in January 1867, the firm then styled W. Turner and Son, cotton manufacturers. That same month, his name appeared in the deed books of Iredell County for the first time: he and his father were named trustees in a mortgage deed from Jeremiah Stack for 110 acres to secure a note of $500 to Wilfred Turner. Stack eventually defaulted on the loan, and Columbus sold the tract, as well as another parcel of 75 acres, to his father for $350 in April 1874.[4]

Mary Jane "Mollie" Graves Turner (1841-1873), the first wife of Columbus Lafayette Turner. The diary her husband kept while serving in the General Assembly in the months following her death palpably reflects the enormity of his grief. Image courtesy of the Iredell Museum of Arts and Heritage, Statesville, N.C.

During that eventful first month of 1867, Columbus Turner took a wife. On January 16, he and Mary Jane "Mollie" Graves were married by the Reverend Joshua Peterkin at St. James Episcopal Church in Richmond, Virginia. The twenty-five-year-old bride, eight months older than her husband, was the daughter of James Henry and Harriet Smith Graves of Culpeper County, Virginia. The couple returned to Turnersburg to live at Cottage Home, a small house on the grounds of his parents' homeplace.[5]

As Lum Turner learned the cotton mill business at his father's side, he decided to follow Wilfred's footsteps and stand for public office. In 1872, he was elected to represent Iredell County as a member of the Conservative Party in the House of Representatives in the General Assembly of 1872-1874. At that time, representatives served two-year terms, and each seating of the assembly consisted of a regular session and an extra session. In 1872, the regular session convened on November 18 and sat until March 3, 1873. The extra session met on November 17, 1873, and adjourned on February 16, 1874.

In the waning days of Reconstruction in North Carolina, the Conservative Party, soon to be officially renamed the Democratic Party, held the balance in both the house (66 to 54) and senate (32 to 18). Still enjoying the exhilaration of their successful impeachment and removal of Gov. William W. Holden in March 1871, the Conservatives were determined to complete the reestablishment of their pre-war political

The mill complex of W. Turner and Son at Turnersburg included a flour mill, which Wilfred Turner began operating during the Civil War. From *Iredell County Landmarks: A Pictorial History of Iredell County*, pp. 144-145.

and social eminence, and to remove the remaining vestiges of carpetbagger rule, personified by the continued presence of superior court judges Albion W. Tourgée and Samuel W. Watts. The legislators of the 1872-1874 assembly were characterized by their "youth and legislative inexperience. A very large number had been in the Confederate army." There were still seventeen African Americans in the legislature, four in the senate and thirteen in the house, and the Republicans retained hold of the governor's office, in the person of Tod R. Caldwell, who had succeeded the ousted Holden and was then elected on his own accord in 1872.[6]

On the opening day of the regular session, thirty-year-old Columbus Turner presented his credentials to the House of Representatives and was qualified. He was assigned membership on the house committee on engrossed bills and on the house branch of the joint committee on the insane asylum. For a freshman legislator, he was relatively active, introducing nine pieces of legislation during the opening session: five bills and four resolutions. His rather inauspicious debut came on

November 26 with the introduction of a bill to levy a tax on dogs. Neither the Committee on Finance nor the Committee on the Judiciary recommended passage of Turner's proposal. His next effort, a resolution of instruction to the Joint Select Committee on Constitutional Reform, was tabled after its second reading. In the meantime, he cast six successive ballots in favor of Zebulon B. Vance in the election in the assembly for U.S. senator, which Augustus L. Merriman finally won on December 3.[7]

The freshman representative from Iredell County strikes a solonic pose, ca. 1872. Image courtesy of the Iredell Museum of Arts and Heritage, Statesville, N.C.

After the assembly reconvened on January 15, 1873, following its Christmas break, Turner made one further attempt to author legislation of statewide application. He introduced a bill on January 17 to amend an act passed in the 1870-1871 session to provide a cheap chattel mortgage. His proviso would declare it a misdemeanor for the maker of a chattel mortgage to "sell, give away, conceal or otherwise dispose of the property mortgaged with intent to defraud the mortgagee." Two days after the Committee on the Judiciary recommended against its passage, Turner moved for a suspension of the rules to have the bill sent back to the committee. Unmoved, the committee again recommended against it on January 25, and there the matter dropped.[8]

Influenced no doubt by correspondence or personal visits from constituents over the Christmas break, the freshman representative from Iredell County turned his attention to matters of local concern during the last month of the regular session. Between February 5 and February 15, he introduced three public-local bills. The first was of particular interest to his immediate family: a proposal to prevent the sale of liquor within one mile of Turnersburg Church. He introduced a similar prohibition for the town of Statesville, as well as a bill to authorize the employment of a police force in the Iredell County seat. The first of these Statesville bills reflected his concern to represent the interests of all of his constituents. Turner drafted the legislation in response to a petition from town leaders to prohibit the sale of spirituous liquors within two miles of the city limits in order to encourage attendance at the town's "flourishing male academy, and one of the finest Female Colleges in the State." After he introduced the measure on February 15, he received a second petition from citizens (including many merchants) of Statesville, opposing the prohibition and requesting that the matter be put to the electorate. On February 15, Turner offered a substitute bill that included the voter-approval requirement. His bill to authorize the town commissioners of Statesville to hire a police force with powers within the town limits commensurate with those of the sheriff and constables was favorably received after amendment by the Committee on the Judiciary. It passed a third reading in the house on February 19. Both of the bills concerning Statesville were enacted, the prohibition of the sale of liquor as a public law and the employment of a police force as a private statute. Turner also introduced a resolution of interest to Iredell County, a proposal to establish a branch of the state insane asylum at either Statesville or Olin.[9]

During the waning days of the session, Turner authored two other resolutions that went nowhere. On March 1, he proposed that the house resolve to investigate the conduct of the notorious carpetbagger, Superior Court judge Albion W. Tourgée. On the final day of the regular session, he recommended that the assembly "inquire into the charges that the Pennsylvania Central Railroad Company and other rings are running papers improperly to influence legislation." Turner also presented a memorial from some of the stockholders of the Atlantic and Ohio Railroad protesting proposed changes to the company's charter.[10]

Portions of the text of two speeches Turner delivered in the house in February 1873 have survived, providing insight not only into his opinions regarding these particular pieces of legislation, but also his

The western face of the North Carolina State Capitol in Raleigh as it appeared in the latter quarter of the nineteenth century. Image courtesy of the North Carolina State Archives, Raleigh, N.C.

vision of the ideal legislator [see Appendixes C and D for full transcriptions of these speeches]. The first, delivered on February 22, concerned a bill to amend the constitutional article that required the assembly to provide care "at the charge of the State" for the deaf, dumb, blind, and insane citizens of the state. The proposal would have limited state-supported assistance to only those families whose holdings were less than the homestead and personal property exemption set by the state constitution. Turner voted against the measure, which failed by one vote to receive the requisite two-thirds majority to amend the constitution. Only the first page of his speech has survived, but these few lines reveal his opinion of the people he represented and his feeling of obligation to express their wishes. He wrote: "I represent a people who when they understand the right, are free to uphold it. They do not wish anything ingrafted into their Constitution that would encourage class legislation." That being the case, he had no choice but to vote against the bill, as "it is my duty to give expression to the wish of a large majority of the people whom I represent, by my vote."[11]

Turner further expounded upon this view in a speech he prepared for the oft-postponed consideration of the amnesty bill by the house on February 26-27. Despite serious reservations about thereby pardoning some very bad people, he voted for its passage. While condemning the excesses committed by secret societies during Reconstruction, he refused to stand in judgment upon any man's "honest political sentiments" honestly expressed. His motto, he said, was "Let every man do just as he pleases provided he does his neighbor no harm." Turner returned to a fuller exposition upon what he believed to be the proper determinants of a legislator's vote on any matter:

> The Aye or No upon many questions is determined by some with a reference to its bearing upon the next political campaign. . . . This is the method of some, whilst others will support a party measure, even though it be grossly wrong. Sir, I trust that I am not one to adapt means to the end whether good or evil. In that sense I am not a politic man, but am "free to confess" that I would be gladly described by that word, if deserved, provided it were taken in its primary sense which is "Exercising sagacity in devising and pursuing measures adapted to promote the public welfare."[12]

Between sessions of the assembly, Turner went back to Turnersburg, where he would encounter another in a number of personal losses to be endured during his lifetime. On September 11, 1873, Mollie Turner died at home of typhoid fever at the age of thirty-two. A newspaper account of her death described her as "a most excellent christian lady, . . . much beloved by the entire community." She was buried in Hollywood Cemetery in Richmond. When her grieving husband returned to Raleigh in November for the extra session, his pain of loss was still fresh, as is obvious in the pages of the diary he kept in 1874. Eleven years would pass before Columbus Turner remarried.[13]

The second session of the assembly convened on November 17. Historian J. G. de Roulhac Hamilton concluded that "the proceedings were of little interest, as no important general law was enacted, and most of the time was consumed in private or local legislation." Four days after the house resumed business, Turner reintroduced his bill to amend the 1870-1871 statute providing for an inexpensive chattel mortgage. While his draft languished in the Committee on Propositions and Grievances, a similar bill was introduced on the floor of the house. Turner offered his version as a substitute, which was rejected. He then joined the majority in approval of the alternate measure.[14]

Turner introduced one other public bill before the Christmas recess, a measure to compel the state treasurer, Republican David A. Jenkins, to pay all lawful warrants and drafts upon the treasury. Jenkins claimed that he was enjoined from doing so by a federal court order in a civil suit against him, *Self et al. v. Jenkins*. Turner's proposal would fine Jenkins $1,000 and imprison him from three to twelve months should he refuse to do his duty. The bill was referred to a joint select committee established to consider the ramifications of the suit in federal circuit court.[15]

In December, the representative from Iredell also presented two bills of local interest, both of which became law. Turner proposed a bill to authorize constable James C. Anderson to collect arrearages of taxes in Statesville for the years 1866 to 1871. The Committee on Finance amended the proposal to make it applicable statewide, which the house approved on December 19. The statute, titled "An Act for the Relief of Sheriffs and Tax Collectors," was ratified on January 19, 1874. The other measure sought to incorporate Centre Presbyterian Church in Iredell County and prohibit the sale of spirituous liquor within a half-mile of the church. The bill was approved by committee with minor amendments and passed by the full house on December 20. It was approved by the senate and ratified on February 10, 1874.[16]

The General Assembly recessed on December 22 for its Christmas break, to reconvene on January 12, 1874. Turner arrived in Raleigh three days late. The following day, January 16, he began keeping a diary, which he backdated to the first of the year. Significantly, January 16 was the seventh anniversary of his wedding, the first since the death of his wife.

THE LEGISLATIVE DIARY OF COLUMBUS LAFAYETTE TURNER, 1874

1874 January 1 Thursday

Had a pleasant drive from Franklinville in Randolph Co. to Mr. O. Palmer's of said county, about 14 miles distant, in company with Mr. P. and two of his daughters, Misses Helen and Decie. Wrote a piece in Mrs. Curtis' Album. She is a daughter of Geo. Makepeace, the founder of the cotton factories at that place. He died in 1872, and his son George now lives at the old homestead.[1] Prevailed upon Miss Emma Taylor a modest young lady of about 18 [?] years to show me some of her original poems which were well conceived and well written. While stopping with Mr. Curtis, a very agreeable gentleman, we visited the factories near, which are on the Deep River, and also the Faith Rock: down which fearful steep Hunter of Revolutionary memory fled from Fanning—he and horse safely escaping.[2] Closed the day at Mr. Oran Palmer's, with his cheerful family & some friends.

[January 2]

[top half of page illegible]

. . . our adieus. Miss Decie played a good piece for me, and bidding the old people a kind farewell—after a short drive with Decie, started for Greensboro. It was cloudy with slight sprinkles of rain—mud abundant. 12 miles from G boys and girls were playing Town Ball—one girl was pitching balls and a big fat one catching "out."[3] Tabernacle Church and Academy are on this road about [torn] miles I think from G.[4] Mr. P [*torn*] sat up till after midnight waiting for the train. Saw a Mr. Robertson of Rockingham with his newly invented tobacco pr. clamps [*In right margin*] good.[5]

Saturday January 3

Took the train at Greensboro about 1 A.M. and had a good disposition for sleep when we reached Salisbury. Changed cars and arrived in Statesville about 6 A.M. Went to Simonton House now kept by Col. Sadler of S.C.[6] Layed down to await breakfast, and barely slept. Engaged horse & buggy to carry me to Turnersburg but J. M. Turner an uncle coming up with me, said he was going there with his buggy and so I went with him.[7] Had pleasant conversation on the way—roads very muddy—some rain and cool. Found my father and Offie and David Stimpson at the store—attending to business.[8] Looked in the P. O. box and found three letters, one written Nov. 18th/72—one from Geo. McCrindell and one from some of my constituents concerning the act of incorporation for Centre Church [torn] on to China Grove [torn] had dinner talked and J. M. T. went on his way home.[9]

Sunday January 4

Did not go to church anywhere. Read some Texas Presbyterian Clergyman's defense of Infant Baptism and Pouring and Sprinkling instead of immersion for Baptism. Phamflet some 80 pages, Usual arguments. This is a vexed question but it seems that the great learning of the age is unable to settle it. It may be on account of prejudices—human preferences and associations. One thing is settled beyond all dispute—the importance of piety. This all can agree upon. When the lust of the eye and the pride of life pass away it may be the same way with religious controversy that is acrimonious discussion. Wrote to Geo. McCrindell and the friends [HP] at Burnt Grove and replied to letter of Nov. 18, 72.

January 5

Examined business letters and sent answers. Began a very busy week, in which we never went home to dinner. Began a general invoice of goods and stock generally.

Tuesday January 6

Close steady work invoicing, except the time occupied with mail and some reading. Rec'd letter from L. L. Lacy regretting that I did not come to Richmond to spend Christmas.[10]

January 7

Engaged invoicing. Cold. Busy, but had to look up now and then, to answer inquiries as to what the Legislature was doing or had done.

Thursday January 8

Invoicing, multiplying and adding up. Sister Addie & husband moved to Cottage Home.[11]

January 9

Occupied in regulating business, & a general summing up of invoice.

Answered the letter of Messrs. J. R. McNeeley, Z. A. McLean, G. J. Houston & Robt. McPherson, showing them that the bill for Centre Church, was drawn so as to cover as nearly as possible and right, all the points contained in their previous letters and petition. They desired two or 3 important things, and now it seems, all they wish is a Liquor Prohibiton Law. They evidently asked that their church be incorporated and furnished me the names of those they wished to be Commissioners & Trustees and also desired the other. The bill is right and passed the House before Christmas, and is now beyond my control.[12]

Saturday January 10

A general oversight and involving such articles as had been missed. Settled with Isaac Gaither col[ore]d up to Jany 8th at $8 per mo. Hired by new concern at $9 per mo.[13]

Took tea with the new housekeeper at my old home and remained all night in the little room which had been nicely fixed up for me with my furniture. The old parlor also reserved for me and mine.

January 11

Rode Dolly to church at Clarksberry. Jennie and Julia Summers went in buggy and drove our old David "the Famous Gray."[14]

Rev. T. Page Ricaud preached. Subject parable of the talents.[15] Handled this subject pretty well. Some sayings and actions quite odd. Some flights very entertaining. A general titter was provoked by the following anecdote. A mule driver wished to marry the daughter of a man of wealth and standing in his community, and in order to effect his purpose he assumed as he thought a high sounding title. At a hotel he registered his name and wrote M. D. after it. The father saw it and said why he is a Doctor and thought much more favorably of the man, who succeeded in marrying the daughter. When the trick was found out the old man, scolded & fretted to think his M. D. should so deceive [*In right margin*] but the man said there was no deception—it stood for Mule Driver.

January 12

Arranged for the disposition of some of my effects, such as horse and harness.

Disposed of 1 Bed Stead [8], 1 Wash Stand [4], 1 Etagere [5], 4 yellow cane bottomed chairs [9], 1 Beaureau [15], l Pr old gears [5], 1 Rocking Chair [3] to W. T. $49.

Turned over to keep for me hair matrass and any needed bedclothing.

Remained Sunday night with W. T. Gaither and family. To day about 9½ oclock he started with me to Turnersburg. Took dinner at China Grove and afterwards went to the factory.[16]

Tuesday January 13

Packed my valise to start to Raleigh. Pa and I went through mud and rain to Statesville. Paid Dr. Campbell $77.[17] Heard of a negro woman at the poor house who was taken there in a dying condition from starvation. Her husband Bill Nichols had deserted her and her baby, and her forlorn condition was not reported or known in time for her to be saved from hungering and starving. Sad neglect in a land of plenty I may say. It too often happens that the col[ore]d people neglect the feeble and suffering.

Took the train at 3 P.M. Met Dr. Ellis Senator from Catawba and Mr. Haynes Rep. from Haywood.[18] Had pleasant converse. Stopped at Boyden House.[19] Took train for Charlotte about 7 P.M. and arrived there about 10.

Charlotte January 14 Wednesday

Called upon Wittkowsky and Rintels to purchase me a neat suit of clothes and overcoat to celebrate my marriage anniversary in.[20]

Obtained a nice suit and fit. Cost including overcoat and two kerchiefs, with Suspenders and cravat is $75.25.

Took meals at the Central Hotel.[21] Highest price for best cotton 14¾. Called upon the Vances. Met there Rev. Mr. Davis of Gaston Co.[22]

Took the train for Raleigh at 7 P.M. Met Bryson Rep. from Jackson, which county he represented as being great for cabbages, having raised a large quantity himself that weighed each 1, 5lbs Good for grazing.[23] Settled down to a restless sleep.

January 15

Reached Raleigh between 7 & 8 A.M. Took omnibus to Mrs. Evans' Cor. Edenton & McDowel Sts. In time for breakfast. Room waiting for me.[24] Weather cold.

Went to House Rep. Recd letters from Geo. McCrindell, W. D. Turner and Eugene B. Drake[25] The latter in regard to bill amending

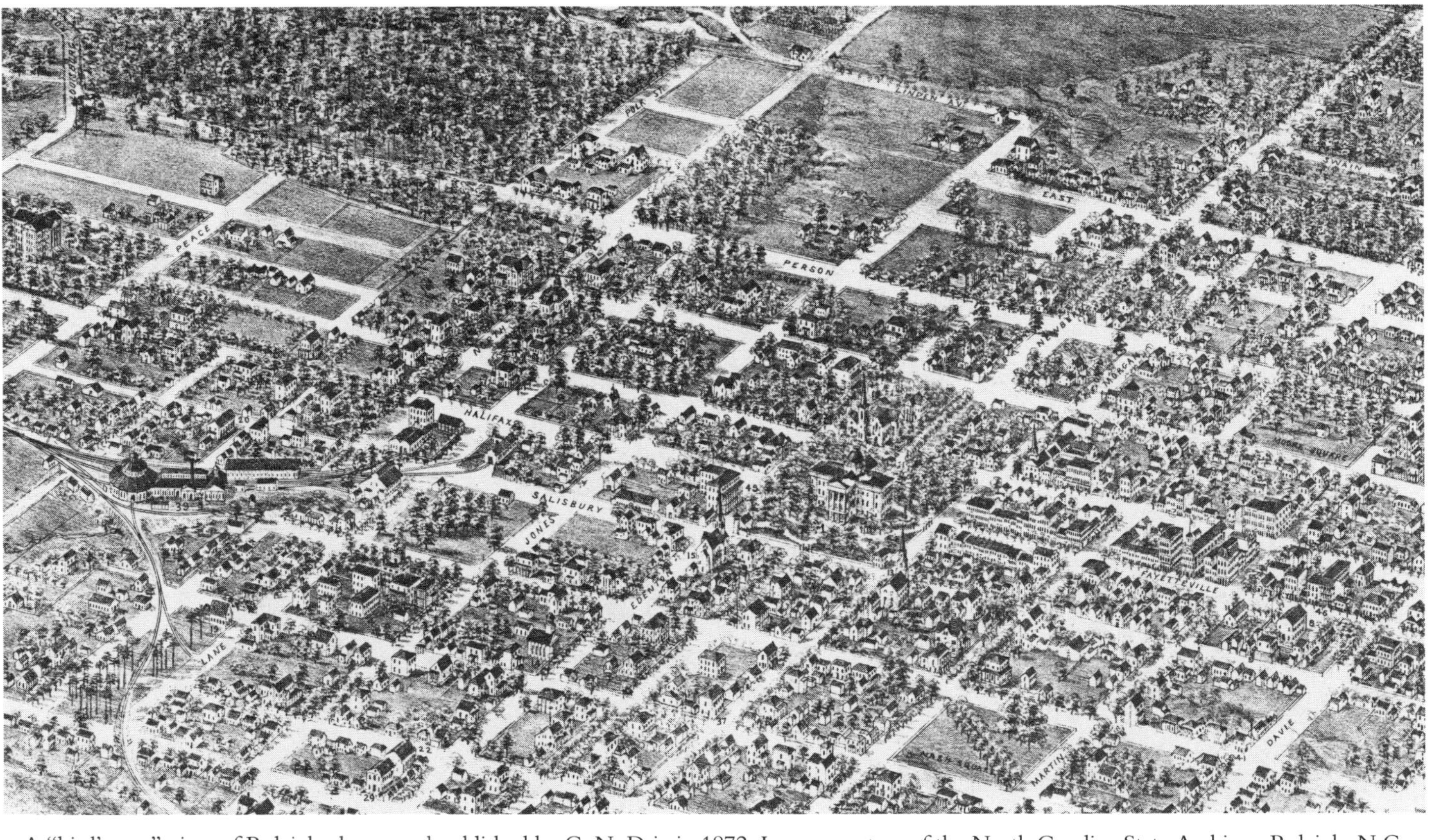

A "bird's-eye" view of Raleigh, drawn and published by C. N. Drie in 1872. Image courtesy of the North Carolina State Archives, Raleigh, N.C.

charter of A. T. and O. R. R. He wishes it amended so as to read, where it regards the sale—"or to any other connecting line" but this bill passed the House before Chmas.[26]

To day the bill preventing the sale of liquor to minors passed. Called Ayes & Noes on it, when a squad of members urged me to withdraw the call, lest some who would vote for it off record would vote against it and defeat it. I did so stating however that I was the same on or off record, but would withdraw on account of the nervous.[27]

January 16

To day seven years ago at 1 oclock P.M. I led a delicate loving amiable sprightly Virginia lady to the nuptial altar in St. James Church Richmond Va. She lived happily—crossed the river of death Sept 11th/73 and is now I trust happier.[28] We always celebrated our marriage anniversary, and tho. I am alone, I wished to honor the day in some cheerful way. Am sorry we are too crowded at this our boarding house for me to have had a dining all together with invited guests. I wore for the first time to day a fine black cass suit,[29] and looked as neat as I could—having shaved and had my hair trimmed—wore my boots smoked a few cigars with some friends, and will don my every day apparel tomorrow. This was in memory of my wifes tidiness, and particularly as to my dress. It happened that we had plenty of turkey for dinner. Wrote the report of Sub. Com. on Insane Asylum.[30] To day began this diary. Rec'd a strange letter. [*In left margin*] Letter to Mr. & Mrs. Lacy & Mrs. C. & W. D. Turner Day pleasant & cool. Showed Mollie's scrap book and obituary.

January 17

Wrote to Ella E. Turner being the last time I will ever write her as a Turner.[31] Long speeches in the Senate on Public Debt—did not hear them.

The House soon after Mr. Houston's resolution, protesting against the passage of the Supplimental Civil rights bill in Congress, was called up, developed itself into a Republican Caucus or Convention, with the Conservative side of the house as Spectators.[32] The latter evidently enjoyed the scene and studiously avoided having any thing to say. "Bad blood" seemed to be in the eyes of the leading white Republicans, on account of the urgency of the Colored members in reference to their rights.[33] There was sharp sparring between the Brethren. Messrs. Trivett, Blythe & Bowman favored the Resolution. Repbs. and Ellison, Dudley and Abbot col[ore]ds. earnestly opposed.[34] Passed the Substitute of similar intent Ayes 75 Nays 24. Wrote on postal card to Julia (sister). [*In right margin*] From whom recd letter to-day urging me to come. Day fine. [*In left margin*] Sister Julia's letter ansd per postal card. My Resolution on J. S. Com. on Adj. introduced.[35]

Sunday January 18, 1874

Up earlier than usual. Took a long walk before breakfast. Read the morning paper containing an account of the Ex-President Johnson–Holt controversy as to where the guilt lies in the execution of Mrs. Surrat said to be an innocent woman. One blames the other, but the article in question heaps the guilt upon both—and I believe both are blameable and very likely feel the lashings of conscience.[36]

Visited the Baptist Sunday School, for the purpose of going into the Infant Department presided over by Mr. & Mrs. Dodd.[37] Exercises creditable to themselves and children. The children are up or down promptly at the sound of the words "one, two." Have been finishing up this diary to date, not having begun until the month was half gone. Visited Cowles & Nicholson Anderson.[38] [*In left margin*] Day beautiful and not quite so cold. 11:15 P.M. Must retire.

January 19

[*In top margin* Sister Ella was to be married today and] In the House to day the bills passed were of a local character such as the laying off

THE MURDER OF MRS. SURRATT.

Blood hath been shed ere now i' the olden time,
Ere human statute purged the general weal;
Ay, and since, too, murders have been performed
Too terrible for the ear. The times have been
That when the brains were out, the man would die,
And there an end; but now they rise again,
With twenty mortal murders on their crowns,
And push us from our stools. This is more strange
Than such a murder is.—[Macbeth.

The recent accusatory, exculpatory and explanatory cards of ex-President Johnson and Judge Advocate General Holt upon the subject of Mrs. Surratt's execution are suggestive of the retributive justice which sooner or later overtakes the cruel and lawless man. In times of high excitement and licentious power, the rights of individuals may be disregarded and innocent blood may flow; but when reason resumes her sway, the loftiest transgressor shrinks, as his misdeeds pass under the calm scrutiny of her searching eye, and the innocent blood will cry out from the ground.

The hand that wrote the appeal of Holt—the hand that penned the reply of Johnson—both have blood upon them—the blood of a helpless woman, who died among the execrations of a mob. Mary E. Surratt has been in her grave for more than eight long years, but "her spirit walks abroad." From the tomb of supposed infamy into which her lifeless body was hissed by a maddened populace, a voice proceeds which will not let her murderers rest. And has this poor, unfriended woman, who swung into eternity with a felon's halter about her neck, power, even in her dishonored grave, to arraign before the bar of public opinion the two most conspicuous actors in the disgraceful and illegal proceedings that culminated in her execution? 'Tis even so. Her spectral finger points to these two central figures in the conscious-smitten group, and the muse of history has so adjusted her photographic lens as to transfer their pictures to the place forever. They may quarrel as to the part each took in the horrible work, and the one endeavor to shift from his own to the shoulders of the other "the deep damnation of her taking off." But they are partners—partners in the trial, partners in the execution, partners in her blood and partners in that undying sentence of condemnation which the solemn voice of posterity will pronounce against the deed. This is a partnership which cannot be dissolved—either by mutual consent, the decrees of courts or the death of parties. They are wasting their time in endeavoring to fix their respective liabilities now. Let them not anticipate the verdict of history. The point they are discussing now is an immaterial and collateral issue, compared with the more solemn aspects of the case. Holt affirms that he laid before Johnson the petition for the pardon of Mrs. Surratt. The position of Holt, if sustained by proof, [and he does sustain it,] falls infinitely below the charge he will be called upon to meet at the bar of posterity. He was the Judge Advocate General; and, as such, was charged by military law with the duty of giving to the military tribunal, that tried Mrs. Surratt, his legal opinion upon all points. If the tribunal undertook to try any individual of whom it had not jurisdiction, it was his solemn duty so to inform them. Such a tribunal had no jurisdiction in Mrs. Surratt's case. The constitution of the United States upon this point is too plain and emphatic for any man who ever read its provisions to doubt about it. Was Judge Holt ignorant of the fact that she was a civilian, and as such could not be tried by a military court? He is too able a lawyer to plead his ignorance on these points, if, indeed, he should desire to avail himself of this defense. The courts of the District of Columbia were open, and he knew it. She could have been indicted by a grand jury and he knew it. She could have been tried by a jury of her peers, and according to the forms of law, and he knew it. The constitution of her country guaranteed to her such a trial, and he knew it. He was the *law officer* of the military tribunal before which she was arraigned, and as such it was a part of his official duty to give the court his opinion in writing if he saw them assuming a jurisdiction which the law did not give them.

Part of the article in the Raleigh *Sentinel* of January 18, 1874, concerning the controversy between Andrew Johnson and Joseph Holt over responsibility for the execution of Mary Surratt. Image courtesy of the North Carolina State Archives, Raleigh, N.C.

and construction of a road from Wilkesboro to Taylorsville, and bills of incorporation.[39] In the Senate bill preventing the selling of cotton between sunset and sunrise in quantities less than a bale passed without a dissenting vote.[40]

Took the train at 4 P.M. for Haywood to see Sister Julia and husband,—observed the form of a lady in front of me which seemed to be familiar and noticed a gentleman walk in and take a seat by her, when it was settled in my mind that it was Miss Emma Taylor and her Curtis whom I met at Franklinville in Randolph Co. Had a pleasant chat until passing through the bridge over Deep River. I was reminded that I was at Haywood and must get off. Hasty leave. Found sister and family quite well. Reported all changes and news from home & retired late.[41]

Tuesday January 20

Up early. Sister Julia provided a good breakfast before leaving. Took the train at 7½ A.M. and arrived in Raleigh about 9½ or 10 in ample time for session of the House Reps. Travelled with Maj. Scott of Haywood.[42] Bill for uniform rate of interest discussed in the Senate, also Worths Bill and the amendments in regard to State Debt.[43] Appointed with Ransom of the Senate to further investigate expenditures for seuport of Insane Asylum and excused by motion of Dr. Luckey from attendance in sessions of House for next day for that purpose.[44]

Bill to make Fee Simple the Homestead exemptions when once layed off passed in the House with only four dissenting votes. Voted for it because it is just as near right as the present law, and because I believe in a small homestead or one of some sort if not large.[45] [*In left margin*] Answered strange letter.

January 21

Resolution requiring the appointment of eight, five on the part of the House and three on the part of Senate, to make investigations, concerning expenditures for support of Insane Asylum, having been passed—thought that myself and Dr. Ransom should be excused from further investigation so as to leave work for that large committee to perform and consequently we awaited the action of the Senate, or that committee. Our previous report gave rise to this resolution in which we showed that butter had cost 41½¢ flour 10.63 Bacon 12½ Syrup 97 and that under heading of Sundries, Provisions and Groceries there was large expenditure not itemised on the books $67,000 & upward had been expended for Support & repairs including $20,700 for wages & salaries of officers.[46] Drew & introduced bill to regulate fees of Justices of the Peace and Constables.[47]

Thursday January 22

The bill appropriating $46,500, to institutions for Deaf, Dumb & Blind was taken up and provoked much discussion. Last session $5000 were appropriated to build an institution for the Col'd Dep't. The Board had gone as far as to require the amount above $40,000, to complete it. Amendments were offered to reduce, which I opposed stating that no plans or specifications for the building were to be found in any act of this Gen. Assembly, and whilst I depricated and earnestly condemned, exceeding powers granted, I believed in the establishment of a building that would answer the purpose, be satisfactory, and creditable to the State, and advised members offering amendment to reduce the appropriation, to back such with informative facts and figures, bassed upon investigation and would [*In left margin*] move to postpone such to give all objectors opportunity to make investigation and be prepared to act knowingly.[48]

Friday January 23

12.20 OClock A.M. Now I will retire. The visit of Josiah Turner at 9 to 10 P.M. of 22d caused me to have to sit up so late.[49] He is anxious to have impeached Judges Watts and Tourgee.[50] Read his petition to House of Reps. which he wants introduced to day, and I preferred someone else to introduce it, and give my support if appropriate, and I believe in the Legislature showing a bold front, and making officers from highest to lowest beware.[51] I had introduced several measures for him heretofore, and other than two of his, I have put forward none but my own, unless it be an effort similar to that in the Senate to compel the Treasurer to pay only audited A/c. Anything that has my own positive sanction I can more freely advocate, and for that it is best to wait, and guess I will freely favor impeachment, but want to be sure of the evidence of guilt. Mr. H backed down from introducing petition & resolution of impeachment. Being of same name myself thought it best for another to introduce etc. Passed election bill.[52] In Senate bill concerning election of officers to take the place of Governors appointees [*In right margin*] discussed at length.[53]

January 24

Bennett of Anson introduced petition of J. Turner Jr., and resolution for impeachment of Judge Watts. He will be impeached I think.[54]

Drew up and introduced bill to incorporate Harmony Hill Camp Ground in the County of Iredell.[55] Sentinel no. Recd letter from Misses Helen and Dora Palmer—Clever ladies. Miss H. said I could put down the joke of Jany 1st., but that page is full & I am sure I will recollect it. I think I will take her middle name as my sobriquet in any public correspondence either with "Our Living and Our Dead" published by Col. S. D. Pool now Clerk of the House or any other paper. "Leroy" is pretty and convenient. I wonder if she spells it that way.[56]

Long debate in Senate on Usury Bill, and no definite conclusion arrived at. This body does not expedite business. There are too many smart men it seems and too much smart alible [?] & without leader.

Sunday January 25 1874

Up early enough to be so late as usual. First up about 4.—took another nap and found time to be as late as ever.

Albion W. Tourgée (*left*) was a favorite target of Josiah Turner (*right*), vituperative editor of the Raleigh *Sentinel*, who lobbied relentlessly for the impeachment of Tourgée and fellow carpetbagger judge Samuel W. Watts during the 1873-1874 session of the General Assembly. Images courtesy of the North Carolina Collection, Wilson Library, University of North Carolina at Chapel Hill.

The First Baptist Church of Raleigh, as viewed from the State Capitol, ca. 1875. Columbus Turner was a frequent visitor to the church during the winter of 1874, taking a special interest in the conduct of its Sunday School classes. Image courtesy of the North Carolina State Archives, Raleigh, N.C.

Col. Dickey and I went to the Baptist Church, and occupied chairs in one of the aisles. Bap. Sec. of Missions Mr. ___ preached from the scripture concer[n]ing Christ's association with publicans and sinners and being a wine bibber and glutton, which the Jews considered the highest reproach they could heap upon him.[57] Went again at night. Mr. Jordan preached from a text in Haggai concerning the time not having come to build the House of the Lord.[58] This the people said. Just after Dr. Pritchard gave the reasons of their mode of Baptism. Four or five were lead, one by one down into the baptistery and immersed—all men or boys. Very large audience.[59] During the evening Capts Horton, Cowls, Todd, Mahler, Dr. Carson and myself walked several miles and Captain H. & I called for a [*In left margin*] short while on a Miss Thomas & my acquaintance Miss Adelaide Boylin. Capt. H. pleased.[60]

January 26

Received Intelligencer containing an account of sister Ella's marriage by L. S. G. This paper ought to be sent to me regularly but Editor seems to neglect it. Why is this.[61]

A Bill asking or rather incorporating a colored lodge of Masons, was strongly opposed by some of the whites, saying they had never been recognized and that it was clandestine. Gudger opposed, and stated that he preferred the institution of Masonry to any other on earth, the Church not excepted, to which he belongs. Dudley col[ore]d only excepted the Church. A call for the Ayes and Noes being sustained the bill passed by only 2 Maj. 38 to 36. Although a large Maj. in fact nearly all of my party voted against it—those who did vote, yet I voted for it, because Masons must settle the question of recognition among themselves, and it is one act of Incor. among a hundred, and if so good a thing its benefits should extend to all races.[62] Took dinner at Mrs Pullens and exercised along the streets with Horton & Anderson of Davie.[63]

January 27

Dickey of Cherokee and myself rose in ample time this morning having slept better because of a free communication of ideas feelings and faults. I had occasion to recount many things concerning the dear departed[.] Bill concerning voting on the question of liquor prohibition in townships, reported favorably by Judiciary Committee with slight amendments.[64] The bill to amend an act concerning the Consolidation of Central N.C. R. R. and others—called forth many amendments and much discussion and feeling.[65] Gudger made a wild speech. Passed several readings but was reconsidered and will come up as unfinished business. Much might be here said—Myself and Capt Horton were invited by Mr. Huston to ride with him to Insane Asylum—also Mr. Mitchell.[66] Went for the ride. Dr. Grissolm showed us through some of the wards.[67] Was cheerfully greeted and recognized by three of Insane ladies. Went to Caucus. Public debt discussed that is all. Mr. Lines of Clay frd of Rep. Anderson has just invited me to his 'room.' Here I go in compliance.[68]

Wednesday January 28

To day the bill of Waugh of Surry came up—to abolish the office of State Geologist. He took the floor and amused the House for some time by his peculiar style—grimaces twitches and turns. He is an old Representative of the old school, and much opposed to new words of many letters and odd pronunciations. He used to say in common with other people "Mu'seum," but now it was "Musē'um," and as to a proposed classification of quadrupeds and reptiles it did not matter with his constituents whether a bullfrog was a quadruped, reptile or "ancipeadae," this latter word not certain. A museum for the exhibition of a stuffed owl, bullfrog, and a petrified monkey foot was too much expense, he thought. A young doctor said to him one time the wind blows very acute and actuatingly, and then inquired for cat Aye de sulpha luntum when he felt [*In right margin*] like hallooing "Table him off." Waugh's bill failed notwithstanding.[69] [*In left margin*] Went to tea at F's according to invitation.

Thursday January 29

A resolution to pay certain citizens $1277.65 advanced Prof. Kerr, State Geologist, to pay his expenses to the Worlds Exposition at Vienna, excited much discussion, as the Legislature had made no appropriation to that end, and it was regarded by the opponents as unauthorized and a case that ought to be made an example of. This resolution passed the Senate, but failed in the House, 61 having voted against it. Bennett sent to the clerks desk to be read as a part of his remarks the letter of Prof K. written at New York just before sailing for Europe. This letter was published, and considered by some to be a reflection upon N. C.[70] Waugh and Moss of Wilson earnestly opposed it. Brown of Mecklenburg and McGeehee of Person advocated it.[71]

The new county of Lillington failed by a vote of 53 to 54 after having passed the Senate.[72] Letter from Sister Ella describing her marriage on the 19th. State debt & New Consolidation bill occupy the Senate's attention. [*In left margin*] At Special session elected 64 University trustees. Recommended E. Hyne Davis of Iredell.[73]

Friday January 30

After taking my seat Rev Mr. Culbreth informed me that my sister Mrs. Wyche was down street shopping, and that she wanted me to come, and would find her somewhere on Fayetteville St.[74] After a search came up behind her wending her way along the St. leading little Bertha.[75] Tapped her on the shoulder when she looked around frightened and ready to scream out or fight. After leaving her to finish her shopping, returned to my seat, when soon the Revenue bill came up. Much discussion took place on amount of exemptions. This I was anxious to secure in a way that would be to the interest of, and satisfactory to the poor and the farming interest but much exemption would be impolitic, and wrong under the ad valorem system, when a small one would meet the case of the poor.[76] Joined Sister Julia at Mrs. Fentress where was her frd. Miss Blanche F. took dinner there as Miss B. was not willing for me to take her away.[77] After a hasty walk the omnibus [*In right margin*] having left we reached the train and I jumped off when the train was pretty well under weigh but being active kept on my feet. [*In left margin*] Went to Quire meeting at Methodist Church, instead of Ball at Yarboro Hotel.[78] Recd letter from Will D. Turner.

Julia Turner Wyche (1838-1878), the sister whom Columbus Turner visited at her home in Chatham County while he was serving in the General Assembly. Image courtesy of Nancy Jones, Burlington, N.C.

January 31

Began the day as usual. Read the morning papers. Senate worked on their new consolidation bill. The House passed the Machinery act for raising revenue. Brown of Mecklenburg had put in a resolution to raise a joint committee on adjournment, which he called up. This was similar to mine introduced before, and action on it was deferred, so that the Public Debt might first be adjusted when a committee could better determine the time of adjournment. It was know[n] too that there was already on hand this resolution, but he as some others, was anxious for a record in this matter, and I gave him opportunity, as it was or amended as to be like mine and would not therefor press the postponement to take it up. "Looks like stealing somebody else's thunder."[79] Wrote to Mr. & Mrs. M. K. Steele. Went with Horton and Marler and called upon Simonton at the Yarboro, & McLeod Turner.[80]

February 1

Went to Sunday School at Edenton St. Methodist Church. Some of the blind carry a piece for the Children. Mr. Best former Secretary of this

The Yarborough House on Fayetteville Street in Raleigh was known as the third house of state government in the latter half of the nineteenth century, serving for twenty years as the unofficial residence of several governors in the absence of an executive mansion. Columbus Turner often called upon visitors to Raleigh who were staying at the Yarborough. Image courtesy of the North Carolina State Archives, Raleigh, N.C.

State has a base voice equal it would seem to about half dozen ordinary voices. He appears to be about 6 ft. 6 in. high and said to be the smallest of five brothers. His daughter seems to be 6 ft.[81]

Went to the Presbyterian Church for the first time this session. Heard Mr. Whaley of Va. from the words "What hast thou done—behold the voice of thy brothers blood cry unto me from the ground." A sensib[l]e practicable sermon in which he depicted the different kind of murderer. A good preacher, but seems to crack his voice rather much.[82]

Went to Baptist Sunday School Singing and Prayer Meeting. A number of new converts spoke asking prayer in behalf of comrades &c. Prayer offered in behalf of Mr. Armstrong [*In left margin*] who is one of their earnest members, and is very sick.[83] Have remembrance.

Monday February 2

Some peculiar but pleasant dreams. Day opened cloudy and rainy which continued all day with accumulations of ice on the trees &c. The Revenue bill was passed on its second reading. Many little amendments were offered which were either adopted or rejected.[84]

Letter from C. A. Carlton recd concerning school law and more especially the usury law, which he thinks would not be beneficial if adopted.

If it is the true interest of the majority of the people of N.C. to have a law and fixed rate of interest, I am for it notwithstanding it may be my individual interest to leave it open to contract as I am more apt to loan than to borrow.[85] Slept after dinner. At Supper Huston found a birthday day present at his plate which he was afraid to exhibit. It proved to be a baby's garment. Jokes and small talk till bed time. [*In left margin*] 12:15 I had better go to bed. Good night Sis.

Tuesday February 3

Received a remarkable letter with a remarkable proposition coming from the source it did. Recd also a letter from my father which I answered and one from A. Holman[86] and a petition from colored citizens near Catawba Church asking the prohibition of the sale of spirituous liquors within one mile of said church and complaining that there was a grocery or grog shop within a few hundred yards. This was recommended by Isaac Harris and other prominent white citizens.[87] The Revenue bill was passed after numerous amendments which were either adopted or rejected. Offered one which recd large majority and failed only because no quorum voted. Took a walk by the R. and G. RR works and on the rail road.[88] Called upon M. L. McCorkle who was rooming with Houston of Catawba here attending on Supreme Court.[89]

Wednesday February 4

Drew and introduced a resolution to secure attendance of nonresidents as wintness concerning impeachment of Judge Samuel W. Watts Col. J. T. Deweese and G. A. Mason or any others.[90] Introduced petition of colored citizens in regard to preventing sale of spirituous liquors within one mile of Catawba Church. The Suplemental Consolidation bill was on its 2d Reading. Much talk and disposition to amend. Gorman's amendment striking at Joe Turner in regard to overdrawing as he supposed for printing was criticized for bad spelling. It was rejected.[91] House adjourned shortly after 2 P.M. Ate a moderate dinner and took an immoderate nap for daytime. Only a small contribution for M. E. C. Sunday S. Library to Mrs. Evans. Dickey of Cherokee and myself went to church at Edenton St. Methodist. Several gentlemen were called upon for their experience. A Mr. Falls in an humble manner regretted the cold way of singing, depending upon the quire.[92] In room of Dickey and Anderson had some revival singing. [*In left margin*] Ansd C. A. Carlton's letter & wrote to W. Turner.

Thursday February 5

The Senate at last agreed upon a bill to adjust the State Debt. Worths bill after the adoption of 3 or 4 amendments offered by himself passed. The N. C. R. R. Construction bonds Amt. $1,800,000. new to be issued, and exchangeable 2 for one, due July 1st A.D. 1904.[93] Moved suspension of rules to take up my resolution concerning attendance of certain nonresidents to testify in behalf of impeachment of Judge Saml W. Watts. Carried. Res. adopted. Bill in favor of Contractors on Marion and Asheville Turnpike adopted. Pays half.[94] February 18th fixed for meeting of University Trustees. Went down street bought some figs for a purpose—had a shave and hair cutting—on return found some married ladies and boys of our house playing croquet and had a game with six. On the prevailing side. My first game in 6 mos. At Marlers room with Armfield and Bryan discussing usury.[95] [*In left margin*] Met Mr. Alston of Warren[96]

Friday February 6

First to breakfast <u>Oh</u>. Postal Card from Julia (sister) wondering why I had not recently put in an appearance at her house. Passed Consolidation bill without requiring conformity to N. C. gauge, and retaining clause preventing Wm A. Smith from being President or Manager, because he refused to testify before Shipp Com. on grounds that he might criminate himself.[97] H. Refused the new County of Jura to be taken from Robeson and Richmond Cos.[98] Had suspended rules and got up my bill to incorporate Harmony Hill camp ground. Passed. Had added to names of trustees that of J. M. Holmes.[99] Appointed Maj. Thos Watts on Conservative Executive Com. in our 10th Judicial District.[100] Wrote to sister Julia and sent letters of Pa, Ellie & N. A. Holman. Wrote to Ch. Standard Cincinnati to stop it and sent check on Jas. S. Woodward & Son to pay up. Dickey B. K. has come to sleep with me as a Mr. McCoombs [*In right margin*] of Cherokee occupies his place tonight.[101] [*In left margin*] Recollections of departed. Night 12 o'clock. We ought to be abed Sis

Saturday February 7

The protest of S. Trivett and others against the passage of a certain clause in the N. C. R. R. Consolidation bill, in regard to excluding any one from a directorship or the holding of an office [in said Co. (~~was read~~)] who had refused to testify or might hereafter before an investigating committee on the grounds that he might criminate himself, was read and ruled out of order by the Speaker on the grounds that it was disrespectful in its language towards the Legislature. Some severe strictures were offered by McGehee and Jones. No reply by Trivett. He redily yielded to the decision of the Chair.[102] Answered remarkable letter. Mr. Dickey lodged with me. He snores as well and sleeps well. A clever well meaning man of robust appearance. Introduced resolution in regard to night sessions.[103]

Sunday February 8

Not in good spirits. Remained in my room all day until five oclock when I walked by the Post Office and depot. Went to Prayer Meeting at Baptist Church about 8½ having remained in Dickey & Andersons room singing for Welch and Blackwell in company with former. Recd a request from room below to sing "There is a fountain filled with blood" signed Stafford & Co. I tell them that Mr. Dickey is pretty good on "storming the skies." His song begins "we'll storm the skies—we will anchor by and by, by and by."[104] Had a lonely time with sad thoughts and actions and retired late.

Monday February 9

First sight was the cheerful face of Mr Dickey looking through the door to know "how is Bro. Turner this morning." We have got up quite a fashion at this house of entitling each other Bro. especially upon the upper floor. Resolution in regard to night sessions adopted amended so as to require a meeting every night, as Senate resolution to adjourn sine die on the 16th Inst. had just been concurred in. By invitation I took tea at Mrs. Fentress' with Capt Haynes of Haywood and Bryson of Jackson. Heard music on piano & guitar by Miss Blanche. Met Mr Gudger a lawyer from Haywood attending Supreme Court.[105] Effie Fentress seems to be a sprightly little girl. Went to the meeting of House 8 P.M. Many bills passed and more layed on table. Horton and I walked to Yarboro and saw different friends.

Tuesday February 10

Bill to prevent sale of liquor in townships where people so determine, after some warm discussion, passed its final reading. Dudley thought the Baptist were the hardest to convert to the use only of cold water, although they believed so much in it for plunging purposes. This brought out old man Blythe, a Bp. preacher from Henderson.[106] Capt Horton and I had already arranged to call on Miss Bettie Blake at 3½ P.M., but a meeting of Senate in executive session prevented him from fulfilling his engagement. I called and rendered apologies. This was for him and he is anxious to be introduced on Thursday next. He has been told that she is the Belle of R. and of course he is anxious to see.[107] Session tonight. Gorman's Militia bill was passed, and Father McNamara's immigration resolution, concerning St. Patrick's day and invitation to Irishmen and others to come here, passed after discussion.[108] Bill to give certain public lands to Burke and Rutherford [*In right margin*] Cos. failed.[109] [*In left margin*] Note from Dr. Grissom.

February 11 Wednesday

Senate passed a bill to make wagoners responsible for damages done by Camp Fires.[110] At night the Senate made ridiculous amendments to Father McNamara's immigration resolutions, and defeated them by a vote of 39 to l. Capt. Horton gave that one vote.[111] In the House a bill to sell vacant state lands in and around the city, proceeds to be invested in U.S. Bonds, and kept as an irreducable fund for University. Passed 2d Re. An amendment was offered to allow four acres on Gallows Hill for the colored people of the State, and freely voted for by many democrats, myself among them. It was carried by a large Maj., but before vote was announced many republicans stampeded.[112] Went with Capt. Horton and Mr Powell Senator from Chatham to call on Miss Adelaide Boylin and Miss Thompson of Pittsboro.[113] Pleasant chat. occupied a chair 100 years old. Mrs. Iredell and Mrs. McKimmon came in.[114] Heaton's birthday 46 years.[115] After tea sat with Mrs Smith, and watch [*In left margin*] having stopped barely missed my vote on election bill at night session having got there at 7.50 oclock.[116]

Thursday February 12 1874

Advocated the rehabilitating of University and proposed offering an amendment to have the State lands in and around Raleigh sold in alternate sections. An amendment was carried to turn over proceeds to Treasurer for the Gen. Educational fund, and afterwards the bill was sustained on motion to table. Much discussion. Bill providing for the election of two Sup. Ct. Judges passed in place of Gov. Caldwells appointees.[117] The Resolution of request to Attorney Gen. Hargrove to render his opinion as to legal effect of disqualifying clause in Consolidation bill, in regard to Wm. A. Smith. President was discussed at great length in the Senate. It failed Ayes 22 Noes 23.[118]

Evening session of both houses at 3½ OClock. The University bill was indefinitely postponed. Many bills were hurried through or tabled.

Each party had a Caucus at night. Our Caucus rather thinly attended. Sentiment of Caucus on public debt Worths bill.

Friday February 13

In the Senate H. B. to pay contractors on Marion and Asheville Turnpike 50¢ on the dollar was after discussion and opposition adopted. 6 in the $100 valuation for Penetentiary purposes was changed to 8. On a motion to concur I voted for it having opposed it before, as 6 cts will about support, without leaving anything for construction. Made an appointment with old Mr. Dickey to call on two of the lady teachers at the Deaf, Dumb & Blind Asylum, and have some nice music from the Blind. He wanted me to sing "Over there," so I took [him] where he could hear it better rendered.[119] Miss Bremley & Miss Shanks were the leading blind singers. Mr Gay and Mr. ___ sang bass. Saw also Miss Narcissa Dupree a blind teacher. Miss Ballinger and Mrs. Ayer two

Tazewell Lee Hargrove (*left*) spent nine months as a fellow prisoner of war with Columbus Turner at Johnson's Island. After the war, he joined the Republican Party and served as attorney general of North Carolina from 1873 to 1877. Image courtesy of the North Carolina State Archives, Raleigh, N.C. Tod R. Caldwell (*right*), one of the founders of the Republican Party in the state, was rewarded with the position of lieutenant governor under William W. Holden. He succeeded to the governor's office upon the impeachment of Holden and was elected on his own right in 1872, but died before completing the term. Image courtesy of the North Carolina Collection, Wilson Library, University of North Carolina at Chapel Hill.

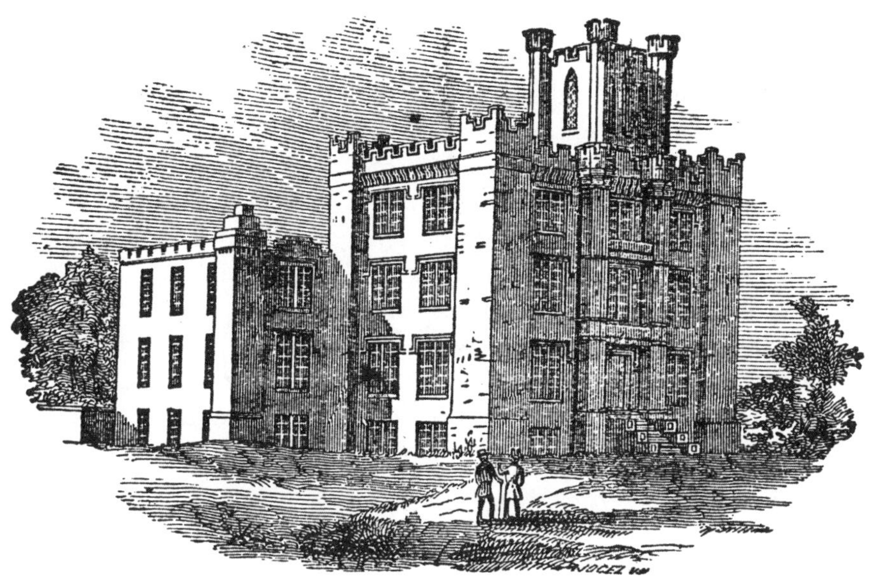

Rep. Columbus Turner occasionally called at the State Institution for the Deaf and Dumb and Blind on Caswell Square, a short walk from his boardinghouse, where he enjoyed the singing of the students and teachers. Image courtesy of the North Carolina State Archives, Raleigh, N.C.

friends are teachers of the dumb.[120] Mr Miller Senator from Cleaveland enjoying it hugely.[121] Miss started for Durham. [*In left margin*] Horton called to go somewhere else, but let him go alone to see Miss A. Boylan.

Saturday February 14

Bill to extend jurisdiction of Justices of the Peace passed both Houses. Allows in cases of petty larceny.[122]

Moring's bill to adjust public debt passed 2d Reading. Lies over till Monday. Dictates terms, 30 20 & 15 on the dollar. New bonds to be issued exchangeable until Jany 1st 1876, when those not returned are to be repudiated. He occupied the floor in quite an able manner for a young lawyer—showing that he deserved success, but in this case he has the wrong bill. Mr McGehee ably replied showing how fallacious it is etc. Johnsons bill to appoint a Commission, after much confusion, passed 2d Reading.[123]

Our night session continued until 12 M. There was a heavy rush of business. S. Bill to secure human life by punishing severely those who sell impure liquor passed. A buyer can have it analyzed, and if found to have poison this shall be evidence.[124] [*In left margin*] voted vs Mooring bill.

Sunday February 15

Went with Mr Dickey to Sunday School at Baptist Church. Joined Strangers class and heard them on Genesis 35th Chap.[125] My object was to visit Infant Department presided over by Mr. & Mrs. Dodd. We were invited in after they were duly organized. The little ones sing in very good time. It seems they have organized a class of young men, who are not users of tobacco, and who will quit it in all its forms. Superintendent J. M. Heck condemned the use of it, saying that all drunkards or nearly so have preceeded this condition by the use of tobacco. Another evil quite as great he thought was the chewing of gum.[126] Dr Prichard preached concerning importance of showing fruit of late revival. Baptism announced for 4 P.M. Called with Horton on Miss Boylan & Miss Thompson. Dr Jordan & Med [?] Leach called.[127] [*In left margin*] Pleasant weather.

February 16

Fine weather. Mild and bright. My resolution to change time of adjournment from 12 to 2 P.M. adopted by making it 3 P.M.[128] Much hurry & confusion. Morings bill failed. Johnsons passed in the House, but failed in the Senate for want of time at exactly 12 M. and the Republicans insisted on complying with resolution just adopted that there was to be no more legislation after 12 M. Guess it would have failed any way. They take much time in Senate to debate and do but little that stands. Tryed to get up from the table a bill appropriating money to Orphan Asylum and reminded the house that whilst they were free to appropriate extra to certain officers and employees this Orphan House should not be neglected—a laudable object but failed. $1.00 to colporteur towards present for Speaker. A Contribution was taken up, which resulted in a seventy five dollar tea service formally presented by Jones of Caldwell and responded to Speaches on adjournment by presiding [*In right margin*] officers.[129] Some weeping as well as hand shaking. [*In left margin*] To my room with many many sad thoughts and feelings. [*Crosshatched*] No wife or children to go home to. Alone. Tea at Prof. Kerr's.

Tuesday February 17

Only two members at breakfast table. Mr Dickey and myself.

Went down town to get the morning papers. Found Joe Turner as ready as ever to talk about rings and impeachment. The Legislature has adjourned and now he appeals to the people. Violent card in paper from Dr. Grissom against Senator Ransom of Tyrrel—the result of certain investigations into the expenditures of Insane Asylum and some stricture on Dr. G. Ransom and myself made first investigation.[130] Dr. G. wrote me a week ago, to know how errors occurred. I did not write him, but wrote to day and think of not sending yet, as errors were perhaps made by others. Mr Dickey as he did last night so again to day, wished me to repeatedly sing Over there and Dont reject Him or Come to Jesus so that he might learn. In my room pretty much all day. [*In left margin*] Dickey gone to call on Mrs Gov. Swain.[131] He will leave to night. [*Crosshatched*] Walked to depot with Dickey. Went to Concert at Peace Institute at night.[132]

Wednesday February 18

What have I done to day worthy of record?—Scarcely any thing. Rather unwell and slept so late in the evening as to miss Chatham train and guess Sister Julia will wonder what is the matter with me. Expect to make the trip to Haywood to morrow. What a forlorn fellow I am.

Met Dr. Grissom and Tim Lee down street.[133] Gave G. the letter concerning investigation of Insane Asylum affairs. Told him I guessed it would not be of much service to him.

Took an evening walk to the depot and back.

Had a chat on general subjects with Mrs. Smith several hours.

Have been sitting here with mind running at large. Would I were settled. Have a free pass to Morehead City, but am so little disposed to use it.[134] 20 min. to 12 M. Good Night. [*In right margin*] Called at P. O. and got wrappers and stamps. [*In left margin*] Some snow— Cloudy all day. Falling.

Dr. Eugene Grissom, Republican appointee to superintend the state insane asylum, had a violent confrontation in the Raleigh *Daily News* with Senator Edward Ransom, who, with Representative Turner, had prepared a report critical of expenditures at the asylum. Image courtesy of the North Carolina State Archives, Raleigh, N.C.

February 19

Sent off to various portions of the County of Iredell and some places in Alexander and Wilkes about fifty copies of Sentinel, News, Examiner and Herald, considering it better to do that than to throw them away.[135]

Took a walk until room could be cleaned up. Numerous Grangers have been pouring into the city. Met P. C. Carlton. They meet to day in convention.[136]

Took the train for Haywood, Chatham Co. at 4 P.M. The day has been cloudy & drizzly.

Had a long conversation concerning house matters—composed letters &c. Dr. Wyche's talks with me on piety, religious disputations, the future state and meekness, brought us to 10½ P.M. when after prayers by the Dr. and a little further conversation retired to my lonely couch to dream &c.

Friday February 20

Began a little cloudy but soon became a bright pleasant day. Dreamed I was in Paris. Had much talk with sister concerning "Mollie dear" and home matters. Heard a few pieces from her on the piano, vizt "Lone rock by the Sea" and "Pass under the Rod." Good old pieces.[137]

Walked with Dr. and Bertha to Mr Farrar's store to weigh.[138] Bertha weighed 39 lbs and Dr. W and I each weighed 156—more than I have since 1865.

Met Mrs. Scott and Mrs. Pitman a lady 70 years old.[139] Sewing machine man called with one of Wheelers and Wilsons.[140] Price $90. Swapped with Julia allowing her $30 for her old machine a 2d handed one for which she paid $35.

The Dr. is fonder of talking on Scripture subjects than any thing else. Had our usual comparison of ideas on Lertinity [?], church differences &c.

Saturday February 21

Up at 6 to eat an early breakfast which sister J had ready, a good meal prepared by herself. She acts independent of her servant, who if not on hand when she wants something done, goes ahead. Reached Raleigh about 9 overcoat in hand too warm for use.

Called on the Auditor.[141] Expected to have seen Dr. Prichard. He invited me early in the session to call on him for the purpose of talking over differences and hindrances in religious matters, but I have had so many talks with different people that I have gotten to think it is useless, so far as being a satisfied Baptist, Methodist or Episcopalian is concerned, or really it seems any other. There are some things among all I like and some I dislike but piety wherever found I admire. Dr. Burrows of Richmond had written to him on the subject.[142]

[*In left margin*] Dr. Mason Rector of Ep. Church here died of Pneumonia.[143]

Sunday February 22

Went to Tucker Hall to see how the new congregation of Episcopalians are getting on.[144] Cabinet organ music good. Pastor a Mr. Rich of Md.[145] Text "Get thee behind me Satan, for &c.["] Day bright and very warm for this time [of] year. Sat out on piazza much of the time. Wrote three notes on postal cards 1 for home 1 to R. and 1 to Willie. Took evening walk to P. Office.

Went to Christs Church at night service read by Bishop Lyman.[146] Sermon by Mr. Rich. The Church is hung with the drapery of mo[u]rning for Dr. Mason descd. Funeral service put off to Tuesday morning at 11.

On return stopped in at Baptist Church and Mr Ivey was concluding a long talk in behalf of Wake Forest College. Then next Dr. P. lead a little boy and young lady down into the baptistery and immersed them.[147]

February 23

Called at Mrs Pullens to see Mrs. Dodd. Day was to[o] pretty to find her at home. Bright and rather warm weather for Feb.

Visited institution of Deaf Dumb & Blind. Saw Mrs. Ayer one of the teachers, and on my return met Mr Gay and Mr Costner, two blind men who sing well, and after expressing a desire to hear them and the other blind sing, was cordially invited to come at 8 P.M. and they would sing until 9. o['clock]. I went a[nd] had the class of blind singers to myself. They were very kind and seemed to think a great deal of me pressing me to come again. Names as follows—Misses Brumley, Shank, T. C. Dettmering, Lilly McCarson, Annie E. Huneycutt, Mary Royall, Master Jackson Massey, and Messrs. Gay J. W., J. M. Costner & J. N. Royall. A. M. Page was not in.[148]

Tuesday February 24

Hurried up my arrangements to leave Raleigh. Made several calls. Attended the funeral of Rev Dr Mason at 11 Oclock. Dr Smedes read

Tucker Hall, Raleigh's first public entertainment hall, occupied the third floor of the Tucker Brothers' mercantile establishment on Fayetteville Street. While Turner was in Raleigh for the 1873-1874 session of the General Assembly, the congregation of the newly formed Church of the Good Shepherd held its first services in Tucker Hall. Image courtesy of the North Carolina State Archives, Raleigh, N.C.

the service Bishop Lyman read the scripture lessons, and Bishop Atkinson pronounced the eulogium, drawing lessons from his exemplary life.[149] The church was crowded to overflowing. Many were on the side walks. Numerous places of business were closed. Clergy attended burial with surplices on.

Went home and packed up my scattered baggage before the dinner bell rang. Ate my dinner took a few strolls, and on return supper was not ready but omnibus was—So I hastily bid good bye and took train at 6.40. Had a broken uneasy slumber part of the way to Greensboro.

Wednesday February 25

About 1½ A.M. got off train at Greensboro to take coffee and a snack. Mr. Woodward of a paper published in New York called The South came up with me, and insisted on paying for coffee & eggs, which I took, he having feasted on oysters.[150]

So began my birthday.[151]

Reached Statesville about 7 intending to go to the Simonton House but the inevitable Shields who always seems to be so good a fellow, insisted on me stopping at the St. Charles.[152] So I let him have my valise & check. At this latter place young Elliot had killed a Mr Neal formerly of Richmond about a week before, and that was my only reason for going to the other House. Habeas Corpus case to day. Hope bail will not be allowed.[153] Expected _____ to send me out. He did not look me up as usual. Slushed through mud & snow in a 2 H Carry all. [*In right margin*] Reached home about 12 M. Went to bed at Statesville till 10.

Thursday February 26

Away from Legislative duties now I must think of my own affairs—which very much need attention. Having stayed at China Grove during the night after conversation. Pa and I went over to the Mill. I took dinner at Cottage Home my former happy home. The things that we used—so many here and there. I hate to arrange and dispose of. Yet I wish they were all except precious souvenirs and articles immediately those of the dear departed were disposed of effectively. Pa and Mother went to W. T. Gaithers this evening. Jennie and I will be happy at China Grove. Miss Drucilla Ward stayed with Jennie.[154]

Columbus Lafayette Turner as a middle-aged businessman. Image courtesy of the Iredell Museum of Arts and Heritage, Statesville, N.C.

AFTERWORD

For several months after he left Raleigh, Columbus Turner continued to faithfully record his activities and private thoughts in his pocket diary. He returned to Turnersburg and his residence in the Cottage Home on his parents' property, spending much of his leisure time and taking many meals at their house, China Grove. He managed the company store, worked on business accounts dating back to 1867, and helped his father attend to the post office. In the evenings, Turner visited relatives in the neighborhood, particularly his eldest sister Betty and her husband, W. T. Gaither, who lived near Harmony, a few miles north of Turnersburg, and his younger sister, Emma Ella, and her husband, Marshall K. Steele, in Olin. He also prepared extracts from his prison journal for publication in *Our Living and Our Dead.* Unfortunately, as he noted in his diary, "some lady took off part of it and would not return it," though it is unclear which part of the journal went missing. The March 11, 1874, issue of the weekly newspaper devoted to firsthand accounts of Civil War battles and events contained an invitation to participants in the Battle of New Bern to submit narratives of the

Betty Turner Gaither (*left*) and Emma Ella Turner Steele (*right*), two of Columbus Turner's sisters whose husbands engaged in business activities with Wilfred Turner. Columbus was a frequent guest of both sisters while a resident of Turnersburg after the Civil War. Images courtesy of Nancy Jones, Burlington, N.C.

battle for publication. Turner noted in his diary on April 7 that he had finished writing such an article, but had laid it aside. Six days later, he mailed the article, signed "Leroy," which was published in the newspaper on April 22.[1]

Back in the little house that he had shared with his wife, Turner continued to mourn her loss. Soon after his return to Iredell County, he lamented: "At business—hard to get through with it here. How changed things are now? Where is that spirit of life and pleasantness that once dwelt here. It left when Mollie dear departed." Returning to the cottage after a social call in the neighborhood, he keenly felt her absence: "How changed with me. A genial loving wife once made these periodical visits and enlivened the company by her vivacious conversation and merry, good natured laughter. It was a pleasure to hear her talk and laugh and behold the intelligent animation of her countenance, and the ease and grace of her manner."[2]

On April 21, Turner departed for Richmond, where he spent two months conducting business for W. Turner and Son, visiting friends and in-laws, and at least once a week tending to his wife's grave in Hollywood Cemetery. On one occasion, he planted a shoot from a plant that Mollie had cared for in their yard at Cottage Home. He apparently stayed most of that time in the household of Leonidus L. Lacy and wife, Emma, the younger sister of Turner's late wife. While in Richmond, "Leroy" prepared and mailed on May 7 a second article to *Our Living and*

Modern-day photograph of Cottage Home on the grounds of Wilfred Turner's homeplace at Turnersburg, where Columbus Turner lived with his first wife until her death in 1873. The cottage has been enlarged over the years. Image courtesy of Wendy Waldron, Turnersburg, N.C.

Our Dead; the first extract from Turner's prison diary was published in the May 20 issue. On June 13, his brother, Wilfred Dent Turner, joined him in Richmond, and nine days later they set out on an extended vacation throughout the northeastern United States and southeastern Canada. The long leisurely trip by railroad, stagecoach, and steamer carried them to Philadelphia, New York City, Saratoga, Niagara Falls, Toronto, Montreal, Quebec, the White Mountains, Portland, Boston, Nantucket, and Newport. Both on the way northward and on the return trip, they stayed with another sister of his deceased wife, Susan, and her husband, George McCrindell, in Bergen, New Jersey. On August 18, the brothers took a train to Baltimore, where they boarded a steamer for West Point, Virginia. Lum Turner spent an additional two months in Richmond before returning home to resume business activities with his father, running the mill store and perhaps the post office while Wilfred supervised the operations of the mill.[3]

There is little record of Turner's activities during the latter half of the 1870s. In September 1879, his father gave him forty-nine acres of the original home tract on Rocky Creek. In February 1880, Turner paid $4,000 for two other parcels on Rocky Creek that totaled ninety-two acres; he also purchased two lots in Olin from sister Ella and her husband. (His father wrote in a letter to his son-in-law, James Willson, on April 8, 1881: "I would not want you to do like Lum secure the lot and then leave.") But even before these transactions were registered, the partnership with his father, W. Turner and Son, was dissolved in January 1881. The mill at Turnersburg continued in operation, but more and more of the daily responsibilities fell to Wilfred's sons-in-law, Laz. T. Stimpson and Marshall K. Steele. In 1890, Wilfred Turner gave the mill property to his daughters Ella and Addie and their husbands. But in the early hours of April 30, 1890, the factory burned to the ground. The damage to the uninsured property, which had been refitted with new machinery only two years before, was estimated at $20,000. The Statesville *Landmark* reported that "the loss, while great, will not fall so heavy upon Mr. Turner, who is one of the wealthiest men in the county, but it is a calamity to the community," putting at least thirty people out of work. The newspaper editor thought it unlikely that the mill would be rebuilt, but sometime prior to Wilfred's death on November 27, 1893, it was.[4]

Lum Turner spent the better part of 1881 traveling to the west. He wrote his father from Richmond in April to say that he was leaving for Tennessee in a few days. He visited relatives and former residents of

Iredell County in Tennessee, Arkansas, and Missouri. Turner stayed several days with a kinsman, Col. A. R. Tomlinson, in Benton, Arkansas, and had a long visit with Capt. A. W. Blackburn, formerly of Iredell, in Pettis County, Missouri. He also called upon his sister, Sallie Holman, at her home in Fayette County, Tennessee, and may have discussed with her a loan or investment in the subsequent purchase of cotton mills in Catawba County. If he was "looking for himself" as his fortieth birthday approached, Turner apparently found his inspiration as he traveled or upon his return to North Carolina.[5]

In the spring of 1882, Columbus and his brother Wilfred Dent Turner, then a twenty-seven-year-old attorney with a practice in Statesville, purchased one of the mills of the Catawba Manufacturing Company, then in receivership. The company's property in Catawba County consisted of two mills, machinery, and acreage about a mile apart on the west bank of the Catawba River. The upper mill was situated near a place in the stream where two islands divided the channel. The Long Island Cotton Mill had been a going concern there since at least 1850, under the direction of Dr. Avery M. Powell. The lower mill at Granite Shoals stood near a thousand-foot-long toll bridge that carried traffic between Statesville and Catawba across the river. A manufacturing enterprise had been in operation there since 1854, when John J. Shuford and sons erected a cotton-spinning mill. Over the next quarter century, the mill was operated by a number of different partnerships. In May 1879, J. A. Claywell sold the Granite Shoals factory and ninety acres to Dr. Powell. A year later, Powell entered into a co-partnership with Pinkney C. Shuford of Catawba County and Joseph Turner and William W. Mott of Iredell County, under the name of Catawba Manufacturing Company. Mott was responsible for the daily operations of the mill.[6]

In 1881, Powell was financially ruined after he stood as surety for longtime sheriff Jonas Cline, who was "caught short of revenues." Powell's bankruptcy entangled numerous partnerships, and several lawsuits were initiated in Catawba County Superior Court to sort out the indebtedness of the various enterprises. On May 3, 1882, the Turner brothers bought the mill at Granite Shoals from the receiver, John L. Cobb. Two months later, Powell's mill property at Long Island, consisting of the factory, flour and sawmills, company store, blacksmith shop, five "tenement houses," and sixteen and a half acres, was also sold at auction by Cobb, presumably to the Turners, though their deed to both mills and acreage was not drawn and recorded until the spring of 1884.[7]

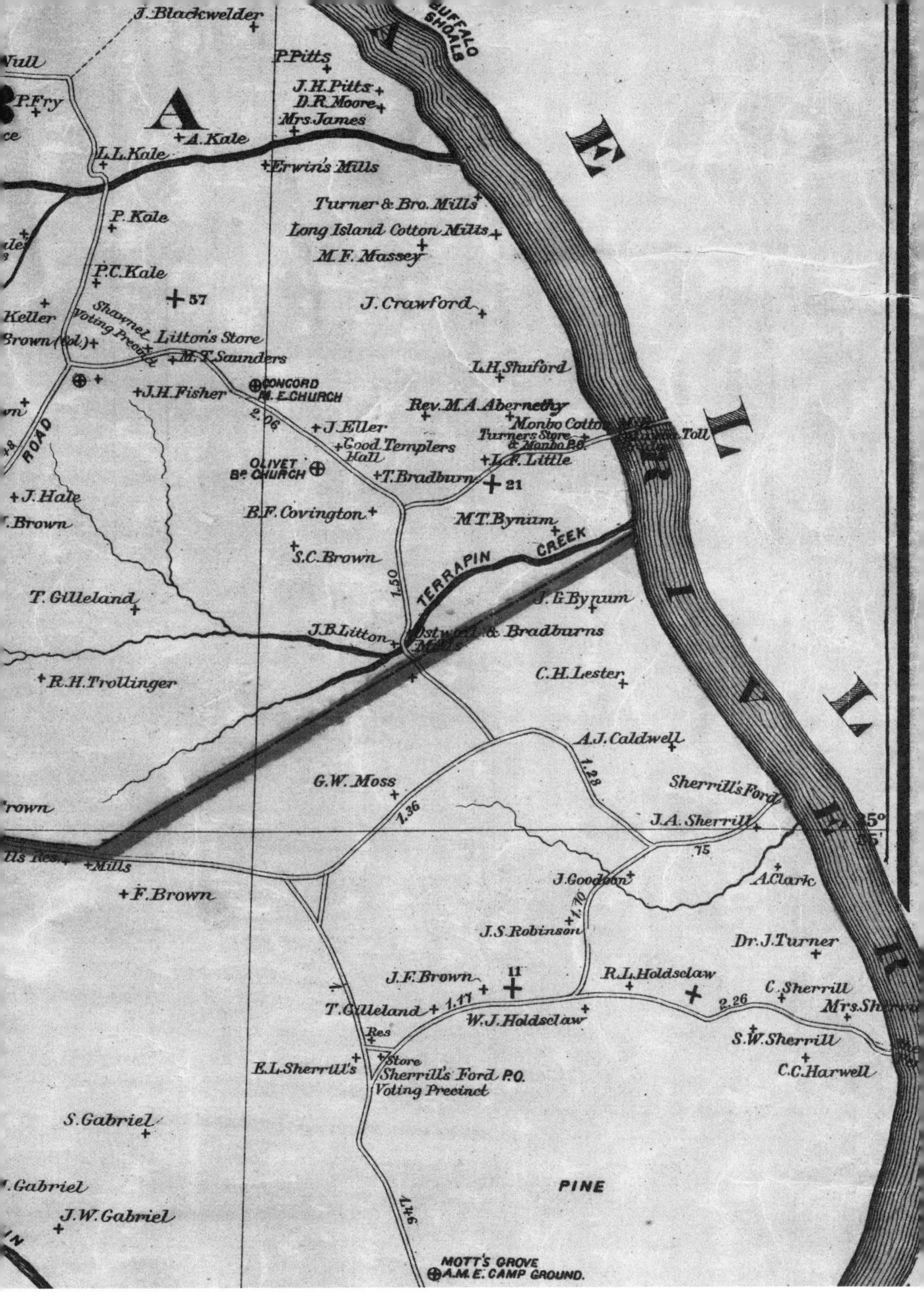

Detail of southeastern Catawba County from the 1886 map by Robert A. Yoder denoting the two mills operated by the Turner brothers. Image courtesy of the North Carolina State Archives, Raleigh, N.C.

While the court-appointed receiver and referees sorted out Powell's tangled financial affairs, the Turner brothers moved to Catawba County to supervise the daily operations of the lower mill. They occupied a large house with a tower, built by noted local architect Charles Henry Lester on a bluff overlooking the mill and river. Lester also constructed the enormous company store, which measured one hundred feet long and twenty-eight feet wide, with two full stories and an attic large enough to host meetings of fraternal orders. Columbus named the house "Mont Beau," from the French for "beautiful mountain." The mill workers corrupted the name to Monbo, which the Turners then applied to the factory, renaming it Monbo Plaid Mills. The mangled name was ultimately extended to the mill village and the post office that opened there on October 13, 1882. Like his grandfather at River Hill and his father at County Line and Turnersburg, Columbus served as postmaster at Monbo until succeeded by his nephew, Samuel Turner, in 1894.[8]

The mill at Monbo contained 1,056 spindles and 42 looms, capable of spinning 1,848 yards of cloth each day. In the first four months of operation under the Turners, the factory turned out 121,790 yards of superior quality plaids and cottonade. A visitor to Granite Shoals in the summer of 1882 reported that the plaid mill, which had been idle since

The cotton mill (*left*) and the enormous company store (*right*) at Monbo, both designed by the noted local architect, Charles Henry Lester. Image courtesy of the Iredell Museum of Arts and Heritage, Statesville, N.C.

Monbo Heights, the Catawba County home of Columbus Turner that was built by Charles Henry Lester on a bluff overlooking the mill and the river at Granite Shoals. Image courtesy of the Iredell Museum of Arts and Heritage, Statesville, N.C.

the previous December, was again running "full blast": "Under the new regime everything works systematically and reflects credit upon the owners, evidencing the fact that they are business men. . . . For industry and morality the operatives are in advance of any I have ever known. They are paid good wages for the services, furnished with comfortable houses and treated kindly by their employers."[9]

In March 1884, with financial backing from other family members, the Turner brothers purchased for $19,800 the mills and machinery of the two factories, and three parcels of land: 16½ acres at Long Island, 104 acres at Granite Shoals, and 8 acres in Iredell County across the Catawba River from the lower mill. The eight hundred spindles of the upper mill were allowed to stand idle, "the owners being content with running the grist mill, cotton gin and press" at Long Island.[10]

Wilfred Dent Turner quickly found that his law practice suffered in his absence and soon returned to Statesville, leaving the running of the Monbo mill to his older brother. In July 1884, he and his wife Ida sold Lum their half-interest in nine acres adjoining the factory at Granite Shoals, formerly the Mott homeplace (presumably occupied by

William W. Mott while he supervised the mill for Catawba Manufacturing Company). Another visitor to the mill, Rev. H. D. Lequer, noted that the business manager, Columbus Turner, was " 'the right man in the right place' ": "His business is so thoroughly systematized that he can tell to a fraction the amount of loss sustained by the raw material from the time it is initiated into the first stages of its manufacture until it is baled and marked for shipment." Turner earned a reputation locally for possessing sound business sense. When he proposed a few years later the organization of a company, underwritten by public subscription, to build a "low-water" toll bridge across the Catawba River near Monbo, the Statesville *Landmark* endorsed the project: "We do not know whether such a bridge is a practical solution of the problem or not, but Mr. Turner is a practical gentleman and since he suggests it we assume that it will meet the demands in an efficient and satisfactory manner."[11]

Lum Turner was a frequent business traveler to Richmond, Virginia, both as a partner of W. Turner and Son and as the representative of Turner Brothers. On one of these trips in the early eighties, he was walking around the city "when he came to a millinery shop and looking through the window, he saw this beautiful young damsel going about her business." He went inside and made the acquaintance of Virginia (Jennie or Lottie) E. Longinotti (née Stansbury), a young widow whose husband had been dead for seven or eight years and the mother of a son, Vincent. Thereafter, Turner's trips to Richmond became even more frequent. Despite a fourteen-year age difference, the courtship culminated in marriage in 1884 (a family genealogical chart gives the date of August 20), presumably in Richmond. The Catawba correspondent for the *Newton Enterprise* may have been referring to Turner, when he reported on June 21: "One of our good looking widowers at Catawba has been barbarized and has entered the matrimonial canvass, and the way he smiles on his return, we have no doubt he is getting more comfort than Blaine and Logan."[12]

Turner returned with his wife and stepson to Monbo Heights, but his days of marital bliss would be few, as his second marriage was to be of even shorter duration than the first. As the pioneer Turners had done when they left Maryland for the North Carolina Piedmont in the early nineteenth century, Lottie Turner cast off her Episcopalian affiliation and joined her husband at Rehoboth Methodist Church near Sherrill's Ford. Vincent attended Rev. Jacob Crawford Clapp's high school for boys in Newton (formerly and subsequently Catawba College). He apparently boarded with a Mrs. Finger, possibly the wife of Sidney M.

Virginia "Lottie" Stansbury Longinotti Turner (1856-1887), second wife of Columbus Lafayette Turner. Image courtesy of the Iredell Museum of Arts and Heritage, Statesville, N.C.

Finger, a teacher at the school in the 1870s before his election to the General Assembly. But Lottie soon contracted an illness all too common in mill villages, gradually wasting away from consumption. She died at home on November 11, 1887, just three weeks after her thirty-first birthday, and was buried in the cemetery at Concord Methodist Church. Despite the brevity of her residence at Monbo, she was known to all as "an amiable and lovable woman."[13]

Earlier that year, the Turner Brothers decided to incorporate their cotton mill business and to bring in additional partners. On May 2, 1887, articles of incorporation for the Monbo Manufacturing Company were drawn up and registered, with a capital stock of $37,000. The five shareholders were Columbus L. Turner (145 shares), Wilfred D. Turner (125), Samuel Turner (40), William W. Turner (30), and James Willson (30). The additional Turners were a second set of brothers, sons of Wilfred's younger brother Henry, and thus first cousins of the original partners. Willson was the brother-in-law of Columbus and Wilfred D., the husband of their sister Jennie. On May 5, the shareholders elected officers and a board of directors: Wilfred D. (on the strength of his brother's 145 votes) was elected president, James Willson vice-president, and Columbus secretary and treasurer. The initial board consisted of the original partners and William W. Turner. Samuel Turner was named clerk or assistant to the treasurer. On May 13, Columbus and Wilfred D. Turner sold Monbo Plaid Mills and its 112 acres to the new corporation for $21,000, as well as their half-interest in Long Island Cotton Factory for $3,000. (At some point, the other pair of Turner brothers had acquired the additional half-interest, which they also sold to Monbo Manufacturing Company.) Columbus continued to manage the daily operations of the factory, and, within the year, he bought an additional twenty acres in two tracts adjacent to the mill property.[14]

Turner was an inveterate traveler who loved to take long trips about the country. Perhaps this was a subconscious reaction to his lengthy confinement during the Civil War. In the summer of 1888, he set out with his brother through the North Carolina mountains, "with the idea that they might wind around through Tennessee and Virginia and take in Gettysburg," where the twenty-fifth anniversary of the battle was being observed. Whether or not they reached Pennsylvania is uncertain, as they reportedly got "hung up" visiting relatives in Grainger County, Tennessee.[15]

Lum Turner did not long remain a widower the second time around. The organist at Rehoboth Methodist Church was vivacious twenty-five-year-old Martha Leonora Sherrill, daughter of Elbert L. and Julia Nance Sherrill, who lived in the family seat at Sherrill's Ford. The twenty-three-year age difference may have caused Nora some hesitation, but she eventually succumbed to Lum's determined courtship. They were married in her parents' home by a Methodist minister on August 26, 1890. After a lengthy honeymoon to Washington, D.C., New York City, and Niagara Falls, the newlyweds returned to the big house on Monbo Heights. Vincent Longinotti, now a teenager, continued to live there until he moved to Washington to take a job in the navy yard. Beginning with the birth of a son, Rodney Wilfred, in July 1891, Nora would give Lum (then forty-nine) the family—three sons and two daughters—that he had wanted for so long. The other children were Rupert, born in 1894; Reginald in 1898; Columbia Dorcas in 1901; and Norma Julia in 1904.[16]

Martha Leonora "Nora" Sherrill Turner (1863-1943), the third wife of Columbus L. Turner and the mother of his five children. Image courtesy of the Iredell Museum of Arts and Heritage, Statesville, N.C.

(*Above*) Columbus and Nora Turner on their honeymoon at Niagara Falls in 1890. (*Left*) The children of Columbus and Nora Turner, ca. 1905: (*standing, left to right*) Rupert, Rodney, and Reginald; (*sitting*) Norma and Columbia. Images courtesy of the Iredell Museum of Arts and Heritage, Statesville, N.C.

After a year of operation, the Monbo Manufacturing Company returned dividends of 10 percent. In March 1888, the corporation sold the Long Island mills and acreage to James Brown of Merchantville, New Jersey, for $5,500. In May, Lum Turner sold five of his shares to A. B. Saunders, who joined the board of directors the next year. Saunders sold the shares back to the company in March 1892. Dividends of 8 percent were returned to stockholders in July 1892. In the summer of 1894, Samuel Turner and James Willson purchased the stock of merchandise and accounts and leased the company store, in which they also operated the Monbo post office.[17]

In 1896, the directors of Monbo Manufacturing Company removed the worn machinery and dismantled the old frame-structured Monbo Plaid Mill at Granite Shoals in order to construct a new, modernized factory. Columbus Turner declined the Democratic Party nomination to represent the district in the state senate that year in order to supervise the operation. During the nine months of demolition and construction, the mill operatives were out of work. A Statesville newspaper reported: "Mr. Turner and wife are very popular among the factory people and were very kind to them during the long time when the mill was idle." The new stone and brick structure had a capacity of 3,040 spindles with

Mill workers at Monbo Manufacturing Company, ca. 1910. Image courtesy of the Iredell Museum of Arts and Heritage, Statesville, N.C.

An elderly Columbus Turner balances on a drum, to the amusement of two of his children. Image courtesy of the Iredell Museum of Arts and Heritage, Statesville, N.C.

motive power supplied by two turbine waterwheels, and electric lights generated by a third wheel. The new mill began operations as Monbo Cotton Mill on March 19, 1897, and by the following July the directors were able to declare a 3 percent return on dividends. In 1900, the capital stock of the company was increased to $50,000.[18]

In his later years, Columbus Turner was able to leave some of the daily responsibilities of the cotton mill to able supervisors, such as Hiram J. Saunders, who became superintendent

Monogram School, a product of Columbus Turner's efforts to improve the quality of public education in Catawba County. Image courtesy of the Iredell Museum of Arts and Heritage, Statesville, N.C.

at Monbo in 1892. He could then devote more of his time to paternal duties and civic affairs. He was a gifted orator and was often called upon to address Confederate veterans and auxiliary organizations, such as the Ladies' Memorial Association of Iredell County on Confederate Memorial Day in 1896, and a group of veterans at Catawba on April 1, 1897 [for the text of these speeches, see Appendixes E and F]. Turner returned to the General Assembly in 1905, representing District 31 in the state senate during the two-month session. He was also active in the development of an improved school system that could provide a better education for his children and the offspring of his mill workers. Along with Osborne Brown, then head of the Long Island Mills, and John Ervin, a large-scale farmer who owned a gristmill on Balls Creek, Turner formed a committee that succeeded in consolidating two adjoining school districts in eastern Catawba County. With the fruits of the combined tax base, a new three-room school building, christened Monogram School, was constructed in the spring of 1907.[19]

Despite violent fluctuations in cotton prices throughout the nineties and early years of the twentieth century, the Turner's cotton mill enterprise continued to flourish. In 1910, Monbo Manufacturing Company expanded across the Catawba River, building a second mill on the eight acres in Iredell County, which developed as East Monbo. The old wooden dam that stretched from the west bank of the Catawba to Goat Island was replaced by a concrete structure that spanned the entire river. On December 14, 1910, Monbo Manufacturing Company was voluntarily dissolved, with Turner acting as process agent to handle claims of indebtedness against the corporation. The two Monbo mills operated thereafter as Turner Mills Company.[20]

But the fruits of all their labors were swept away by capricious nature in the summer of 1916. A pair of "tropical cyclones" (what today would be labeled hurricanes with Christian names) pounded western North Carolina in swift succession. On July 8 the first storm passed through the Gulf of Mexico and moved northeastwardly into Mississippi, Alabama, and Georgia, then directly over the crest of the Blue Ridge Mountains of North Carolina, dumping heavy rains into swollen rivers and creeks throughout the Southeast. Three days after the first had subsided, a second storm out of the Atlantic made landfall on July 13 just north of Charleston, South Carolina, and swept up the Catawba River valley (tracing the path Hurricane Hugo would follow in 1989). In western North Carolina, rain fell in torrents for three days and could not be

The two mills of the Turner Mills Company as viewed from the Iredell County bank of the Catawba River, ca. 1910. East Monbo Mill is in the foreground. At the far end of the new concrete dam stands the original Monbo Mill. Turner's home, Monbo Heights, is barely visible on the ridge in the middle distance. Image courtesy of the Iredell Museum of Arts and Heritage, Statesville, N.C.

absorbed by ground already saturated from the downpour of July 10. Hickory recorded more than thirteen inches within a forty-eight-hour span. On Sunday, July 16, the river overran its banks from its watersheds in Burke and Caldwell counties to the flatlands downstream in Catawba, Iredell, and Mecklenburg. Every bridge and railroad trestle across the river in Catawba County, including the Buffalo Shoals toll bridge and the Southern Railway bridge east of Catawba, were swept away. When the half-completed dam at Lookout Shoals gave way, a six-foot-high wall of water roared downstream towards the mill communities at Buffalo Shoals, Long Island, and Monbo. Already inundated by heavy rains, Monbo Mill was totally destroyed. An eyewitness reported that " 'when the building began to give it wailed and made noises like it was human.' " The large company store near the front entrance of the mill was also completely wrecked by the flood. On the Iredell County bank, the waters rose to the top of East Monbo Mill before receding.[21]

The extent of the destruction to the eastern Catawba County mill communities cannot be overstated. Hundreds of workers lost their

Eighteen-year-old Reginald Turner stands amid the ruins of the mill at Monbo in the wake of the catastrophic flood of July 1916. Note the trademark tower at the front entrance of the mill still standing in the wreckage. Image courtesy of the Iredell Museum of Arts and Heritage, Statesville, N.C.

livelihoods, while the mill owners suffered thousands of dollars worth of damages. The Turners estimated their loss at nearly $200,000: $70,000 to the property at Monbo; $45,000 at East Monbo; $34,975 worth of cotton; and $50,000 worth of lost business. In effect, "it was the end of the Monbo industries on the Catawba County side of the river."[22]

In the obituary that he wrote upon the death of his father-in-law, Wilfred Turner, in 1893, James Willson reported that when Turner awoke one morning in the spring of 1890 to learn that his factory had burned during the night, "he felt like a great burden had rolled off of him, and he rejoiced that it burned down as his own property." It is doubtful that Wilfred's sons felt the same sense of relief after their extensive cotton mill operation was destroyed by the flood of 1916. The brothers threatened legal action against the Southern Power Company for the damages caused to their property by the wall of water unleashed by the collapse of the half-built dam at Lookout Shoals, but the utility company took out options on the wrecked mills at Monbo and Long Island in partial settlement. The Turner family continued to operate the mill at East Monbo until December 1919, when the Turner Mills Company sold for $475,200 the factory and six tracts of land encompassing 230½ acres on either side of the river at Monbo, as well as an island in the channel, to Superior Yarn Mills.[23]

Cruel fate would deal Columbus Turner one more tragic hand, this last a double blow. On September 28, 1918, his first-born child, Rodney Wilfred Turner, died of a severe case of sinusitis, at the age of twenty-seven. Rodney's wife Mattie was then pregnant with their third child and approaching full term. The child, a son, was born the night after his father's funeral, but lived only three hours. Rodney Turner Jr. was buried beside his father in the Concord Methodist Church cemetery near Monbo.[24]

A few weeks later, Columbus Turner suffered a stroke while walking up the steep hill to Monbo Heights as he returned from the mill at East Monbo. He lingered for several days, hearing of the armistice that ended the war in Europe, before dying in his bed on the afternoon of November 19, 1918. He was seventy-six. Turner was buried beside his son and grandson in the churchyard of Concord Methodist Church.[25]

APPENDIX A

THE BATTLE OF NEWBERN

CO. A. 33D N. C. REGIMENT.

(FROM *OUR LIVING AND OUR DEAD*, APRIL 22, 1874)

The booming of the enemy's cannon from his gunboats was heard in Newbern on the 13th of March, 1862, when the 33d N.C. regiment was ordered to leave its camp at the Fair Grounds and proceed to a place near our upper line of works about four miles below the town. Being yet weak from the effect of a long spell of typhoid pneumonia, an officer kindly offered to carry part of my luggage, and I was forbidden to go upon picket duty with the company the following dreary night, and thus escaped a very unpleasant experience. Having slept soundly in one of the vacant tents of the 26th N.C. regiment and being greatly refreshed, hurried away to join my company, early on the morning of the 14th. Soon the rattle of musketry began. We were only a short time in reserve; company A, with four other companies, was sent just to the right of the railroad. The former was sent to occupy a position in advance of the balance of the regiment. Over a cleared rising ground this company first heard the whizzing of minie balls near their ears. They pressed forward over a ravine and and [*sic*] an abattis of trees, to high ground nearest the railroad, where a ditch had been dug and the dirt thrown on the wrong side, thereby affording a great deal less protection.

The men fell to work in good earnest loading and firing with great rapidity. The trees had been cut down in front and behind them; in the low ground the enemy were thickly posted, and kept the air vocal with minie balls. Here the enemy lost in killed many men. They were afterwards carried and piled up under the shed of the old brick kiln. Here, also, company A, lost heavily in killed, but must have compensated the loss, in one respect, of every man, by the slaughter of not less than two of the enemy. A Massachusetts corporal boldly walked in front, along a rising ground, when a bead was drawn upon him and he was shot dead—the ball passing through his loins, the place aimed at. The exclamation was "There, you fetched him." The men loaded and fired with such eager zeal that when the militia broke ranks and retreated, or even after some of the regular forces had retired they could not believe the enemy were gaining the field. They kept their position until they were well nigh surrounded, and continued to fire after the entire left had given away.

An order was given for five or six men to jump over the mound, behind which the company lay, and in the face of a fearful tornado of bullets, and take a certain position with the hope of being better able to get deliberate aim at the enemy. Lieut. Joseph Saunders, of Chapel Hill, and Privates John M. Lazenby, John Murchison, John Sherril, Jake Halterman and Samuel Whitaker, of Iredell county, immediately responded, but after finding they could not gain the object of their bold undertaking, returned in full view of Yankee sharpshooters who made the dirt play all around and bullets sing about their heads. The constant firing of their comrades must have saved them.[1]

The casualties in this company testify that it was not in a warmer place during the war, notwithstanding the numerous battles the regiment was afterwards engaged in. The following were killed: Sergt. Stanley, of Cabarrus county. The ball entered his mouth. He passed safely through the Mexican war, but fell thus early in this. Privates Holliman, Seaman, Whitaker, Sheeler, Beaver, Mahoney and two others.[2] The severely wounded were Sergt. Phifer, of Cabarrus, whose daring was conspicuous; Corporal Kelly, who lost his right arm. Private Lazenby (who still carries an ounce ball in his right lung), Joe Stamper, and six others whose names I cannot now accurately mention.[3]

Fortunate Capt. R. V. Cowan had on a tall hat, as a ball passed directly through without injury to his head, the marksman not having aimed quite low enough.[4] Fortunately I said—and so a certain private thought when on the march and a gun in the hands of a careless man in front of him, fired sending a ball through the crown of his hat, and a comrade said "I tell you it was lucky you had on a high hat," he said, "I'll *swar* it was."

A large number of the enemy passed to our rear, before we left our position and those who escaped being captured, had to do it by fast running. A number became prisoners, and were put in the old brick kiln, where the sharp points of numerous brickbats became their easy chairs and downy couches. A little log hut served as a hospital where arms and legs were quickly amputated and thrown away. Obtained permission with a detail of men, to bring in our wounded and gave them the best attention circumstances would allow, answering their calls for water and changing their position. A schoolmate by the name of Tysor was brought into the old kiln, badly and painfully wounded through the thigh. He was a noble man—gentle and kind. He died trusting in a common Saviour.[5]

Col. Avery was captured, and soon after beset by a yankee woman, who was apparently half attired in male and half in female garb, who urged him to allow her to cut off one of his brass buttons, but I believe without success.[6] Some of the yankee officers boasted that they had captured Newbern and six thousand prisoners, which number dwindled down to about 200 of the regular forces. The losses of the two armies were, I think, on the part of the Confederates 68 killed and 101 wounded, and on the part of the Federals 137 killed and about 500 wounded.

Within a few days we found ourselves huddled together on an old transport called the "Albany," which was anchored in the middle of Neuse River. Our *delightful* experience here—our *delectable* trip North over the breakers of Hatteras Inlet—our *gorgeous* state rooms, and the beauties of prison life at Governor's Island, Pea Island, Point Lookout, Fort Henry, and a slight experience of twenty months at the far-famed "United States Hotel" on Johnson's Island, must be reserved for description in future numbers, under the head of "Extracts from Leroy's Prison Journal."

It is entirely unnecessary for me to attempt any account of the part other regiments or companies took in the battle of Newbern. Able reports have been made. I have written concerning a company I know most about.

LEROY.

APPENDIX B

Introduction to the prison journal of Columbus Lafayette Turner (as published in *Our Living and Our Dead*, May 20, 1874.)

"EXTRACTS FROM THE PRISON JOURNAL OF A CONFEDERATE"

In the middle of Neuse river the "Albany" lay anchored about one month. All the room on it was occupied by prisoners. It was a steam transport, old, rickety and ungainly in appearance. When on deck we barely had elbow room. When night came on we had to go below in the dark, foetid gloom of the hold of the vessel and sleep on broad shelves which were made one above the other. Here beneath the water, crowded together, we slept and dreamed as best we could, fully testing the luxury of the "soft side of a plank," of which we had heard so much. Here we were literally "laid on the shelf." Here, too, was our only retreat during the day when tired of standing or lolling on the crowded deck. Here, for the first time, I observed some of that pestiferous tribe of insects afterwards so universally known in both armies. Two or three of the advanced scouts had no sooner made their attack than, seized with loathing and disgust, I imprudently, as it afterwards proved to be, drew off a good shirt—almost an only shirt—and threw it overboard. From this time forward it became necessary to keep up a ceaseless warfare, to secure anything like freedom from their depredations. Some of the men actually surrendered. It would seem that they could not do otherwise, being without change of raiment, and the opportunity of using scalding water. It seldom happens in civilized life that one has to go without while his washed clothes are drying, yet many both in prison and camp life, have had just such experience. Some have washed their clothes and put them on to dry. Others never parted company with dirty clothes, and every regular soldier, officer or private, has been compelled at some time or other, by the force of circumstances, to wear badly soiled clothing.

Of course in this steamer we were without chairs, divans, sofas or settees. We were without benches, tables, plates, cups, saucers, spoons, knives, or forks. Pocket knives were scarce. Mine was captured on the battlefield by a yankee who claimed to be acting under orders. There was not room sufficient for issuing rations, especially the soup, which was served in buckets and tubs. Beneath the hatchway in a narrow passage a wash tub was set down in the hold of the vessel, and a horse bucket was filled with the soup from a large boiler and let down by means of a rope, emptied, drawn back, and the same process repeated. Getting to the tub was not easy and eating the soup without spoon or cup was worse. Went without soup rather than push and crowd around such a bowl or tureen, and in unison with some take my hands or a stick to it. Here was a picture that beat Harper or Leslie, some of the men would have eagerly dipped it up with their hands but it was generally too hot. Wooden spoons became numerous or would have been so if sufficient raw material, and suitable implements could have been obtained. Many sticks were whittled into a more convenient shape. around the tub pale lines of soup could be seen where it had drained back from sticks, fingers and wooden spoons. Looking on, I beheld a forcible reminder of times gone by when a tray of dough was cast to or set down for a large flock of chickens. I happened to be able to start fifteen cents of "old money," with which was obtained a tin cup, and thereafter my share of soup was fairly secured and highly appreciated. However, it was often too late to have my cup replenished after cooling and emptying it the first time. The cup was useful to more than one, and was sometimes the fortunate receiver of coffee. Fat meat and hard bread were also used. We could relish the meat very well without cooking—could handle it better.—When cooked the grease would drip from it like water from a dish rag. Upon that crowded vessel, in its narrow aisles and dark main-hold, emitting offensive odors, some might think we did not relish our food, but we did. We did not, however, enjoy eating soup without a spoon.

It is now time to weigh anchor, both for a voyage to Governor's Island in New York harbor, and for closing this extract. The former will be speedily disposed of in the next—bringing us by a near cut to Fort Delaware, concerning which, much may justly be said.

LEROY

APPENDIX C

"Remarks of C. L. Turner of Iredell in the House of Representatives on the bill proposing to amend Section 10 of Article 11 in regard to the Insane and the Deaf Dumb and Blind of the State, which failed to pass its third reading Feb. 22d 1873"

[EDITOR'S NOTE: Introduced in the senate on February 3 by the chairman of the Committee on Constitutional Amendments, the proposal would amend the constitutional article that required the assembly to provide free care for the deaf, dumb, blind, and insane citizens of North Carolina. The measure would have restricted public assistance to members of families whose holdings were less than the homestead and personal property exemption set by the North Carolina Constitution. Turner voted against the measure, which failed by one vote to receive the two-thirds majority necessary to amend the state constitution.]

Mr. Speaker—I had said that I expected to vote for all the proposed amendments to the Constitution, because they have been so long published, and have been so well canvassed before the people and because I recognize the fact that in a case of this kind, it is my duty to give expression to the wish of a large majority of the people whom I represent, by my vote. In making that assertion a short while since, I overlooked the amendment now under consideration. This was not discussed before the people—I have no evidence that they desire its adoption. I am sure they do not want it, unless it is right. I represent a people who when they understand the right, are free to uphold it. They do not wish any thing /ingrafted/ in/to/ their Constitution that would encourage class legislation. They do not wish any improperly draw[n] line of demarkation between the poor and the rich &.

APPENDIX D

[EDITOR'S NOTE: Representative Turner prepared these remarks for delivery during the discussion of the amnesty bill in the House on February 26-27, 1873. The bill was introduced in the senate on January 21 by William A. Allen of Duplin County. It was received by the House ten days later, but consideration by the lower chamber was repeatedly postponed. When the bill with several amendments appended finally came to a vote, the House approved it by a vote of 57 to 50, Turner voting in its favor. Ratified on March 3, the Act for Amnesty and Pardon forgave all crimes except rape, murder, arson, burglary, larceny, robbery, and embezzlement from a railroad company committed prior to September 1, 1871, by members of secret societies on both sides of Reconstruction-era violence in the state. These organizations included the Ku Klux Klan, Red Strings, Heroes of America, Loyal Union League, and Governor Holden's North Carolina State Troops and militia. *House Journal 1872-'73*, 303, 390, 434, 473, 517-518, 531-534, 555, 600; *Senate Journal 1872-'73*, 190; *Laws and Resolutions, 1872-'73*, Public Laws, c. 181, pp. 298-300.]

Mr. Speaker. If the bill now under consideration had been put upon its passage ~~only a few days ago~~ /not long since/, I should have promptly voted No. If the vote had been taken ~~on yesterday Tuesday~~/Tuesday before last/, I would have been in a state of doubt, and might have felt a disposition to dodge. But dodging questions or a vote upon them is not my custom. All I ask is to be certain of the right, and when the question is put an emphatic Aye or No will be, and has been my immediate answer. The Aye or No upon many questions is determined by some with a reference to its bearing upon the next political campaign. The mental query at once arises—Will it be popular? can I make capital out of it before the people?—If so right or wrong I will vote pro or con, just as the case may be to suit ~~the above~~ /such/ reasoning. This is the method of some, whilst others will support a party measure, even though it be grossly wrong. Sir, I trust that I am not one to adapt means to the end whether good or evil. In that sense I am not a <u>politic</u> man, but am "free to confess" that I would be gladly described by that word, if <u>deserved</u>, provided it were taken in its primary sense which is "Exercising sagacity in devising and pursuing measures adapted to promote the public welfare." In that sense then is this a politic measure?—would it be wise? would it be right? I have striven Sir, to conjure up as it were the future workings of this measure, in all its bearings, and am compelled to think that its adoption would promote the peace and welfare of the country. I had thought that this Amnesty bill was rather sweeping in its provisions, and did expect to offer an amendment excepting wilful murder and arson from the pardon herein provided; but just here a difficulty presented itself. If there have been any cases of <u>wilful</u> murder and arson, they are few, whilst hundreds, including numerous inocent people, would be implicated, and a trial necessitated, to ascertain whether or not they belonged to the excepted class. I am exceedingly anxious to reach the heartless and bloodthirsty evildoers, and see them summarily punished, but do not with to hazzard the peace of communities and bring down the severe penalties of the law upon the innocent, the unwary, the deceived and misled.

Under an ~~a decision of the Supreme Court~~/opinion held by some of the courts/ all the members of certain secret organizations are ~~held to be~~ /regarded as/ accomplices or accessories before or after the fact. Would not many in this way be implicated whose feelings are foreign to the commission of crime? Would it not be highly impolitic to punish members of the Ku Klux Klan, or Loyal League or any other secret organization in Currituck for crimes committed by members of the same order in Cherokee? Would it be right to punish the good men of any community for the evil done by the bad men thereof? Is it right to allow fear and anguish to torture the minds of the Mothers wives and daughters of our land, simply because their fathers husbands and brothers happened to belong to an order, which at the time of their joining they considered to be proper for their protection? Shall all of them suffer for the ~~crimes~~ deeds of imfamy and brutality perpetrated by the few? I hope not.

I have sir in private and public earnestly condemned the foul and heinous deeds of all these organizations. All secret societies of a political nature have at all times when I have expressed myself received my unqualified disapproval. The honest political sentiments of any one have received no persecution at my hands. I stand upon the broad catholic ground of freedom of speech—the liberty of the press /& conscience/—and the safety and welfare of the citizen. My mottoe is and has been—Let every man do just as he pleases provided he does his neighbor no harm.

But Mr. Speaker, the madness of politics and the generally disordered state of society consequent upon the war produced those deplorable results, the last remembrance of which it is the object of this Amnesty Bill to cover up, so far as the law is concerned. /Should this bill pass/ Some bad men may escape the punishment justly deserved, but hundreds of innocent will be relieved from unnecessary Molestation, ~~and~~ the peace and welfare of society promoted and the designs of some evil men frustrated.

Waters both sweet and bitter, or water both salty and fresh will not and cannot gush forth from the same fountain. You cannot gather "grapes of thorns" or "figs of thistles." Like begets like and evil produces evil. ~~One~~ /The/ secret organization of one party produce~~d~~ /s/ fear and suspicion, especially so when party passion runs high, and cursings and threatenings are common. A counter movement results and violence on the one hand produces retaliation on the other.

These things ought not so to be, but it is natural—it is usual and we have had a clear illustration here in North Carolina. Are not these assertions confirmed by the facts of history? Have there not been occurrences in every clime and country which vindicate this position? Every man in the State I suppose inclined to or associated himself with one of the two great political parties, and partook in some degree the fear or excitement of the hour. Partisan zeal together with numerous evils which followed in the train of a devastating civil war, gave to the once peaceful Old North State a disordered and unsettled condition of society. Out of this sprang hatreds, strifes false accusations, violence retaliations criminations and recriminations. Innocence and virtue were profaned and trampled upon, dwellings were rumaged, robberies were committed, barns were burned and murders /were/ frequent. The ignorant were led into evil ways, and incited to the commission of crimes. Violators of the law were allowed to escape. Disturbers of the peace of society went unpunished. Some boasted the privilledge of doing violently with immunity from punishment. The organization of one party seemed to be so complete, both as to officers of the law and otherwise, and a determination so apparent to stand by each other right or wrong, that a feeling of uncertainty possessed the minds of communities in certain parts of the State. What was naturally the result is very well known by every member upon this floor. Another long train of evils followed. Another secret order was instituted. Summary punishment was administered in some instances, where the outraged sense of the people sanctioned it, but in other instances, it was deserving of severe condemnation. Just so it will happen among secret order or vigillence committees that cruelties and barbarities will be practiced. Lynch ~~now~~ /law/ will be improperly administered, and is of itself wrong. States North East South and West have had some experience in this respect. Civil law and Lynch law have both had a decidedly improper administration here in North Carolina.

APPENDIX E

MEMORIAL DAY ADDRESS

Delivered in Statesville Saturday, May 9th, 1896 by C. L. Turner, Esq.

[From the Statesville *Landmark*, May 15, 1896, transcribed in Irene Clanton Black, comp., *Newspaper Transcripts from the* Landmark *Statesville*, 3 vols. (Statesville: privately printed, 1993-1995), 3:107-111. Reprinted with permission.]

Ladies of the Memorial Association of Iredell County, Ladies and Gentlemen:

I remember that in the first brick church the Presbyterians of this place had (they now have the third), the North Carolina Conference held its annual session that years, and Rev. D. McFerrin remarked that it was "hard to plow in rooty ground all week, with a stubborn mule, and preach on Sunday."[1] So, you may readily imagine, that it is equally difficult for a man of business to be engrossed with all the detail of his daily occupation, and come before this intelligent audience, on such an occasion, and properly entertain his hearers. But, my friends, there is some inspiration in being called by the ladies of this Memorial Association to unite with them in keeping sacred and memorable the names and deeds of our own departed braves. All honor to them who for each year since our mighty struggle, in spite of all the cares of life, have come up on the 10th of May or Memorial Day, to spread garlands upon their graves, and call to remembrance the names of those who have passed away. Today marks their 30th celebration. Thirty one years now since the war, and our heroes—privates and all—still remembered, still honored. This is gratifying; giving promise that the lapse of years shall not drown their memories. It promises also that our just pride in the glory and renown of our beloved Southland shall be unfading.

I remember that many years ago, and since the war, Henry Ward Beecher declared the time would come when a Southern man would be ashamed to stand by the grave of a Confederate soldier.[2] Almost a generation since the war and it is not so yet. Your acts and presence today eloquently contradict it. May it never be so. I am sure it will not be. Shall the gold ornament be ashamed of the diamond that glitters and sparkles from its gilded centre?

We are not ashamed of our soldiery or the record the Confederacy made, or the history the south has made in letters of living light, both in war and peace—nor is any part of this great Union.

Shall the star-bedecked crown of night be ashamed of the silvery moon riding in serene loveliness tho are of the heavens? Or to use a stronger figure: Shall the cerulean vault above be ashamed of the glorious sun of day, rising up from the orient, and going on up with increasing power and brilliancy to the zenith of his glories; then descending with continuing brightness to the occident, sinking beneath the horizon, but shedding back haloes of glory and spreading to the gaze of admiration pictures of gold and ineffable beauty?

So my friends, the Confederacy arose, when the world fixed its wondering gaze upon a new giant among the nations which from the start displayed Herculean might and shed increasing lustre upon Southern arms. On, up, up, with increasing brilliance and power, till reaching its culmination at Gettysburg, it went amid brightness down, down to Appomattox—when its sun set forever, but left behind grand panoramas of beauty. The sun of the Confederacy set in glory to revive and reassure the greater glory of our common country—to be "one and inseparable, united and indivisible." Old Glory waves above us. We came back to our own. The old flag that Southern valor had so often carried to victory, and beneath whose folds the South, perhaps more than any other section, had won battles and added wide empires to our domain. I am not here to decry and condemn any section. There is fame for all. I wish to promote a laudable pride among our immediate people. I would also stir up your hearts to a genuine love of the Old North State, whose soldiers, so numerous in our late war, so sturdy and self-sacrificing, so obedient to the commands which involved the greatest dangers, so bold and daring, that they have rendered forever famous and honorable the name Tar Heel.

"Carolina, Carolina, Heaven's blessings attend her;
While we live we will cherish, protect and defend her.
Hurrah! Hurrah! the Old North State forever;
Hurrah! Hurrah! For the good Old North State."[3]

The tocsin of war was sounded in 1861 and it became a question of State or nation. The former involved homes and firesides, our immediate people and kindred, and so circumstances were such that notwithstanding our pride in the Union of States and the glory of wide domain and past history, we stood up and fought for North Carolina and the sunny South.

The men of North Carolina in legion and phalanx, from the lowlands of the east, the table lands of the centre, and the highlands of the west, poured forth to meet greater numbers on the battlefield. They endured the chill and bleakness of winter, the dust and heat of summer, hunger, thirst and fatigue, lack of clothing, shelter and other comforts, the trying march and the furious onset of battle. In all these things they showed themselves well worthy of remembrance and of the tribute of praise and honor we give them this day. Not only this day but at all times they deserve our consideration.

It has been customary with me to support for offices, such as sheriff, clerk of court, register of deeds and other offices for which they were adapted, and in common, too, with many of the people of Catawba county, the one-armed and one-legged soldiers. For these I feel sincere sympathy and the highest respect and consideration, as also for others who have been unfortunate by reason of wounds and the casualties of war.

Many of these unfortunates have passed away, but so many are still hobbling along on the shores of time that at this late day it reminds us in emphatic language of what a wonderful record North Carolina made in the great conflict; showing that she was well to the front in posts of danger and death.

Only a few weeks ago I was in the town of Newton; had just entered town, and the first object of interest and of greatest interest to me, was three or four one-legged soldiers standing near each other and looking as if they had nothing of which to complain. I stopped, saluted and said: "Well, this is certainly interesting. So many peg-legged soldiers right here together. What is up? Some special meeting?" No. And just then another peg-legged fellow walked up. The interest grew. I went on and pretty soon I saw still another with only one leg. I halted and told him what had just happened, and before leaving I met the old clerk of the court and former Representative and Senator from Catawba. He looks as if he had two legs, but he has only one.[4] This made, I think, the seventh one legged soldier I saw that day. The others were what I call a peg-leg, similar to J. M. Patterson, Esq., of Iredell, whom you have seen.[5] I met also that day in Newton two men with one arm each. Upon all these and their kind may Providence pour rich blessings, dealing gently with them in their single-handed and one-legged march to the tomb.

But time would wail me to speak in turn of all the different kinds of suffering and misfortune. Those who lost the sight or hearing of one or both eyes and ears, who lost both arms or legs, who received various and bruises, who are carrying minnie balls in their person, those who have deep wounds in their bodies and suffer to this day. Many of them have passed away since the war and all, all, whether living or dead, deserve our kindly remembrance.

And now I come to those who fell in the hurly-burly of battle, in the skirmish, on the dangerous picket line, or on the march; or who, wounded, languished and died upon the ensanguined field or in the hospital. And we all come this day to honor and ennoble their names. Would it not be appropriate for me to speak more especially here and on this occasion, and before the ladies of the Memorial Association of Iredell county, of Iredell's fallen heros? Would it not be eminently appropriate for me to call by name some of these, and all if I could?

You have heard the refrain, "Where are the friends of my youth?" Whilst many have passed away since the great struggle, and some are still living and scattered here and there, yet there were others who were slain in battle. Among the latter now appears to my mind, with such vivid distinctness, the form of W. H. H. Weaver, that if I were an artist I could draw a good picture of him. Hal Weaver, as we usually called him. He was a native of Iredell and lieutenant in one of your companies. He was tall of form and quick to act. He was frank and kind-hearted and as "bold as a lion." In the heat of that fiery struggle at Sharpesburg he jumped in front of his company, and said, with sword aloft, "Men I don't say go—I say come." Then and there he was shot dead. Hearing this of Hal Weaver, I thought it was so much like him. I would like to tell some anecdotes illustrative of his character but the amusing part might appear unseemly on an occasion like this. Shade of the departed brave! May it ever rest in peace, and may we meet again.[6] Boon companions of his in their school days were Boone Perry and Jackson Anderson of Davie, and John B. Turner of Iredell. A bold and daring quartette, and all lost their lives.[7] His brother, Lieut. G. Washington Weaver, had a foot shattered at Chancellorsville by a shell, and lost his life.[8] In this action also, culling from memory, I give the names of Humphrey and Robert Summers, brothers, who were killed near each other and about the same time.[9] Also Wm. Campbell, whom I learn was found dead, squatted, with eye sighting along the gun barrel which pointed towards the enemy.[10] I remember the last three when I was a mere boy. They were fine marksmen and accustomed to shoot squirrels and turkeys with a rifle. In death no doubt they were drawing a fine bead, just as they once did when they saw a squirrel in a high tree.

From this same neighborhood I would mention the names of Noah Ward, John Tharpe and others killed in battle.[11] Sharpe Tomlin who died of disease and John A. Turner, who, as a cavalryman, rode so near the enemy and, refusing to surrender, was shot from his horse, and after some months confinements at Point Lookout died.[12]

I have often remarked that you might point from the place where I was raised in north Iredell to any home near in any direction—and that home had lost a son, as also had the home from which would be pointing.

And now let me mention the tall and commanding form of Col. R. V. Cowan, the rattle of whose musketry was among the last to be heard at Appomattox, and who, I learn just before the terms of surrender were arranged, met General Custer, of the Federal army, on the lines, and who was a schoolmate at West Point, whom you will remember in a battle with Indians since the war was slain and all his men except one or two who escaped. Cowan and Custer met with demonstrations of friendship abusing each other for their red heads, and not knowing when to quit fighting—too ready to fight. Col. Cowan went to the war as captain, being at the time a West Point student.[13] Just over the way there the first section of his company was gathered. With these I went to the war, fresh from commencement at Trinity College. Going as private, I ended as lieutenant, but spent the latter half of the war in prison, having been captured at the close of the last charge at Gettysburg. Capt. Cowan took us into camp at Graham, where we drilled, and soon afterwards went to Raleigh, where recruits came to us from other counties. Cowan's company became Company A of the 33d N. C. Troops. Gen. L. O'B. Branch was the first colonel. Cowan's company received its first baptism of fire at New Berne. Here it occupied an advanced position to the right of the railroad and immediately on the same. The space was open and we were placed behind the dirt of a ditch thrown on the wrong side. Well do I remember that I was just gaining strength from the effects of a serious and protracted spell of typhoid- pneumonia and Capt. Cowan would not allow me to go on picket duty the dark and drizzly night before the battle, and had Abel York to stay with me.[14] I slept well in one of the deserted tents of Col. Z. B. Vance's regiment. Guided by the firing next morning, we soon joined our company. Soon Sergeant Stanley was killed. He had been in the Mexican war, but was killed thus early in this. The ball entered his mouth. The other killed in this company were Privates Holliman, Seaman, Whitaker, Speeler, Beaver, Mahoney and two others. There were nine killed and ten wounded. In unusual proportion of killed to wounded.[15]

I have thus referred to the first battle of this Iredell company in order to show how they heeded only what was in front of them, fighting until well nigh surrounded, and our little army had retreated, justifying in some measure Custer's pleasantry with Cowan at the end of the war, and also in order to give the names of the fallen; and also to relate that during the heat of action Capt. Cowan ordered Lieut. Saunders, with a few men, to jump over the mound and get in the ditches so as to secure better aim at the enemy. Immediately he was followed by Private John M. Lazenby, John Murchison, John Sherrill, Jake Halterman and Samuel Whitaker. In going and returning they must have been saved by the fierce firing of their comrades. The casualties of this battle were Confederates killed, 68; wounded, 101; Federal killed, 137; wounded, 500.[16]

Time and patience would fail me to follow this company through its various and trying experiences. I have wished to do as good part as I could by my comrades, drawing only from memory, avoiding detailed history or a discussion of the causes that led up to the war. I do not detain you with arguments to show that we were right or wrong. I know upon which side my lot was cast and I know that I was with and for my own people. It hath been said

"Breathes there a man with soul so dead,
Who never to himself hath said,
This is my own, my native land?"[17]

So! to day I ask, Breathes there a man to the manor born, with soul so vile, who would decry and discredit his own native land, our own beloved North Carolina or our Southland! But, my friends, I am digressing from my main purpose.

When a single file of our command stood in the open on the railroad at Fredericksburg to receive the on-slaught of double columns of the enemy, and when looking them in the eye at the track on the other side, we were ordered to fall back to reserves in the wood. With rapid speed we did so, but Orderly Sergeant Washington Shields received a shot almost centrally in the back. He urged that he be not left. Two soldiers carried him out. He bemoaned his sad fate at being shot in the back and said, "Captain, haven't I always been a good soldier?" "Yes, yes, you have." He died that night or next morning. And so went out the life of one of the bravest of the brave. His brother, William Shields, also an orderly sergeant, fell with his face to the enemy in the last charge at Gettysburg.[18] Here also fell another of Iredell's heroes in whom you are specially interested, many of you at least. I heard the thud of the ball that smote his breast, and saw him fall like Shields—face to the enemy. Like myself he was young, but more ambitious for glory. He was appointed as a lieutenant to act with the guard detailed for service in the rear, and could have honorably missed the last and fatal charge at Gettysburg. So he was with us when the serried ranks swept across the wide open, amid hurtling, bursting bombshells, into the hailstorm of bullets, and amid the roar of five hundred cannon, and, looking the enemy in the face, he went down to death. So passed away Lieut. Thos. A. Cowan, brother of Col. R. V. Cowan.[19] Here also Capt. H. H. Baker fell. Just before the charge he was smoking, pleasantly talking, and said he did not "expect to get killed in there."[20] Lieut. Burton Summers, who was wounded by a piece of shell before the charge, became captain on the death of Capt. Baker.[21] I have often thought how noble the few Federals looked who stood in line to receive our charge when their ranks had been so thinned by injuries, and especially by those who fled. The idea seemed to be with them, "Come they will;" and I am sure we would have routed them in our front but for our flank being uncovered at the supreme moment and the men being conscious of it. Our right having gone down to death or been driven back, left us in the last moment unprotected on the flank. The crisis of battle had come. The Southern Cross and Constellation was about to wave in triumph, but "reinforcements appearing" again saved the union force from complete rout. Upon this gage of battle depended the establishment of a new nation. It was decided against the Confederacy, and so the latter, after all its triumphs, began to wane; but, as before stated, it struggled with varying results and went amid brightness to find its setting sun at Appomattox.

I cannot conclude this address without reference to Iredell County's professional soldier—a hero in the Mexican war—Col. Reuben Campbell, the gallant commander of the gallant seventh North Carolina. His color bearer having been shot down he gathered up the flag and with the stars and bars waving in his hand, he went down to a brave soldier's death.[22] His fearless brother, Mansfield, is also numbered among the slain.[23] Also I must mention Lieut. Col. Junius Hill, the "brave and gentle," as denominated by Gen. Jas. H. Lane.[24] If the Confederacy had towers of strength in her Hills, who were generals, so old Iredell had her in Hills that were colonels and captains and lieutenants. And so I mention in association with the fallen Junius Hill, Col. Clinton Hill, also Lieut. Hugh A. Hill, of Cowan's company, and Dr. M. W. Hill.[25] As I go forward names like that of Major Ab. K. Simonton, who fell at Seven Pines quite early in the war, come up;[26] and so if I had refreshed my memory and consulted history and friends by letter or otherwise, you will see if I had attempted to speak of all of Iredell's heroes by name, the latest minute of the day would be gone and the half would not be told.

So the men of Iredell, ladies of Iredell county, supplement what I have said by filling in here and there—now and then. Listen also to the demands that may be made upon you by the ladies of this Memorial Association to commemorate their names and their deeds. Let a grateful people rear on high the monumental pile, so that the enduring granite may tell the story to coming generations. Or else let the memorial be a monumental institution, recording their names and deeds, preserving history, relieving suffering and diffusing knowledge.

Men of North Carolina, ladies of the Old North State, citizens of the native land of such men as Generals Branch, Pender, Pettigrew, Anderson, Gordon of Wilkes, Ramseur, Polk and McCulloch, who fell in the late war, and Generals Grimes, Robert Ransom, Scales, Tucker (who was born and raised in Iredell), Bragg and Loring, who have passed away since; and also Generals Hoke, Cox, Mat. Ransom and some others who yet live: I call upon you to be exercised by a proper and commendable State pride. This list I have mentioned because it is short in comparison with that of gallant colonels, and the list of the latter is short when compared with that of heroic captains, lieutenants and noncommissioned officers, and the list of all the braves who were officers is short in comparison with the legion of bold and daring privates. Will a vast army of brave men make you proud? No greater was furnished by any State to defend the Confederacy or the Union.

Giants of war on both sides made a great history for our common country. The whole nation now glories in the record made. Old animosities have passed away. In common the whole country celebrates the 4th of July. The Blue and the Gray meet on common ground. Concord prevails and they say by their acts that the war is over, we are citizens of the same great nation and partakers together of her glory. Our pride passes beyond State limits and includes the whole country. North, South, East and West have become one.

As I contemplate the difference in the conduct of our war and the methods pursued in the island of Cuba I see how far in advance we are in civilization and enlightenment and rejoice that instead of being a Spaniard I am an American. This comparison makes me feel more kindly towards all sections of our great country. Peace and liberty here prevail. Liberty's defenders here reside, and all the jarrings of fool politics cannot destroy their patriotism. Union and liberty—not license—are the watch words. And so our hearts go out to the struggling patriots of Cuba, Queen of the Antilles, key to the Gulf, and, if necessary, in the securement of her liberties, may she yet be joined with the South in swelling the grand chorus of this Union. I have no desire to see our country involved in war, but our earnest sympathies must be with that tormented and oppressed people, tyrannized over by a cruel foe, whose acts confirm in my mind the history of cruelties in the Spanish Inquisition. Behold the reports of numerous conflicts emanating from Spanish censorship, wherein few or many Cubans were killed and one or a few Spaniards wounded, and when the truth leaks out it is found that the Spanish have simply murdered *pacificos,* or peaceful citizens, and some times children. Also when Spanish officers too chivalrous to murder have sent captives to Havana they have had a sham trial and a speedy execution. The American people have spoken in resolutions, backed by all parties, that belligerent rights should be granted to the Cuban patriots, and may the stage of their success soon be such as to induce this administration to go ahead, let the consequences be as they may, and thus, in the interest of fair play, civilization and Christianity, stop many horrors that are being enacted.

Think not that I have digressed from the subject or subjects appropriate to the day in speaking of Cuba. The tyranny and cruelty exercised there are worse than our own revolution, when, more than one hundred years ago, our forefathers struggled seven long years. Spain is an old number and behind the enlightenment and civilization of the present, and so this comparison, if made by our people generally, would relieve us of much of the pessimism and complainings of the present and inaugurate a higher ideal of our own country. Such optimistic view is the heritage of the Confederate soldier. Though defeated, he turns his reassured gaze to the opportunities offered by the great union of States and hopes to realize the greater victories of peace. The crowning triumph is coming. What was not accomplished by war will be done through the instrumentalities of peace. The soldiers returning from the war, to devastated homes and fields, did not sit down to repine but went to work, rebuilt the waste place, tilled the soil, restored commerce and manufactures, and now the new South is making rapid strides to reach the van of the marching hosts which are moving forward in science, art, civilization and improvements.

So, after all, it cannot be said that the fallen heroes of Iredell county, of North Carolina, of the Southland, died in vain. Spread garlands upon their graves. Sleep, soldier, sleep.

"Soldier rest; thy warfare o'er,
Sleep the sleep that knows not breaking.
Dream of battlefields no more.
Days of danger, night of waking."[27]

APPENDIX F

Speech given by Columbus L. Turner, at Catawba, N.C., April 1, 1897

"Victory lost, Victory won"

Veterans, Ladies and Gentlemen

Does it not happen now and then in the course of human events, that the cause struggled for, and apparently lost eventually becomes established upon an enduring foundation? It also seems to be the order of Providence that we shall contend earnestly for what we believe to be right, and sometimes fail, and yet be rewarded in the future with a victory, either securing to us what was contended for, or giving to us something better[.] In art, in science, in religion[,] in government, there have been evolved from the conflict of contending forces discoveries and principles, which have been of beneficial and far reaching consequences. Labor, contention, struggles and suffering have been a law of our being ever since the first of human kind were excluded from the terrest[r]ial paradise, and of the class who will enter the celestial it will be said, "these are they, who came up through great tribulation."

So then it is work, it is struggle, it is suffer in order to the accomplishment of any great end. Struggling peoples for the right of self government, have gone down in disaster, but their cause lived on and again there would be another outbreak to again be overwhelmed by treachery or superior numbers, but on and on the cause lives, for "the eternal years of God are hers." The victory may be lost but afterwards it is won, by renewed effort or by such a combination of events as to give success wherein war failed. /Men/ Veterans of Co. I 49th N.C. Regt.[1] I say to you, that if victory you lost in war, you have since gained /it/ in peace. Did you contend for the right of local self government? If you did we have as much of it to-day, I verily believe, as you would have had otherwise. but of course we find ourselves contending for its maintenance "by eternal vigilance" which "is the price of liberty." Had the confederacy been established it would have required thousands of men to guard an illy defined border thousands of miles long, and ever and anon, difficulties would have arisen between the two nations and ere this we might have had war. We have had peace for near a third of a century and now we /have/ the galaxy of forty ~~six~~ five states to swell the grand "Chorus of the Union." The Stars & Bars, or the Southern Cross and Constellation we will ever cherish as the emblem of the South's glory and honor, for under its folds we battled manfully and lost all except these.

The principle for which we fought is eternal and we expect to see it maintained beneath the ample folds of the Stars and Stripes. To this flag Southern valor and statesmanship had given great honors and renown before the tocsin of civil war was sounded. It is our flag[.] Also these—Southern valor and Statesmanship had added wide empires of territory to our vast domain. It had defended our borders, it had won victories, it had given power and fame to the great republic. Yes it is our flag and now long may it wave as the emblem of strength, liberty & justice.

May the Lost Cause of the South—the victory lost, when her ever honorable flag was furled—be ever secured or won under the banner of the Union. I believe that Providence intended that our defeat should result in our ultimate triumph by the establishment on an enduring basis the leading principle of the Confederacy. Was it that the shackles might be bound tighter on an ignorant and enslaved race that you fought and continued to fight? Oh! no. Only about one fo[u]rth mil[l]ion of our people owned slaves. It is true ~~most~~ many of them, the slaveholders were selfish and wanted to make slavery a cornerstone of the new republic and had their influence when most of our people, led by Gen. Lee and others wanted to set the slaves free. He wanted to make soldiers of them, but he wished them to be free. This small selfish element owning the slaves were guided by a narrow policy, but I in common with many others, felt in the last year of the war, that the slaves would be free, which ever side won. I believe that was the order of Providence.

Let it be said to the credit of the negroes as a race, that they followed the paths of peace, took care of women & children, cultivated our fields and reaped our crops, while we were fighting each other, and God was fighting their battle for them. So let their footprints still be in the way of peace and Providence will do greater things for them.

Soldiers! from this place you went to the war surrounded by your mothers fathers wives and sweethearts, and cheered on by them. In imagination I can see the white handkerchiefs fluttering in the breeze. I can see the tear of fear and hope. As your train sped on, from windows, doors piazzas, farm yards and fields and way sides, other white emblems waved, and sweet voices cheered. Around and up went your hats and the embryo rebel yell. The camp you first pitched was a pleasant one compared with the last. You had good clothes and good food at first. You set your tents in rows and had covering for your heads. You had pleasant visits from well dressed people. You drilled, you were organized into a regiment, and joined to Ransom's famous brigade.

You were ordered to the front and began the active and trying duties of a soldier. You endured fat[i]guing marches in dust and heat and cold. You slept upon the bare ground with arms in your hands. You kept the weary vigils of the night. Hark, a solemn sound. It is the deep intonation of distant cannon prepare to march. You hear the command all along your campfires. Fall in. Fall in, then Forward March and by fou[r]s goes the long line until a swift flying courier meets your commander with orders to file right or left as the case may be at some given point. You are brought into line and faced the direction of the enemy who is somewhere near. Other troops hurry along to your right or left flank. A reserve force is posted in your rear.

A big general dashes along the line a cheer starts when silence is ordered lest you make known your position. Some more shifting of position, ah listen an exploding bomb shell and some of the pieces fall around you. Cannon on both sides begin to play. The word attention sounds out, the command Fall in. You dress up together in long line, the charge may be sounded by a comcannon [*sic*] or other signal, and Forward, Sounds from numerous Colonels & Captains up and down the line. The host moves forward in serried rank like some mighty serpent, the cannon roars, and as you pass out of the skirt of woods you see the enemy in line, on on you go myriad muskets open fire on you the balls whiz by, now and then a man falling, but on on the column sweeps. The rattle of musketry deepens the big guns belch forth their missels [*sic*] of death with a roar that makes the hills reverberate, on you go, a shell explodes in the line, men are blown up around it and fall dead or badly wounded. Musketry grows fierce killed and wounded fall around more rapidly, the spirit of the column revives with the long loud terrific rebel yell, the enemy knows by that ~~they~~ you will come on, he wavers. You press up to his lines, he gives back the yell deepens, he flies victory is you[r]s. On the occasion of the enemy being driven back at the famous battle of the crater your daring Col. /John A./ Flemming ~~mounted~~ flushed with triumph mounted the works, waving sword & was killed.[2] You suffered long in the muddy trenches ~~of~~ /around/ Petersburg, you endured want, fatigue, hunger, thirst. Often your couch was the cold /damp/ earth, your covering the high canopy of heaven. After a long and patient defense of Petersburg with the resources of the Confederacy constantly dwindling, the number of your comrades constantly decreasing you took up your mournful march toward Appomattox, where the incomparable Lee surrendered the remnant of a once magnificent army worn out by superior numbers, a long war by victor~~y~~ies turned into defeats, by numerous battles, by disease and want and constantly failing resources. You wended your way home, and by your return brought /some/ sunshine into the prevailing gloom. My father was /quite/ sick abed when I walked in. Immediately after the first salutations he put on his clothes and got well at once.

Manfully you went to work to restore the waste places. You had suffered and lost, but you did not sit down to repine. To the fathers and mothers of that period well may it have been said

"Welcome with shouts of joy & pride
Your veterans from the warpaths track
Your gave your ~~sons~~ /boys/ untrained, untried
Your bring them men and heroes back"

My friends, after all the victory of peace is greater than the victory of war. It is not tear down, but build up. It is not devastation slaughter and blood shed, but happiness and prosperity. It is not to lay waste the country but to improve it. It is not to burden the hearts of mothers with the loss of their sons, but to fill their being with joy and hope. It is not to bring down with sorrow to the grave, the gray hairs of our fathers, but to fill the evening of their lives with sublime faith. It is not to sunder husband and wife, but to join them in more joyous union. It is not to make orphans, but to be the nursery of romping bounding happy childhood.

It is not to blast character, but to rear men of sturdy habits, and women who are the hope and stay of our land. It is not the desolation of lovers, but the promotion of union and strength. It is not the demolition of homes, but their improvement and permanency. It is not the promotion of disease and anguish, but the relieving of it. It is not the mas[s]acre of men and horses, but the advancing column marching on to the redemption of the world. Light and progress are the watchwords of the age and developments have been made in the last score of years exceeding man's fondest expectations. As the poet said

"Come bright improvement on the car of time
And rule the spacious earth from clime to clime."

and so, united with the Evangels of God it will redeem renovate and regenerate the world. Onward to final triumph. Victories to win—Victory won.

ENDNOTES

INTRODUCTION

1. Columbus L. Turner, Memorial Day address, May 9, 1896, reported in the Statesville *Landmark*, May 15, 1896, transcribed in Irene Clanton Black, comp., *Newspaper Transcripts from the* Landmark *Statesville*, 3 vols. (Statesville, N.C.: privately printed, 1993-1995), 3:109.

2. Reginald Turner, untitled memoir, ca. 1970, chapter 7, copy in Turner Family Papers, North Carolina State Archives, Raleigh.

3. James R. Turner, "Turner Family History," unpublished manuscript, 1997; Locke Turner Clifford, "Turners," unpublished manuscript, n.d., transcript in possession of James R. Turner, Greensboro, N.C.; Jethro Rumple, *A History of Rowan County, North Carolina* (Baltimore: Regional Publishing Company, 1974 reprint), 313-314. Rev. Jethro Rumple offered the opinion in 1881 that the Episcopal Church missed a golden opportunity to sprout in the fertile soil of Rowan, had Dent chosen to remain and been "ordinarily zealous and successful in his ministrations."

4. Turner, "Turner Family History"; Iredell County Record of Deeds, 1821-1919 (microfilm), North Carolina State Archives, Raleigh, K:97-99, L:346-348, N:405, O:29, 363, P:379-380; *The Heritage of Iredell County* (Statesville, N.C.: Genealogical Society of Iredell County, 1980), 318; Seventh Census of the United States, 1850, Slave Schedule: Iredell County, North Carolina State Archives, Raleigh.

5. Clifford, "Turners."

6. Statesville *Landmark*, November 30, 1893, in Black, *Newspaper Transcripts*, 3:25; Davie County Record of Deeds, 1840-1860 (microfilm), North Carolina State Archives, Raleigh, 1:387, 2:255, 261, 269; Iredell County Record of Deeds, W:228; James W. Wall, *History of Davie County* (Mocksville, N.C.: Davie County Historical Publishing Association, 1969), 367.

7. Iredell County Record of Deeds, D4:288, 373-374, D5:716-717; Notley D. Tomlin Collection, Rare Book, Manuscript, and Special Collections Library, Duke University. Durham; Eighth Census of the United States, 1860, Slave Schedule: Iredell County, North Carolina State Archives, Raleigh.

8. John H. Wheeler, *The Legislative Manual and Political Register of the State of North Carolina for the Year 1874* (Raleigh: Josiah Turner Jr., 1874), 257; Statesville *Landmark*, November 30, 1893, in Black, *Newspaper Transcripts*, 3:25-26; editor's analysis of Wilfred Turner's transactions in Iredell County Deed Books, K-Z, and D1-D63. The African Americans who bought land from Wilfred Turner were Frank Belt, Alexander Insley, Alfred Neely, Alexander Nichols, Aug. Nichols, Sicily Nichols, Binum Patterson, Austin Smith, and Ben Stevenson.

9. Iredell County Record of Deeds, D4:369, D6:63, 87-88, D11:499-500; unidentified newspaper clippings, n.d., in Turner Family Papers in possession of Nancy Jones, Burlington, N.C.

10. Tenth Census of the United States, 1880, Population Schedule: Iredell County, North Carolina State Archives, Raleigh; Julia Wyche Cherry, notes on her grandmother, Julia Louisa Turner, n.d., in possession of Pamela Cherry Lee, Sierra Vista, Ariz.

11. Unidentified newspaper clippings, n.d., in Turner Family Papers, Burlington.

12. Louis H. Manarin et al., comps. *North Carolina Troops, 1861-1865: A Roster*, 15 vols. to date (Raleigh: Office of Archives and History, Department of Cultural Resources, 1966-), 2: 676; Compiled Service Records of Confederate Soldiers, Seventh Confederate Cavalry (microfilm), North Carolina State Archives, Raleigh; Columbus L. Turner, Memorial Day address, May 9, 1896, in Black, *Newspaper Transcripts*, 3:108. While Gus Turner was a prisoner of war, his company was transferred to the Sixteenth Battalion, North Carolina Cavalry.

13. Iredell County Record of Deeds, D10:292, D14:453-454.

14. Manarin, *North Carolina Troops*, 10:193, 257; paper read by Jimmy Turner at the Turner Historical Association meeting, August 10, 1986, and unidentified newspaper clippings, n.d., in Turner Family Papers, Burlington.

15. Iredell County Record of Deeds, D6:58-60, D8:706, D11:81-82, D14:452-453, D23:57-58.

16. William S. Powell, ed., *Dictionary of North Carolina Biography*, 6 vols. (Chapel Hill: University of North Carolina Press, 1979-1996), 6:68; Statesville *Landmark*, August 29, 1899, in Black, *Newspaper Transcripts*, 3:200.

17. Walter R. Turner, "Columbus Lafayette Turner and Turner Family Involvement with Olin High School," unpublished research article, enclosed in letter to editor, July 5, 2007; Homer M. Keever, article in unidentified newspaper, n.d., in Turner Family Papers, Burlington; letter from C. L. Turner to Henry A. Chambers in Statesville *Landmark*, April 13, 1915.

18. Walter R. Turner, "Columbus Lafayette Turner and Turner Family Involvement with Olin High School"; Olin High School Papers, 1859-1865, Rare Book, Manuscript, and Special Collections Library, Duke University, Durham. An undated circular (A. Haywood Merritt was then principal) in the Olin High School Papers at Duke University noted that the cost of boarding was $7.50 to $8.00 per month. Alfred Turner was a half-brother of Wilfred, a son of Samuel by Clarissa Nichols Turner.

19. Nora Campbell Chaffin, *Trinity College, 1839-1892: The Beginnings of Duke University* (Durham: Duke University Press, 1950), 42-251.

20. Columbus Lafayette Turner Notebook, 1859-1861, 1865, in possession of James R. Turner, Greensboro, N.C.; Trinity College, *Catalogue of Trinity College, 1860-'61* (Greensboro, N.C.: Greensborough Times Office, 1861), 13, 21.

21. Walter R. Turner, "Columbus Lafayette Turner's Years at Trinity College," unpublished research paper, enclosed in letter to editor, September 1, 2007; Thomas F. Harkins, associate university archivist, Duke University Archives, e-mail to Walter R. Turner, historian, North Carolina Transportation Museum, August 22, 2007; Chaffin, *Trinity College*, 221; Columbus Lafayette Turner Notebook.

22. Manarin, *North Carolina Troops*, 9:112, 123; Columbus L. Turner, Memorial Day address, May 9, 1896, in Black, *Newspaper Transcripts*, 3:108; C. L. Turner to Wilfred Turner, January 1, 1862, original in possession of James R. Turner, Greensboro, N.C.; John G. Barrett, *The Civil War in North Carolina* (Chapel Hill: University of North Carolina Press, 1963), 102-105.

23. Manarin, *North Carolina Troops*, 9:112, 123-135; *Our Living and Our Dead*, April 22, 1874; Columbus Lafayette Turner Diary, 1874, in Turner Family Papers, North Carolina State Archives, Raleigh, March 14, 1874; *Catawba County News*, April 27, 1904; Columbus Lafayette Turner, Memorial Day address, May 9, 1896, in Black, *Newspaper Transcripts*, 3:109. Turner gave the casualties in Company A as nine killed and ten wounded, but an

analysis of the individual service records in *North Carolina Troops* yielded the figures above. The same source indicated that thirteen soldiers in the company were definitely captured at New Bern, with the suggestion that another four or five may have been.

24. *Our Living and Our Dead*, April 22, 1874; Manarin, *North Carolina Troops*, 7:571.

CIVIL WAR PRISON JOURNAL

1. Formed in present-day Durham County by the juncture of the Eno and Flat rivers, the Neuse flows southeastwardly through central and eastern North Carolina, past Raleigh, Smithfield, Goldsboro, Kinston, and New Bern to empty into the lower Pamlico Sound.

2. *Harper's Weekly*, 1857-1916, and *Frank Leslie's Illustrated Newspaper*, 1855-1922, were two of the most popular illustrated publications of the day.

3. Maj. Gen. Benjamin Franklin Butler was nicknamed "Spoons" for allegedly stealing silverware from Southerners. Before the war, he was an astute criminal lawyer and politician. On the strength of his political connections, he was commissioned a brigadier general of Massachusetts militia on April 17, 1861, and major general of U.S. Volunteers on May 16. As commander of the District of Annapolis, his troops occupied Baltimore on May 13. He led the expedition that captured Forts Hatteras and Clark on the North Carolina Outer Banks in August 1861. Butler commanded the infantry that occupied New Orleans on May 1, 1862, after David G. Farragut had reduced the city's defenses. Here he earned his reputation as "the Beast" for such misdeeds as hanging William Mumford for pulling down the Stars and Stripes from the U.S. Mint and issuing the infamous "Woman Order" of May 15, 1862. Jefferson Davis declared him a felon, to be immediately executed if captured. In late 1863, Butler was assigned command of the Department of Virginia and North Carolina, subsequently the Department of the James. His army was virtually "bottled up" at Bermuda Hundred. After he failed to capture Fort Fisher near Wilmington in December 1864, Butler was finally relieved of command. He was elected to Congress in 1866 and governor of Massachusetts in 1883. He died in 1893. Mark Mayo Boatner III, *The Civil War Dictionary* (New York: David McKay Company, 1959), 109-110; Charles W. Sanders Jr., *While in the Hands of the Enemy: Military Prisons of the Civil War* (Baton Rouge: Louisiana State University Press, 2005), 145-146.

4. Only one page has survived of what may be the second draft; titled "Extracts from my Prison Journal," the revision covered the first paragraph and the first sentence of the second paragraph, as follows:

"It was with pleasure that we saw the anchor of the old transport Albany weighed to begin a trip somewhere. On this vessel in the middle of the Neuse River, the prisoners from the battle of Newbern had remained one long tedious monotonous month. It was a gloomy abode, and every object had been so often seen that it would have been a great relief to fall asleep, and continue to slumber until prison life should end.

After anchoring at Hatteras Inlet for the night, where a wild waste of water and sand bars with high rolling billows were presented to the view, we passed out to sea. The vessel seemed to be in a regular swing—prow low, stern high—stern low, prow high. It creaked and rolled. Many of the prisoners became very sick and crawled about on deck and to the sides of the vessel like lizzards. The salty dampness of the ocean the press on board, our dingy quarters and in fact every thing connected with the voyage were highly disagreeable, until we came in view of the Narrows, where a bright panarama of high cliffs, fine structures, beautiful gardens and yards, caused a feeling of cheerfulness to"

5. Hatteras Inlet flows between Hatteras Island to the north and Ocracoke Island to the south, a passage from the lower Pamlico Sound to the Atlantic Ocean. The inlet was formed by a storm in 1846.

6. The Narrows is the tidal strait that separates Staten Island from Long Island and connects the upper and lower sections of New York Bay. It is the principal maritime entrance to New York Harbor.

7. Fort Lafayette was erected in 1822 on a small rock island near the eastern (Brooklyn) shore of the Narrows between the lower end of Staten Island and Long Island, opposite Fort Hamilton. Originally named Fort Diamond, it was octagonal shaped, with eight-foot-thick walls that rose twenty-five to thirty feet high. The fort was first used as a military prison in July 1861, under the command of Lt. Charles O. Wood. Fort Lafayette was razed in 1960 to make way for the Verrazano Narrows Bridge. Sanders, *Hands of the Enemy*, 56.

8. Castle Williams, named after its builder, Lt. Col. Jonathan Williams, was constructed between 1806 and 1811, as part of the Second System of American coastal fortifications. The circular stone fort sits on the southern tip of Governors Island in Upper New York Bay at the mouth of East River, off the southern end of Manhattan Island. Its walls are forty feet high and eight feet thick. Beginning in the late summer of 1861, enlisted Confederate prisoners of war were held there. Following the arrival of Confederate prisoners from Hatteras Island, the fort was filled beyond capacity, and conditions rapidly deteriorated. Sanders, *Hands of the Enemy*, 56-58; http://www.nps.gov/history/history/online_books/founders/sitea22.htm.

9. Fort Columbus was the earliest permanent fortification on Governors Island, situated at the northern end of the island. It was built in 1794-1798 and named Fort Jay after Chief Justice John Jay. The fort was razed and rebuilt between 1806 and 1808, and renamed Fort Columbus after Jay fell out of public favor. The brick fortification is pentagonal shaped, and its four bastions could support one hundred cannons. Confederate officers were confined there. The original name was restored in 1904. http://www.nps.gov/history/history/online_books/founders/sitea22.htm.

10. At the Battle of Roanoke Island on February 8, 1862, approximately 2,700 Confederates from North Carolina and Virginia under the command of Brig. Gen. Henry A. Wise surrendered to a Federal force of approximately 13,000 infantry led by Brig. Gen. Ambrose E. Burnside and supported by nineteen warships and numerous gunboats. At the Battle of New Bern, March 13-14, 1862, 413 Confederate officers and soldiers were reported as captured or missing, including 144 from the Thirty-third North Carolina. Fort Pulaski was on Cockspur Island near the mouth of the Savannah River, fifteen miles east of Savannah, Georgia. Begun in 1830 and completed in 1846, the fort's eight-foot-thick masonry walls were no defense against rifled artillery. The 384-man Confederate garrison commanded by Col. Charles H. Olmstead surrendered after a thirty-hour bombardment, April 10-11, 1862. Barrett, *Civil War in North Carolina*, 74-84; *The War of the Rebellion: A Compilation of the Official Records of the Union and Confederate Armies*, 150 vols. (Washington: Government Printing Office, 1880-1901), ser. 1, 9:247; Manarin, *North Carolina Troops*, 9:112.

11. Originally conceived as the *Leviathan*, the enormous steam-powered vessel of 22,374 tons remained the largest ship in the world until the construction of the *Lusitania*. It was designed by Isambard Kingdom Brunel to compete with clipper ships on the Far Eastern and Australian routes. Construction of the ship in England between 1854 and 1858 nearly bankrupted the Eastern Steam Navigation Company. The *Great Eastern* briefly engaged in transatlantic runs in the 1860s but could not profitably compete with the faster clipper ships. By 1865, the company was bankrupt and the ship laid up. It was leased in 1866 to lay the first

transatlantic cable, a service it again rendered from 1869 to 1872. In 1885, the vessel was leased as a floating amusement park; three years later, it was sold for scrap. www.cwhistory.com/history/TeacherPack/Tppart3.html.

12. Turner decided to adopt the nom de plume, "Leroy," the middle name of eighteen-year-old Helen Palmer of Randolph County, whom he met while passing through the eastern part of the county in January 1874. Turner vowed to use the name "as my sobriquet in any public correspondence," which he did on at least three occasions. Turner Diary, January 1, January 24, April 13, May 1, 1874; *Our Living and Our Dead*, April 22, May 20, 1874.

13. Pea Patch Island is located in mid-channel of the Delaware River near the entrance into Delaware Bay. According to local folklore, a boat carrying a load of peas grounded on the swampy shore of the island, and a crop of peas soon sprouted up. The State of Delaware ceded the island to the federal government in 1813 for the purpose of building a fort to guard the river approach to Wilmington and Philadelphia. The island is one mile long, comprising approximately seventy-five swampy acres. Construction of the first fort on Pea Patch Island began in 1819, but the structure was destroyed by fire in 1831. Construction on the Civil War-era fort—"a brooding granite structure"—began in 1848, directed by engineer Maj. John Sanders and chief designer Col. Joseph Totten. The engineers first had to drive in more than six thousand giant piles to provide a stable footing on the swampy island. The second fort was completed in 1859. It was assigned a military garrison under the command of Capt. Augustus A. Gibson in the spring of 1861, and the installation of seacoast artillery commenced. The island was an ideal location for a military prison: "remote enough to hinder escape, strong enough to withstand any attack by the weak Southern navy, and near enough to the Southern states to facilitate the business of prisoner exchange." The first Confederate prisoners of war arrived in July 1861. The following April, construction began on shanties outside the walls of the fort to accommodate an additional two thousand prisoners. According to a recent study of the Civil War prison systems, "The clapboard shanties . . . were not fit for habitation, the rations supplied the captives were unappetizing and unwholesome even by prison standards, and the medical care provided the sick was spotty at best." After Gettysburg and Vicksburg in July 1863, more than 12,500 new arrivals flooded the island. Sanders, *Hands of the Enemy*, 101-102.

14. The engagement at Hanover Courthouse, Virginia, on May 27, 1862, also known as Kinney's Farm or Slash Church, was a sidelight of the Peninsula Campaign. Elements of Brig. Gen. Fitz-John Porter's Federal Fifth Corps attacked Brig. Gen. L. O'B. Branch's brigade, protecting the Virginia Central Railroad. Porter drove the Confederates back towards Ashland and took (he claimed) 730 prisoners. Branch reported 243 casualties and Porter 355. Branch's brigade, which included Turner's Thirty-third North Carolina, had been organized at Kinston on March 17, after the Battle of New Bern. Boatner, *Civil War Dictionary*, 373.

15. Capt. Augustus A. Gibson, an 1839 graduate of the U.S. Military Academy and a veteran of the War with Mexico, was in command of Fort Delaware from February 7, 1861, to July 31, 1862. He held a regular army commission as captain in the Second Artillery, but was appointed colonel of the 112th Pennsylvania Volunteers (Second Heavy Artillery) on June 25, 1862. He commanded a brigade of artillery in the defenses around Washington for much of the war. He was promoted to major on July 25, 1863, and to lieutenant colonel after the war. www.library.ci.corpus-christi.tx.us/MexicanWar/gibsonaa.htm.

16. Brandywine Creek is a tributary of the Christina River, which it joins about two miles upstream of the river's confluence with the Delaware River. The creek rises in Chester

County, Pennsylvania, and flows about twenty miles through southeastern Pennsylvania and northern Delaware.

17. The Battle of Seven Pines (or Fair Oaks) on May 31 and June 1, 1862, was the climax of a bungled Confederate attempt to destroy two of Gen. George B. McClellan's advancing corps that were isolated south of the abnormally high Chickahominy River. Maj. Gen. James Longstreet apparently misunderstood the verbal marching orders of Gen. Joseph E. Johnston and deployed his columns on the wrong road, delaying the advance of other elements of the assault. As a result, rather than the envisioned three-pronged envelopment of the Federal corps, Maj. Gen. Daniel Harvey Hill's division alone attacked the enemy position at Seven Pines, belatedly assisted by brigades from the divisions of Longstreet and Brig. Gen. W. H. C. Whiting. Johnston was wounded during the battle and succeeded by Gen. Robert E. Lee. Confederate losses were estimated at 6,134. Boatner, *Civil War Dictionary*, 272-273.

18. The negotiations to which Turner refers were between Maj. Gen. John A. Dix and Maj. Gen. Daniel Harvey Hill to work out an arrangement for the exchange of prisoners of war. They met at Haxall's Landing on the James River on July 18 and in one day came to an agreement. Sanders, *Hands of the Enemy*, 116.

19. Native to India and China, ginger was introduced to Jamaica about 1525, and soon Jamaican roots were widely regarded as the best variety. Medicinal uses of ginger include diaphoretic (induces sweating), carminative (breaks up intestinal gas), and as a remedy for congestion. http://botanical.com/botanical/mgmh/g/ginger13.html.

20. Secretaries of War Edwin M. Stanton and George W. Randolph approved the Dix-Hill compact as drafted, and it was signed and ratified on July 22, 1862. Sanders, *Hands of the Enemy*, 116-117.

21. Willoughby's Point on the southerly shore at the mouth of Hampton Roads was named for a local landowner, Thomas Willoughby. The point was formed during a storm in the 1660s. Sewell's Point on the southeastern shore of Hampton Roads was apparently named after Henry Seawell, who cleared 150 acres for planting there about 1634. It was the site of the Jamestown Exposition of 1907. The Rip-Raps, a shoal at the mouth of Hampton Roads between Hampton and Norfolk, was so named for the sound of the rippling water as it passes over. http://www.norfolkhistorical.org/highlights/03.html.

22. Hampton Roads.

23. On August 2, Federal forces from Harrison's Landing on James River reoccupied Malvern Hill, site of the bloody final engagement of the Seven Days Battle on July 1. There was a "light engagement" there on August 5 and more skirmishing on August 6. On the seventh, Federal infantry withdrew from the hill. E. B. Long and Barbara Long, *The Civil War Day by Day: An Almanac, 1861-1865* (Garden City, N.Y.: Doubleday, 1971), 246, 248, 249.

24. Aiken's (or Aikin's) Landing on the north bank of James River, southeast of Richmond and close to the site of the first courthouse of Henrico County (Verina), was specified in the Dix-Hill cartel of July 1862 as the point of delivery for exchanged prisoners of war in the eastern theater. But because of superior accessibility by railroad, City Point on the south bank was soon substituted. After City Point was occupied by the Federals in the summer of 1864, the exchange point was moved to Boulware's and Cox's Wharves, near Fort Harrison on the north bank of the river above Aiken's Landing. Turner was part of the first prisoner exchange under the new cartel. On the morning of August 3, two ships, one Union and one Confederate, docked at Aiken's Landing. The Confederate prisoners were from Forts Warren and Delaware, the Federals from camps throughout the South. "Shortly after

docking, officers from each of the ships disembarked, traded rosters of the prisoners, and, in accordance with the table of equivalents stipulated in the cartel, began to work out the details whereby each of the men would be exchanged." Sanders, *Hands of the Enemy*, 118.

25. Compiled Confederate Service Records of Confederate Soldiers Who Served in Organizations from the State of North Carolina, Thirty-third Infantry; Manarin, *North Carolina Troops*, 9:113-115, 123; Columbus Lafayette Turner Prison Journal, Chapter 8 (August 1863), Turner Family Papers, North Carolina State Archives, Raleigh; Columbus Lafayette Turner, Memorial Day address, May 9, 1896, in Black, *Newspaper Transcripts*, 3:109. Ironically, if Major Saunders was the disagreeable association that Turner sought to avoid by resigning his commission, they were soon to be more closely confined in even more disagreeable circumstances. Saunders was wounded and captured at Gettysburg and imprisoned at Johnson's Island from late August 1863 to mid-March 1865.

26. Turner refers to casualties in Company A, Thirty-third North Carolina Regiment. Capt. Henry Hyer Baker of Halifax County was promoted to captain on May 3, 1863, and was killed on July 3. Before the Confederate charge, Baker was "smoking, pleasantly talking," saying he did not expect to be killed that day. Third Lt. Thomas A. Cowan of Iredell County, younger brother of Robert V. Cowan, enlisted at age eighteen on March 1, 1862. He was appointed third lieutenant on June 1, 1863, and was killed on the third day at Gettysburg. Turner later recalled the "thud of the ball that smote his breast." Though a few months younger than Turner, Cowan was "more ambitious for glory." He had been assigned that day to the guard detail in the rear of the army but chose to participate in the attack. First Sgt. Robert W. Shields was born in Mecklenburg County, resided in Gaston County, but enlisted in Iredell County. He was captured at Fredericksburg, December 13, 1862, and exchanged four days later. He, too, was killed in the charge on July 3. Pvt. William H. Bowers was a resident of Orange County who entered Confederate service from Person County. He was wounded and captured at Gettysburg and died in a hospital there on July 10. Manarin, *North Carolina Troops*, 9:123, 125, 132; Columbus Lafayette Turner, Memorial Day address, May 9, 1896, in Black, *Newspaper Transcripts*, 3:109.

27. Maj. Gen. Isaac Ridgeway Trimble was born in Pennsylvania in 1802. He was appointed to West Point from Kentucky. On August 9, 1861, he was commissioned a brigadier general in the Confederate army. Trimble was severely wounded at Second Manassas. During his recovery, he was promoted to major general on April 23, 1863, to rank from January 17. He returned to the field in time for the Gettysburg campaign but was without a command. He was appointed to lead a division of the Third Corps after Maj. Gen. William Dorsey Pender was wounded on July 2. The next day, Trimble was also wounded, resulting in the amputation of a leg, and captured. He was a prisoner of war until exchanged in February 1865. Boatner, *Civil War Dictionary*, 849.

28. Second Lt. John C. C. Cowper of Company E, from Gates County, was wounded in the left lung and captured at Gettysburg on July 3, 1863. He was hospitalized at Gettysburg and Baltimore, and then imprisoned at Fort McHenry, Fort Delaware, and Hilton Head. He died of pneumonia in the hospital at Morris Island, South Carolina, on October 14, 1864. Second Lt. Samuel C. Watson of Company F, from Hyde County, was appointed second lieutenant on September 9, 1861. He was wounded at Chancellorsville but returned to duty, only to be wounded again and captured at Gettysburg on July 3. He died in a hospital near Gettysburg on or about July 6, 1863. Second Lt. John Caldwell of Company E, from Burke County, enlisted as a private at age eighteen on May 3, 1863. That same day, he was appointed second lieutenant. He was killed at Gettysburg two months later. He was the only son of Tod Caldwell, governor of North Carolina when Turner served in the state House of Representatives in 1873-1874. Second Lt. William H. Gibson of Company C was from

Caldwell County but enlisted in Wake County on October 24, 1861. He was promoted to regimental sergeant major on November 1, 1861. Gibson was appointed third lieutenant and transferred back to his company on September 3, 1862, and promoted to second lieutenant on January 14, 1863. He was also killed at Gettysburg on July 3. During the Gettysburg campaign (including the Battle of Falling Waters), the Thirty-third North Carolina lost ten killed and fifty-three wounded. Manarin, *North Carolina Troops*, 9:116, 147, 172, 185.

29. Westminster, Maryland, the railhead of a branch of the North Central Railroad, was approximately twenty-five miles northwest of Baltimore. The Second Pennsylvania Cavalry Regiment (Fifty-ninth Pennsylvania Volunteers) served as provost guard for the Army of the Potomac from July to December 1863. http://www.civilwararchive.com/Unreghst/unpacav1.

30. Turner refers to Littlestown, Pennsylvania, and Westminster, Maryland.

31. The Fifty-first Massachusetts Regiment was organized as a nine-month regiment at Worcester during September-October 1862. The regiment had been on duty in North Carolina since late November 1862, marching with Maj. Gen. John G. Foster's expedition to Goldsboro in December and to Trenton and Pollocksville in January 1863. The regiment left New Bern on June 24 and arrived in Baltimore about July 1. It was mustered out of service on July 27. Fort McHenry is a star fort located at the tip of Whetstone Point, a small peninsula between two branches of Petapsco River. It was built between 1798 and 1800 to protect Baltimore Harbor. Named for Secretary of War James McHenry, the fort is best known for inspiring the writing of the "Star Spangled Banner" by Francis Scott Key during the British attack on Baltimore, September 13-14, 1814. During the Civil War, the fort was used as a transfer prison and generally held between 250 and 350 prisoners. After the Battle of Gettysburg, the prisoner population briefly swelled to nearly 7,000. The fort housed three classes of inmates: Confederate prisoners of war, civilian prisoners of state, and Union soldiers convicted of crimes. http://www.civilwararchive.com/Unreghst/unmainf4.htm:51st; Sanders, *Hands of the Enemy*, 58-59.

32. In this instance, the Federal soldiers spoke truthfully. On July 4, 1863, Gen. John C. Pemberton surrendered his besieged army of thirty thousand Confederates to Gen. Ulysses S. Grant.

33. At the end of June 1863, there were 3,737 Confederates imprisoned on Pea Patch Island. By the end of July, the number had risen to 8,982. Fort Delaware was then commanded by Brig. Gen. Albin F. Schoepf (1822-1886), a native of Hungary who immigrated to the United States in 1851. He secured appointments to the coast survey and the patent office. On September 30, 1861, Schoepf was appointed brigadier general of volunteers and commanded a division at the Battle of Perryville. He assumed command of Fort Delaware in April 1863. Schoepf was nicknamed "General Terror" by the Confederate prisoners. After the war, he was appointed principal examiner in the U.S. Patent Office. Wharton J. Green described him as "lately a waiter in the dining-room of Willard's hotel, and a more pretentious, over-wheening upstart I have never seen." Samuel Asbury referred to Schoepf as a former porter in a Washington hotel, and described him as "destitute of every feeling of humanity and imbued with so much selfishness and tyranny that he can hardly show mercy to his own soldiers." Sanders, *Hands of the Enemy*, 181; Boatner, *Civil War Dictionary*, 726; Wharton J. Green, *Recollections and Reflections: An Auto of Half a Century and More* (Raleigh, Edwards and Broughton Printing Company, 1906), 180; www.herbertasbury.com/asburycivilwar.asp.

34. The quotation is from Cicero's first oration against Cataline, 63 B.C. The literal translation is: "O the times! O the customs!" meaning, "these are bad times."

35. Turner refers to Confederate casualties at Fredericksburg (December 1862) and Chancellorsville (May 1863).

36. Chuck-a-luck is a game of chance involving three dice. A player bets on a number (one through six) and is paid according to the number of times his number appears on a roll of the dice. Keno is a lottery-type game in which a player places a wager upon one or more numbers on a card containing eighty numbers. If his winning number is announced, he must quickly take his card to a keno booth to collect before the next game begins. Faro is a betting game involving a deck of cards. Players place their bets upon which card they think will be turned up by the banker.

37. The transfer of officers imprisoned at Fort Delaware was part of a Federal initiative to consolidate all captured Confederate officers at Johnson's Island. See *War of the Rebellion*, ser. 2, 6:13, 93, 119, 157-158.

38. Delaware City is approximately one mile west of Pea Patch Island on the west bank of Delaware River, incorporated in 1851. The town was the eastern terminus of the Chesapeake and Delaware Canal. Havre de Grace, Maryland, not Newcastle, Delaware, was sacked and burned by the British during the War of 1812. In revising his diary, Turner realized his error and corrected the name of the town, but not the incidental information. Havre de Grace is located at the mouth of Susquehanna River, where it empties into Chesapeake Bay.

39. In 1852, Leonard B. Johnson purchased the island in Lake Erie, approximately one-half mile wide by one mile long. In the fall of 1861, he leased for $500 a year forty acres of cleared land near the southern end of the island facing Sandusky City (approximately 2.5 miles distant) to the Federal government for a prisoner-of-war camp. The site had been selected in October 1861 by the newly appointed commissary general of prisoners, Lt. Col. William Hoffman. The Sandusky firm of Gregg and West began construction in November, and "in only six weeks the facility was almost completed." The prison compound encompassed 16½ acres containing 13 blocks (one a hospital), each of which was two stories high, approximately 130-by-24 feet. The facility was designed to hold 2,500 prisoners. It was the first prisoner-of-war depot constructed by the U.S. since the War of 1812. The first prisoners arrived in April 1862; most were exchanged that September. According to prisoner Col. Thomas S. Kenan, the grounds were surrounded by a "strong plank fence twelve or fifteen feet high," patrolled by sentinels. Another prisoner from North Carolina, Col. Robert F. Webb, noted that the island was a limestone formation, and the three wells that supplied drinking water to the camp were very shallow. Sanders, *Hands of the Enemy*, 69-70, 72-73; Walter Clark, ed., *Histories of the Several Regiments and Battalions from North Carolina, in the Great War 1861-'65*, 5 vols. (Goldsboro, N.C.: Nash Brothers, 1901), 4:668, 689.

40. The first commandant of the Johnson's Island prison, Lt. Col. William S. Pierson, was an attorney and former mayor of Sandusky. "It was probably this political connection that led to his selection" by Col. William Hoffman, commissary general of prisoners. The 400-man "Hoffman Battalion," organized in December 1861, served as prison guards from the spring of 1862 to January 1864, when six more companies were added and a regiment organized as the 128th Ohio Volunteer Infantry, commanded by Col. Charles W. Hill. Sanders, *Hands of the Enemy*, 72; John G. Barrett, ed., *Yankee Rebel: The Civil War Journal of Edmund DeWitt Patterson* (Chapel Hill: University of North Carolina Press, 1966), 125.

41. The steamer, *Island Queen*, plied the lake trade out of Sandusky. Joseph Mason Kern noted in his diary that the vessel made two trips each day between the island and the mainland. The vessel was regularly used to transport Confederate prisoners to Johnson's Island. Ironically, the ship was seized, scuttled, and sunk near Pelee Island in Lake Erie on

September 19, 1864, in an abortive attempt (the "Lake Erie Conspiracy," led by John Yeats Beall) to free the prisoners of war. Joseph Mason Kern Diary, 1861-1865, Joseph Mason Kern Papers, #2526, Southern Historical Collection, Wilson Library, University of North Carolina at Chapel Hill, 55.

42. Turner refers to baseball, which was supposedly "invented" before the war by Abner Doubleday, but more likely gradually evolved from town ball and similar bat-and-ball games. The sport was popular during the Civil War in both armies, in camp and in prison.

43. The Peripatetics were followers of Aristotle. The name is from the Greek word for walking about, derived from the philosopher's habit of teaching while walking through the lyceum at Athens.

44. The surgeon in charge at Johnson's Island was Dr. T. Woodbridge, regimental surgeon of the 128th Ohio. The steward was E. S. Keith, a Federal soldier. *War of the Rebellion*, ser. 2, 6:366.

45. "The Doxology" was written by Thomas Ken in 1674 and set to the music of the "Old 100th" of the Genevan Psalter of 1551, attributed to Louis Bourgeois. It is actually the last verse of a longer hymn, "Awake, My Soul, and With the Sun":

Praise God, from Whom all blessings flow;
Praise Him, all creatures here below;
Praise Him above, ye heavenly host;
Praise Father, Son, and Holy Ghost.

http://www.cyberhymnal.org/htm/p/r/praisegf.htm.

46. The order that limited prisoners to one suit of clothing was improperly attributed to Maj. Gen. Ambrose Burnside, who at that time was commander of the Department of the Ohio, which included the prisoner-of-war camp on Johnson's Island. It actually originated with the commissary general of prisoners, Col. William Hoffman. On July 31, 1863, Hoffman, expressing the wishes of his superior, Secretary of War Edwin M. Stanton, informed Lieutenant Colonel Pierson, commander at Johnson's Island: "You will hereafter permit no purchases of clothing by rebel officers prisoners of war, except such as are absolutely necessary. One suit of outer garments and a change of underclothes is all they require, and if they have this they will not be permitted to purchase anything more." Pierson posted a copy of Hoffman's directive in the sutler's store. *War of the Rebellion*, ser. 2, 6:161, 184.

47. Only short letters were allowed because they had to be read by censors, and they were so numerous. According to Henry E. Shepherd, prisoners' letters were limited to twenty-eight lines. Robert F. Webb reported that a new order was issued at Johnson's Island on June 8, 1864, limiting letters *received* by prisoners to half a page. Henry E. Shepherd, *Narrative of Prison Life at Baltimore and Johnson's Island, Ohio* (Baltimore: Commercial Printing and Stationery Company, 1917), 17; Clark, *Histories of Regiments*, 4:682.

48. Now archaic, meaning "I believe, think, or suppose."

49. In a letter dated September 3, 1863, Turner's father Wilfred listed some of the Northern firms that he might call upon for assistance: "some names of Prominent Houses in N. York and Philadelphia of whom I had bought goods . . . George A. Fuller N.Y. upon whom I send you a draft, same I did once before but which you did not receive. Boosman Seller & Co. N.Y. Scull & Thompson N.Y. David & Springs Phil., Faust & Winebrimer Phil. Wescott & Hallowels Phil. and many others I might name with whom I have formerly been acquainted and bought goods from them for myself and for the firm of Turner & Tomlin many of them I think are Southern by birth, and I trust & hope would be disposed to render you assistance i.e. furnish you money &c on the assurance I or you would return it whenever the war ended

or an opportunity was offered." W[ilfred] Turner to C. L. Turner, September 3, 1863, in possession of Wilfred Turner, New Bern, N.C.

50. Gutta-percha is a tough, plastic-like substance derived from the latex of certain evergreens of East Asia, particularly of the sapodilla family of Malaysia. It resembles rubber but contains more resin. A milky fluid collected by felling or girdling the tree evaporates, and the latex that coagulates is washed and purified. After its introduction to the western hemisphere in the mid-nineteenth century, one of the first applications of gutta-percha was in the manufacture of golf balls. Prisoners at Johnson's Island filled their days by fashioning jewelry and trinkets out of gutta percha rulers and buttons.

51. Brig. Gen. James Jay Archer (1817-1864), a native of Maryland, attended the College of New Jersey (Princeton) and the University of Maryland and was a lawyer by profession. A veteran of the Mexican War, he re-entered the regular army as a captain in the Ninth U.S. Infantry in 1855, but resigned on March 14, 1861. He was commissioned colonel of the Fifth Texas and appointed brigadier general in the Confederate army on June 3, 1862. He commanded a brigade during the Peninsula Campaign, at Cedar Mountain, Second Manassas, Antietam, Fredericksburg, Chancellorsville, and Gettysburg, where he was captured. Archer was held in Northern prisons, including Johnson's Island, for more than a year. On June 21, 1864, he was among the Confederate officers (the "Immortal Six Hundred") ordered to be sent to Charleston Harbor and placed under Confederate artillery fire in retaliation for alleged mistreatment of Union prisoners. He was released ca. August 1864. Archer died in Richmond on October 24, 1864, and was buried in Hollywood Cemetery. Boatner, *Civil War Dictionary*, 23.

52. Lt. Col. William Groves Morris of Gaston County enlisted in Company H of the Thirty-seventh North Carolina at age thirty-six. He was appointed second lieutenant on October 6, 1861, elected captain on March 29, 1862, and promoted to major, July 30, 1862. He was wounded at both Fredericksburg and Chancellorsville and promoted to lieutenant colonel on May 29, 1863. He was captured at Gettysburg and confined at Fort Delaware, then transferred to Johnson's Island, July 18, 1863, the same day that Turner left Pea Patch Island. Morris was paroled ca. March 14, 1865, and exchanged at Cox's Wharf on James River, ca. March 22, 1865. Third Lt. Jeremiah Coggin, Company C, Twenty-third North Carolina, of Montgomery County enlisted on May 27, 1861, aged twenty-three. He was mustered in as a sergeant and elected third lieutenant on April 16, 1862. He was wounded at Seven Pines and Sharpsburg and captured at Gettysburg on July 1, 1863. He, too, was initially confined at Fort Delaware and transferred to Johnson's Island, where he arrived with Turner and Morris on July 20. Coggin was among the four hundred prisoners transferred to Point Lookout, ca. Feb. 9, 1864. From there he was sent to Fort Delaware, Hilton Head, Fort Pulaski, and finally back to Fort Delaware, where he died of chronic diarrhea on March 15, 1865. First Lt. Samuel L. Asbury of the Forty-fifth Mississippi Regiment was wounded and captured at the Battle of Murfreesboro on the last day of 1862. He was a prisoner at Fort Delaware when the Confederates captured at Gettysburg arrived there and was transferred with them to Johnson's Island. Asbury left a prison diary, a copy of which is now in the Western Historical Manuscript Collection, University of Missouri, Columbia, Mo. Manarin, *North Carolina Troops*, 7:165, 9:468-469, 566; www.herbertasbury.com/asburycivilwar.asp.

53. Goold Brown (1791-1857) of Rhode Island was a prominent American grammarian during the first half of the nineteenth century. He published *Institutes of English Grammar* in 1823 and *A Grammar of English Grammars* in 1851. His systematic approach to grammar found an appreciative audience, and his books sold quite well. Turner probably had a copy of the 1851 text. http://www.famousamericans.net/gooldbrown/.

54. Both quotations are from the Book of Ecclesiastes. "Vanity of vanities, saith the Preacher, vanity of vanities; all is vanity" is in both Ecclesiastes 1:2 and 12:8. "All is vanity and vexation of spirits" also appears twice in the Old Testament book: "I have seen all the works that are done under the sun; and, behold, all is vanity and vexation of spirit" (Ecclesiastes, 1:14). Perhaps more in keeping with Turner's situation is the line from Ecclesiastes 2:17: "Therefore I hated life; because the work that is wrought under the sun is grievous unto me: for all is vanity and vexation of spirit."

55. Turner's reading list included Sir Walter Scott's Waverly novels: *Waverly*; *Castle Dangerous*; *The Surgeons' Daughter*; and *The Antiquary*. *Jacob Faithful* is a novel by Capt. Frederick Marryat, published in 1834. The book relates the adventures of a small boy born and raised on a lighter in the Thames River in the early nineteenth century. Marryat (1792-1848), who retired from the British navy, was a prolific and popular writer of the day. www.athelstane.co.uk. *The Actress: or Under the Spell* is unidentified.

56. Translated "While I breathe, I hope." It was adopted as the state motto of South Carolina in 1776.

57. The quotation is from W. R. Spenser, quoted by Sir Walter Scott at the beginning of Chapter 10 of *The Antiquary*. Turner garbled the third line, which should read: "No bloodless shape my way pursues." http://etext.library.adelaide.edu.au/s/scott/walter/antiquary/chapter10.html.

58. According to his compiled service record, Turner was sick in General Hospital No. 4 from June 11 to 18, 1863, under the care of Dr. James P. Reed, surgeon-in-charge of the hospital for commissioned officers on Tenth Street, between Marshall and Clay, in downtown Richmond. Compiled Confederate Service Records, Thirty-third North Carolina.

59. The three deceased siblings were Laura Catherine (1848-1863); Tobitha Olivia (1837-1862), who died of typhoid fever six weeks after her marriage to Dr. John R. Anderson; and William Graham (1843-1845). The nine still living in August 1863 were Mary Elizabeth "Betty," born 1835, who married William T. Gaither in 1853; Julia Louisa, born 1838; Sarah "Sallie" Elizabeth, born 1840, who married Newton Holman in 1859; Columbus Lafayette, born 1842; John Augustus, born 1845, who enlisted in the Seventh Confederate Cavalry in June 1863; Adaline "Addie" Dorcas, born 1847; Virginia "Jennie" Ann, born 1851; Emily Ella, born 1853; and Wilfred Dent, born 1855.

60. President Jefferson Davis declared August 21, 1863, a day of fasting and prayer in the Confederate States of America, one of several days so designated over the course of the war. At the request of Gen. James J. Archer, the sutler at Johnson's Island prison closed his shop in observance of the day. Ironically, that was also the day of the brutal sacking of Lawrence, Kansas, by Confederate guerrillas. Kern Diary, 57.

61. The Reverend Mr. Sherrill is unidentified.

62. The Island Prison Debating Society certainly selected timely topics for discussion. Clement Laird Vallandigham (1820-1871) was the leader of the Peace Democrats (Copperheads) of Ohio. Before the war, he was a lawyer, editor of the Dayton *Empire* (1847-1849), state legislator (1845-1846), and U.S. representative (1858-1863). In 1863, he was arrested for delivering an inflammatory anti-war speech, purposefully challenging Gen. Ambrose Burnside's General Order No. 38, issued to intimidate Confederate sympathizers in the Department of the Ohio. Vallandigham was tried and convicted in a military court and sentenced to two years in prison. On May 19, 1863, President Lincoln commuted the sentence to banishment behind Confederate lines. Vallandigham was passed

through the lines south of Murfreesboro, Tennessee, but the Confederates soon sent him off to Canada. He returned unmolested to Ohio in the summer of 1864. In June 1871, he accidentally mortally wounded himself while demonstrating to a group of lawyers how the victim in a murder case (he represented the defendant) might have shot himself. www.civilwarhome.com/ vallandighambio.htm.

During the American Civil War, a joint expeditionary force of French, British, and Russian troops was sent to Mexico to enforce the collection of European debts. In 1863, "France assumed leadership of the coalition and gave evidence of more than monetary interest." By June, French troops had captured Mexico City. But Napoleon III had no real interest in establishing an empire in Mexico. He simply wanted to use Mexico as a pawn in European power politics, hoping to trade his Central American possession to Austria for territorial concessions in Italy. Emory M. Thomas, *The Confederate Nation, 1861-1865* (New York: Harper and Row, 1979), 186-188.

Congress passed a law on March 2, 1807, forbidding the further importation of African slaves, effective January 1, 1808. The Confederate Constitution (Art. I, s. 9) likewise prohibited the slave trade, to the great disappointment of Robert Barnwell Rhett and other members of the South Carolina delegation to the constitutional convention. Thomas, *Confederate Nation*, 63.

63. On September 5, 1863, while engaged in sketching prison scenes, Joseph Mason Kern was approached by a member of the company of the "Island Minstrels" and asked to prepare a playbill for the troupe's second weekly concert. Kern noted that the troupe also served as the orchestra at the first performance of the "Rebel Thespians" three weeks later. The musicians included Charles L. Stout, who also served as manager, on tamborine; pianist D. L. Dunham; T. F. Mitchel on guitar; J. C. Ward, flutist; William H. Harriss on violin; "Ole Bull" Livingstone; "Paul Julien" Hanrahan; "Joe Sweeney" Cronin; and "Triangular" Decker. Kern Diary, 21, 59.

64. While Vallandigham was exiled in the South, the Peace Democrats of Ohio nominated him for governor. His opponent, John Brough (1811-1865), was, like Vallandigham, both an attorney and a newspaperman. He was the publisher, owner, and editor of the Cincinnati *Enquirer* (1844). He had also served in the state legislature (1838-1839) and as state auditor (1839-1845). Although Brough was a Democrat, he was solidly behind the war effort and was nominated for governor by the Ohio Republicans. He soundly defeated Vallandigham in the fall 1863 election, 288,000 votes to 187,000, but died before the expiration of his term. www.ohiohistory.org/onlinedoc/ohgovernment/governors/brough.html.

65. The Rebel Thespians debuted on September 25, 1863, with a performance of the farce, *Slasher and Crasher*, which Joseph Mason Kern characterized as "somewhat of a failure," though he conceded that the "female characters were very good." The players included Lt. T. D. Houston of Virginia, Lt. A. J. Peeler of Florida, Capt. John Cussons of Alabama, Capt. John McLochlan of Kentucky, Capt. John R. Fellows of Arkansas, Capt. J. W. Youngblood of Tennessee, Capt. E. F. Lamar, a Captain Washington of North Carolina, Col. Jack Brown of Georgia, a Major Cook of Mississippi, and Maj. George McKnight of Louisiana, whose poetry and prose written under the pseudonym, Asa Hartz, was widely read North and South. By April 1864, the theatrical club was presenting two shows weekly. Among the group's repertoire were *Box and Cox*, *The Secret* (a farce), and *The Toodles* (a comedy). Robert F. Webb considered it "a very good troupe, and if one is not too far gone with the blues he can enjoy a hearty laugh." Kern Diary, 18, 59; Clark, *Histories of Regiments*, 4:677.

66. Wharton J. Green related this (or a similar) incident and identified the officer who got stuck as a Captain Cole of Arkansas. According to Green, Cole remained trapped in the

tunnel all night and did not call out till morning, in hopes of allowing the other two to escape. He was taken to Gen. Alexander Shaler, who treated Cole like a hero. Green also wrote of this incident in *Our Living and Our Dead.* He described the hole in the basement floor as six or eight feet deep, and the tunnel as fifty feet long, extending beyond the fence where the sentries stood. In this account, three prisoners got through the tunnel before Cole got stuck. If this was the same escape attempt described by Turner, Green was mistaken about General Shaler, who did not arrive at Johnson's Island until January 1864. But it would seem out of character for Lieutenant Colonel Pierson to treat a prisoner who tried to escape as a hero, regardless of the circumstances. Green, *Recollections and Reflections,* 183-185; *Our Living and Our Dead,* vol. 2, no. 3 (May 1875), 297-298. One wonders if this was the same Captain Cole (Charles H.), an officer from Nathan Bedford Forrest's command, who escaped from Johnson's Island in July 1864 and returned to the island in September to orchestrate the failed plot to free the Confederate prisoners.

67. Robert F. Webb noted that soon after his arrival at Johnson's Island in late November or early December 1863, the "sutler business was broken up." For two months, prisoners could not buy anything, but on the recommendation of Lieutenant Colonel Pierson, the embargo was lifted to permit the sale of tobacco, stationery, and postage stamps. By April 1864, the sutler was back in business, though his prices were exorbitant. At the urging of Pierson, who "appears greatly interested in Johnson's affairs," General Henry D. Terry appointed Leonard B. Johnson, owner of the island, as sutler, in partnership with one Finnegan, when the operation resumed. By mid-May, the Confederate dollar was worth only seven cents American in the camp store. Clark, *Histories of Regiments,* 4:669, 676, 678; *War of the Rebellion,* ser. 2, 6:654, 1014-1015, 7:122, 681-682.

The closure of the sutler's operation and the discontinuance of the express service were manifestations of a hardening of attitudes towards the treatment of prisoners of war in late 1863. After the exchange cartel completely broke down earlier that year, following a series of "disputes and successive rounds of retaliation [that] progressively reduced the number of men being exchanged," conditions in prisoner-of-war camps North and South rapidly deteriorated as a result of overcrowding. Prominent among the causes of these disputes were the Southern attitude towards captured African American prisoners of war, whom Confederates considered unsuitable for exchange, and excesses by certain Union officers, most notably Benjamin Butler, towards captured Southerners. As reports of conditions in the prisons became widely disseminated in mid-1863, "the men who directed the prisoner-of-war systems became increasingly hardened to the pitiful plight of the men in the camps. Military and civilian leaders, with full knowledge of the consequence of their actions, began to implement policies that dramatically increased the incidence of sickness and death among the captives under their control. They also came to embrace the notion that massive retaliation against helpless prisoners was a just and warranted response to charges that their own men were being systematically mistreated in enemy camps." On November 9, 1863, Secretary of War Edwin M. Stanton codified the new Federal policy in a directive to Maj. Gen. Ethan Allen Hitchcock: "You will please report what measures you have taken to ascertain the treatment of United States prisoners by the rebels at Richmond, and you are directed to take measures for precisely similar treatment toward all prisoners held by the United States, in respect to food, clothing, medical treatment, and other necessities." When the War Department learned of food shortages in Confederate prison-of-war camps, Federal officials retaliated by cutting prisoners' rations in half and eliminating such staples as coffee, tea, and sugar. Prisoners could no longer receive food from home nor buy it from the sutler, though they could still purchase tobacco, paper, and ink. Colonel Hoffman recommended that the prisoners at Johnson's Island, at that time comprised solely of Confederate officers, might be made an effective example. He wrote to Stanton on April 29, 1864: "I respectfully suggest as a means of compelling the rebels to adopt a less barbarous policy toward the prisoners in their hands that the rebel officers at Johnson's Island be allowed only half-rations; that their clothing be reduced to what is only sufficient to cover their nakedness, and that they be denied the privilege of purchasing the articles allowed to other prisoners." Six weeks later, Robert F. Webb noted in his diary: "They have stopped our rations of sugar, coffee and candles. We get nothing but bread and meat with a few beans." On August 28, he added: "In our prison many petty things are done to make us feel the sting and degradation of prison life. Late orders from the Secretary of War forbid the selling of any kind of clothing to us; also provisions, vegetables, etc., and no one is allowed to send us anything." He understood that exchanges had been halted by the U.S. government, despite the suffering that that meant for its own soldiers in Southern prisons, and commented: "This is a burlesque on civilization and a lasting disgrace to the Federal Government." Sanders, *Hands of the Enemy*, 164, 179-180, 195-196, 310-313; *War of the Rebellion*, ser. 2, 7:81; Clark, *Histories of Regiments*, 4:679, 681, 685.

68. The term, "Hard-Shell Baptists," was used during the nineteenth century to designate primitive, fundamentalist, uneducated Baptists. The Primitive Baptists, also called Old-School or Anti-Mission Baptists, constituted a sect opposed to missions, Sunday Schools, and, in general, human religious institutions. They arose about 1835 and numbered approximately 126,000 communicants. www.answers.com/topic/baptist; www.newadvent.org/cathen/02278a.htm.

69. The entire passage from Zechariah reads: "But it shall be one day which shall be known to the LORD, not day, nor night: but it shall come to pass, *that* at evening time it shall be light." Lt. Col. Levin M. Lewis of the Sixteenth Missouri Infantry Regiment was, by all accounts, one of the most widely liked and respected leaders among the Confederate prisoners at Johnson's Island. Before the war, he was a Methodist preacher and an early secessionist. In the prison camp, he taught Bible classes and was president of the "Masonic Association." He generally delivered his sermons outdoors because none of the blocks was large enough to accommodate his audience. Lt. Edmund D. Patterson of the Ninth Alabama described Lewis as "a very eloquent speaker, and everybody likes him." When Lewis was the beneficiary of a special exchange and left the island on September 16, 1864, Patterson wrote in his diary: "He will be missed more than any one else who has ever left this prison. He has wielded a powerful influence for good during his stay and those who have enjoyed the benefit of his society will never forget him. Always foremost in every good work he had endeared himself to all who knew him." Robert F. Webb noted: "It is a great privilege to have such a good man among us. . . . We part with him with regret, but our well wishes go with him." After Lewis was exchanged, he was selected to fill the vacancy as senator from northern Missouri in the Confederate Congress, but declined to serve. Barrett, *Yankee Rebel*, 134, 194; Clark, *Histories of Regiments*, 4:679, 686.

70. Littleberry Woodson Allen (1803-1871) was a volunteer aide-de-camp on the staff of Maj. Gen. John B. Magruder. He was born in Henrico County, Virginia, and before the war served as a Baptist preacher in Caroline County, Virginia, and at Louisville, Kentucky. Lieutenant Patterson mentioned Rev. L. W. Allen preaching to a large congregation in the prison on December 27, 1863. Joseph Mason Kern referred to a Captain Allen, "a baptist minister of Caroline Co. Va.," involved in the debating society at Johnson's Island. Robert E. L. Krick, *Staff Officers in Gray: A Biographical Register of the Staff Officers in the Army of Northern Virginia* (Chapel Hill: University of North Carolina Press, 2003), 60-61; Barrett, *Yankee Rebel*, 151; Kern Diary, September 4, 1863, 58.

71. Isaiah 55 begins, "Ho, every one that thirsteth, come ye to the waters, and he that hath no money; come ye, buy, and eat; yea, come, buy wine and milk without money and without price." Col. Benjamin Everidge Caudill (1830-1889), commander of the Thirteenth Kentucky Cavalry, was a Baptist preacher before the war. He was captured at Gladeville (now Wise), West Virginia, on July 7, 1863, and imprisoned successively at Kemper Barracks, Camp Chase, Johnson's Island, Baltimore, Fort Delaware, Fort McHenry, and Hilton Head, where he was one of the "Immortal Six Hundred." He was exchanged on August 3, 1864, and returned to his command. After the war, Caudill settled in Alleghany County, N.C., and resumed preaching. He moved back to Kentucky in 1879. "His ministry was not without controversy as he spent much of the decade of the 1880s attempting to convert 'missionary' Baptist churches throughout Kentucky to the doctrines of the Old Regular Baptist denomination." http://groups.msn.com/CaudillGenealogyGroup/general.

72. Probably Second Lt. John M. Harris, Company C, Twenty-sixth North Carolina, from Wilkes County. He enlisted at age twenty-two on June 12, 1861, and was mustered in as a sergeant. He was elected second lieutenant on April 21, 1862. Harris was captured at Bristoe Station on October 14, 1863, and confined at Old Capitol Prison, then transferred to Johnson's Island on November 11, 1863. He was released on June 12, 1865. Manarin, *North Carolina Troops*, 7:494.

73. The reference is to Psalms 19:10: "More to be desired are they [God's judgments] than gold, yea than much fine gold; sweeter also than honey, and the droppings of honeycombs."

74. Much of the original text is illegible because of the "blotches" that reflect Turner's subsequent reinterpretation of his dream.

75. Charles Rollin (1661-1741) was a French historian best known for *The Ancient History of the Egyptians, Carthaginians, Assyrians, Babylonians, Medes and Persians, Macedonians, and Grecians* (1730-1738), *Roman History*, and *Traité des études* (1726-1731), which contained an innovative system of education. Two-volume editions of his *Ancient History* were published by George Conclin of Cincinnati in 1842 and 1848. The English historian, Sir Archibald Alison (1792-1867), is best remembered for a fourteen-volume *History of Europe from the French Revolution of 1789 to the Accession of Napolean III.* He also wrote *Principles of Population* (1840), *Free Trade and Fettered Currency* (1847), *Life of the Duke of Marlborough* (1848), a collection of essays (1850), and an autobiography that was published posthumously in 1883. Alison was the subject of a recent biography by Michael Michie, *An Enlightenment Tory in Victorian Scotland: The Career of Sir Archibald Alison*, published by McGill-Queen's University Press in 1997. Thomas Babington Macaulay (1800-1859) was the author of *The History of England from the Accession of James the Second*, published in four volumes between 1848 and 1855. http://gdl.cdlr.strath.ac.uk/mlemen/mlemen001.htm.

76. Turner may be referring to *The History of the Glorious Life, Reign, and Death of the Illustrious Queen Elizabeth*, by Samuel Clarke (1599-1682), published in the year of his death.

77. The parable is recorded in the Book of Matthew 13:45, 46: "The kingdom of heaven is like unto a merchantman, seeking goodly pearls, who, when he had found one pearl of great price, went and sold all that he had, and bought it."

78. Point Lookout, Maryland, was the site of a notorious Federal prisoner-of-war camp. Turner's younger brother John Augustus died there in February 1865. Robert F. Webb noted in his diary on February 14, 1864: "Last week about four hundred men were sent from this prison, their destination, we supposed, being Point Lookout, as we are confident that they are not to be exchanged. They were taken alphabetically by name and the same number will leave again as soon as they can cross the lake, which at this time is impracticable on account of the ice." On January 5, Colonel Hoffman had instructed Lieutenant Colonel

Pierson to divide the prisoners into groups of five hundred, "taking a proportional number from each grade and make duplicate parole-rolls . . . with a view to transferring them South," and to arrange for transporting the groups under guard to Sandusky at forty-eight hour intervals. Clark, *Histories of Regiments*, 4:670; *War of the Rebellion*, ser. 2, 6:815.

79. Clark, *Histories of Regiments*, 4:697-702.

80. William Mason, "Christian Preacher," to "any Congregation of the Faithful Bretheren [*sic*] in Christ," February 14, 1865, document folded in Columbus Lafayette Turner Notebook. The Brethren in Christ Church developed along the Susquehanna River in southeastern Pennsylvania during the last quarter of the eighteenth century. The Germanic founders of the movement were deeply affected by the revivals of the Great Awakening and influenced by the disparate strains of Anabaptism, Pietism, and Wesleyanism. They stressed the importance of a genuine personal conversion experience and shunned the trappings and rituals of organized denominations. The Brethren favored simplicity in dress and appearance, and eschewed such worldly activities as politics and card playing. By 1788, a group of the Brethren had immigrated to Canada and during the early years of the nineteenth century spread throughout the American Midwest. The North American Church of the Brethren in Christ organized into a general conference in 1879. http://www.bic-church.org/about/history.asp.

81. Compiled Confederate Service Records, Thirty-third North Carolina.

82. This incident is mentioned in several other prison diaries. Lt. Edmund D. Patterson gave the date as Saturday night, July 23. According to Patterson, it was the fifth time that sentinels had fired into the blocks, but the first time anyone had been hit. Lt. Col. John Washington Inzer of Alabama likewise recorded the incident on the same date. He noted that Dillard and "Ingram" of Block 5 "were seriously wounded" by the "shameful cowards." Webb noted in his diary on July 29: "A great outrage was committed last Saturday night by the sentinels on post. Without any provocation they fired into one of the blocks and severely wounded two officers. The commander expressed much regret and assured us that there would be no repetition of such a cowardly action." Lt. Aaron A. Inman of Company D, Eighteenth North Carolina, was born in Robeson County, where he enlisted on May 18, 1861, aged twenty-one. He mustered in as a sergeant but was later reduced to the ranks. He was again promoted to sergeant on October 10, 1862, and appointed third lieutenant on December 13, 1862. He was captured at Gettysburg and initially confined at Fort Delaware, then transferred to Johnson's Island on September 14-16, 1863. Inman was exchanged at Cox's Wharf, Virginia, on March 22, 1865. Lieutenant Dillard of Virginia is unidentified. Barrett, *Yankee Rebel*, 182-183; www.archaeology.org/online/features/civil/words/inzer.html; Clark, *Histories of Regiments*, 4:684; Manarin, *North Carolina Troops*, 6:344.

83. The commandant of the prison in July 1864 was Col. Charles W. Hill, commander of the 128th Ohio Volunteers. He succeeded Brig. Gen. Henry Dwight Terry, who had replaced the incompetent Pierson on January 14, 1864. Terry, who led a division in the Sixth Corps of the Army of the Potomac, had been sent with one of his brigades (that of Brig. Gen. Alexander Shuler) to the island on January 6 after repeated requests from the thoroughly rattled Pierson for reinforcements. Even the addition in November 1863 of four companies of cavalry, a company of light artillery, and a heavy artillery battery, and the presence of the armed revenue steamer *Michigan* offshore, were insufficient to assuage his fears of a massive prisoner uprising. Pierson had also permitted sanitary conditions in the camp to deteriorate. According to Wharton J. Green, a "badly decimated brigade" under Gen. Alexander Shuler was sent from Virginia to relieve Pierson, after which conditions improved. Robert F. Webb reported in his diary on February 25, 1864, that they were now under the command "of one

General Shaler." He noted on April 5: "Everything here lately under the direction of the commander, has undergone a change decidedly for the better." On May 14, he reported: "During the greater part of the winter and spring we had a part of Sedgewick's [*sic*] Corps to guard us. They were very kind to the prisoners and we received many favors at their hands, and we were all sorry when they left for the front, for they left us in the hands of the cold blooded militia of this State, whose acts of cruelty will long be remembered." Shaler's brigade was composed of the 65th, 67th, and 122nd New York, and the 23rd and 82nd Pennsylvania. Green, *Recollections and Reflections,* 183; Clark, *Histories of Regiments*, 4:672, 676, 678; *War of the Rebellion*, ser. 1, 33:359; ser. 2, 6:841, 853-854, 7:140-141. For the correspondence between Pierson and Col. William Hoffman that resulted in the change of commandant, see *War of the Rebellion*, ser. 2, 6:333, 385-386, 395-397, 448-450, 490-491, 500.

84. Capt. Henry James Hawkins (1833-1901), a twenty-six-year-old merchant in Cowan, Tennessee, enlisted as a third lieutenant in the Tullahoma Guards of Coffee County on April 29, 1861. He was elected captain of the company, then Company I, First Tennessee (Turney's) Infantry, on April 27, 1862. He was captured at Gettysburg on July 3 and confined at Johnson's Island. Hawkins was transferred to Point Lookout, Maryland, for exchange on March 14, 1865, and paroled on April 1. Capt. John Moore of Company E, Eighteenth North Carolina, was from New Hanover County. He enlisted at age thirty-one on May 17, 1861, was promoted to corporal, September-October 1861, elected first lieutenant at an unspecified date, and promoted to captain, January 13, 1863. He was captured near Falling Waters, Maryland, on the retreat from Gettysburg, ca. July 14, 1863. He was confined at various prisons, including Johnson's Island, to which he was sent on December 9, 1863. Moore was released on January 11, 1865, after taking the oath of allegiance. Capt. Alfred A. Moffitt, Company F, Eighteenth North Carolina, from Randolph County, enlisted on June 1, 1861, at age twenty-two. He mustered in as a sergeant and was promoted to captain, November 28, 1862. Moffitt was wounded in the thigh and captured at Gettysburg, July 3, 1863. He was first hospitalized at Chester, Pennsylvania, and then transferred to Point Lookout on October 4, 1863, and to Johnson's Island three weeks later. He was paroled and exchanged at Cox's Wharf, ca. March 22, 1865. Capt. James B. Williams, Company C, Twentieth North Carolina, was a native of Robeson County, but enlisted in Columbus County on April 23, 1861, at age twenty-four. He mustered in as a corporal, was promoted to sergeant on June 17, 1861, and to captain on June 27, 1862. He was wounded at Malvern Hill and captured at Gettysburg. With Turner, he was confined at Fort Delaware before being transferred to Johnson's Island, where he arrived on July 20, 1863. Williams was sent to Point Lookout on March 21, 1865, to Fort Delaware on April 28, and released on June 12. Second Lt. James M. Kendrick, Company H, Twenty-third North Carolina, enlisted at age twenty-two in Gaston County. He was captured at Gettysburg, July 1, 1863, and confined at Johnson's Island until paroled ca. March 14, 1865, and exchanged at Cox's Wharf, ca. March 22. First Lt. James Elijah DeVaughn, Company F, Second Georgia Cavalry, was a native of Jonesboro, Georgia. He was responsible for the provost detail that on June 27, 1862, hung the Federal "Anderson Raiders" of the "Great Locomotive Chase" near Big Shanty, Georgia. He was captured at Sugar Creek, Tennessee, on October 9, 1863. He may have been promoted to captain prior to his capture. DeVaughn died on July 13, 1908. Manarin, *North Carolina Troops*, 6:355, 367, 456, 7:218; John Randolph Poole, *Cracker Cavaliers: The 2nd Georgia Cavalry under Wheeler and Forrest* (Macon, Ga.: Mercer University Press, 2000), 7-8, 185-196.

INTERLUDE: FROM JOHNSON'S ISLAND PRISON TO THE NORTH CAROLINA STATE HOUSE, 1865-1873

1. Col. Silas A. Sharpe of Iredell County commanded the Seventy-ninth Regiment of North Carolina Militia, his commission dated July 1, 1863. *Catawba County News*, April 27, 1904; undated note, quoting Wilfred Dent Turner, in Notley D. Tomlin Collection; Adjutant General's Office, Roster of the Militia of North Carolina, 1861-1862, 1864, North Carolina State Archives, Raleigh, 214-215.

2. Columbus Lafayette Turner Diary, March 20, 1874.

3. Columbus Lafayette Turner Notebook; Reginald Turner memoir, chapter 1. In the Turner Family Papers in the possession of Nancy Jones, there is a report card of Jennie Turner's progress at Olin High School for the "session" ending June 7, 1866, but it is unclear when the term commenced. The courses she studied, such as music, Bible recitations, history, and deportment, were much more extensive than those taught by her brother.

4. *Catawba County News*, April 27, 1904; Iredell County Record of Deeds, 3:391, 6:92. In the 1870 census, his occupation was listed as "merchant," so presumably he was still running the mill store at that time. Ninth Census of the United States, 1870, Population Schedule: Iredell County, North Carolina, North Carolina State Archives, Raleigh.

5. In the account of the marriage in the (Salisbury) *Carolina Watchman*, March 4, 1867, she is referred to as "Mollie J. Graves, of Raleigh."

6. Jeffrey J. Crow et al., *A History of African Americans in North Carolina*, rev. ed. (Raleigh: Office of Archives and History, Department of Cultural Resources, 2002), 233-235.

7. *Journal of the House of Representatives of the General Assembly of the State of North Carolina, at its Session of 1872-'73* (Raleigh: Stone and Uzzell, 1873), 61, 66, 75, 86, 108-109, 125, 135, 157; *Laws and Resolutions of the State of North Carolina Passed by the General Assembly at its Session 1872-'73* (Raleigh: Stone and Uzzell, 1873), Public Laws, c. 123, pp. 198-199, Private Laws, c. 62, pp. 459-460.

8. *House Journal, 1872-'73*, 225, 249, 263, 271; House Bills, General Assembly Session Records, November 1872-March 1873, North Carolina State Archives, Raleigh.

9. *House Journal, 1872-'73*, 339, 407, 412, 452, 456, 466; House Bills, General Assembly Session Records, 1872-1873.

10. *House Journal, 1872-'73*, 405, 574, 595.

11. Remarks of C. L. Turner in the House of Representatives, February 22, 1873, original in possession of James R. Turner, Greensboro, N.C.; *House Journal, 1872-'73*, 403-404, 492; Senate Bills, General Assembly Session Records, 1872-1873.

12. Remarks of C. L. Turner in the House of Representatives, [February 26 or 27, 1873], original in possession of James R. Turner, Greensboro, N.C.

13. Obituary in the (Raleigh) *Daily Sentinel* (copied from the *Charlotte Observer*), September 16, 1873.

14. J. G. de Roulhac Hamilton, *Reconstruction in North Carolina* (New York: Columbia University, 1914), 597; *Journal of the House of Representatives of the General Assembly of the State of North Carolina, at its Session of 1873-'74* (Raleigh: Josiah Turner Jr., 1874), 53, 75-76, 97.

15. *House Journal, 1873-'74*, 63, 66; House Bills, General Assembly Session Records, November 1873-February 1874, North Carolina State Archives, Raleigh.

16. *House Journal, 1873-'74,* 166, 192, 203, 222-223, 243, 250, 255; House Bills, General Assembly Session Records, 1873-1874; *Laws and Resolutions 1872-'73,* Public Laws, c. 52, p. 72; *Laws and Resolutions of the State of North Carolina Passed by the General Assembly at its Session 1873-'74* (Raleigh: Josiah Turner Jr., 1874), 380-381.

LEGISLATIVE DIARY

1. Franklinville is situated on the Deep River in eastern Randolph County. The town was incorporated in 1847 as Franklinsville, named in honor of Gov. Jesse Franklin (1760-1823). In the 1870 federal census of Liberty Township, Randolph County, O. A. Palmer was listed as a farmer, age 57. Also in the household were Sylvania, 46, keeping house, and seven children "attending school": Bascom H., 21; Gustavus, 17; Anna C., 15; Helen, 14; Decimus H. [male], 12; Dora S., 10; and Conrod, 9; and Emma O Connor, 22, a schoolteacher. Turner probably meant Dora rather than Decie, most likely the nickname of the twelve-year-old son. Dennis Curtis was listed in the 1870 census of Franklinsville Township as a 40-year-old merchant and manufacturer of domestic cotton goods. His wife was 30-year-old Lucy Ellen Makepeace Curtis. He administered the estate of his father-in-law, George Makepeace, who died in October 1872. Makepeace was listed in the 1870 census as 71 years old, a manufacturer of cotton yarn and domestic sheeting. He was one of the original directors and stockholders of the Island Ford Manufacturing Company at Franklinville, organized in 1846. His wife was 58-year-old Lucy A. Makepeace, and his son was George Henry Makepeace. According to his widow's petition for a dower, the homeplace consisted of approximately 141 acres. William S. Powell, *The North Carolina Gazetteer* (Chapel Hill: University of North Carolina Press, 1968), 182; Randolph County Historical Society, *Randolph County, 1779-1979* (Winston-Salem: Hunter Publishing Company, 1980), 76, 102; Estate of George Makepeace, 1872, Randolph County Estates Records, North Carolina State Archives, Raleigh; Ninth Census of the United States, 1870, Population Schedule, Randolph County, N.C.

2. Faith Rock is on Deep River, south of the bridge at Franklinville. Andrew Hunter, a prisoner of the British who had broken parole, was recaptured on May 1, 1782, by the forces of Col. David Fanning (1755-1825). Leader of the Loyalist militia in the North Carolina Piedmont, Fanning had established a fortified base at Cox's Mill on Deep River after the Battle of Guilford Courthouse. Hunter escaped on Fanning's horse, Bay Doe. Several days later, while being pursued by Fanning's men, Hunter evaded capture by riding Bay Doe down the steep slope of Faith Rock and across the river. *Randolph County,* 37.

3. Town ball was an early form of baseball that evolved from the game of rounders.

4. Tabernacle Academy for white males and females opened in the 1870s on the grounds of Tabernacle Methodist Protestant Church in southeastern Guilford County, about ten miles south of Greensboro on the Liberty Road. Principal Martin H. Holt brought wide recognition to the school but left in 1879 because of a lack of community support. The school closed in 1930. National Register of Historic Places Registration Form, Tabernacle Methodist Protestant Church and Cemetery, Greensboro, Guilford County. State Historic Preservation Office, Raleigh; John E. Batchelor, *The Guilford County Schools: A History* (Winston-Salem: John F. Blair, Publisher, 1991), appendix [p. 271].

5. Mr. Robertson is unidentified.

6. The Simonton House in Statesville, also called the Carolina Hotel, was built by Robert F. Simonton before the Civil War. Colonel Sadler is unidentified. Homer M. Keever, *Iredell Piedmont County* (Statesville, N.C.: Iredell County Bicentennial Commission, 1976), 318.

7. Wilfred Turner's younger half-brother, James Martin Turner (1836-1885), was the son of Samuel and his third wife, Clarissa Nichols Turner. He was less than six years older than his nephew, Columbus. He was a member of the board of commissioners of Iredell County in 1874. J. M. Turner was listed in the 1870 federal census of Turnersburg Township of Iredell County as a 33-year-old farmer, with wife Emeline, 29, and four children. He was listed in the 1860 census as Mark Turner, 24, schoolteacher, with wife Emeline, 20, and son William, 1. His wife was Emiline Juliana Gaither, born 1840. Wheeler, *Legislative Manual for 1874*, 257; Eighth Census of the United States, 1860, Population Schedule: Iredell County, N.C., North Carolina State Archives, Raleigh; Ninth Census of the United States, 1870, Population Schedule: Iredell County, N.C.

8. Columbus Turner's father operated a cotton mill complex at Turnersburg, which included a company store, cotton gin, and gristmill. David H. Stimpson, a 28-year-old farmer, is listed in the 1880 federal census of Turnersburg Township with his wife Etta, 23, and son Luther, 4. Offie Stimpson is unidentified. Tenth Census of the United States, 1880, Population Schedule: Iredell County, N.C.

9. Columbus Turner and George McCrindell married sisters. McCrindell wed Susan Margaret Graves (1833-1914) "before 1860." She was eight years older than her sister, Mary Jane. China Grove was the name given Wilfred Turner's homeplace. http://www.gravesfa.org/gen836.htm.

10. Leonidus Littlepage Lacy also married a sister of Mary Jane Graves. Emma Huldah Graves (1844-1888) was three years younger than her sister. She and Lacy were married ca. 1869 in Richmond. http://www.gravesfa.org/gen836.htm.

11. Turner's younger sister, Adaline Dorcas Turner (1847-1895), married Laz. Theophilus Stimpson (1843-1916) in Iredell County on November 20, 1873. Cottage Home is located on the grounds of Turner's parents' home in Turnersburg. Columbus lived there with his wife until her death in 1873. Both the main house and the cottage still stand.

12. On December 15, 1873, Turner introduced a bill (HB 304) to incorporate Centre Presbyterian Church in Iredell County, which was passed by the House on December 20 and ratified on February 10, 1874. On January 16, he offered an amendment to HB 76 (an act to prevent the sale of liquor in certain localities), inserting Centre Church and Coddle's Creek Church and Academy, which was adopted by the House. The statute as ratified included Centre Presbyterian Church in a long list of localities at which "it shall be unlawful for any person or persons to sell or in any manner give away any intoxicating liquors, or either directly or indirectly to receive any compensation for the same within four miles of." *House Journal 1873-'74*, 203, 255, 288; *Laws and Resolutions 1873-'74*, Private Laws, c. 70, pp. 380-381, Public Laws, c. 137, pp. 216-219.

13. Listed in the household of C. L. Turner, twenty-eight-year-old merchant, in the 1870 federal census of Turnersburg Township is Isaac Gaither, twenty, a black domestic servant. Ninth Census of the United States, 1870, Population Schedule: Iredell County, N.C.

14. Clarksbury Methodist Church, formerly known as Irvin's Old Meeting House, was established in 1832. It is located approximately five miles due east of Turnersburg. Wilfred Turner's church, Mount Bethel, formerly Prather's Meeting House, is the oldest Methodist congregation in the county (1797). It stands between Clarksbury and Turnersburg. A Matthew Summers owned a store at Turnersburg in 1860. In the 1870 federal census of Turnersburg Township, a Vira Summers, 35, female, is listed as the head of a household that also includes Lulia, 10, and Julia A. E., 7. Ten years later, Julia A. Summers, 18, lived with her mother, Elvira C., 46, in the household of her stepfather, Melmoth Holmes, 55. Iredell County American Revolution Bicentennial Commission, *Iredell County Landmarks: A*

Pictorial History of Iredell County (Statesville, N.C.: Brady Printing Company, 1982, reprint), 78-79; Keever, *Iredell Piedmont County*, 140; Ninth Census of the United States, 1870, Population Schedule: Iredell County, N.C.; Tenth Census of the United States, 1880, Population Schedule: Iredell County, N.C.

15. Rev. Thomas Page Ricaud (1817-1900) was born in Baltimore and joined the Methodist Conference in Norfolk in 1847. He died in Durham and is buried in Wilmington, where he served as minister of the Fifth Avenue Methodist Episcopal Church. The parable of the talents is recorded in Matthew 25:14-30. A master went away on a trip, leaving different amounts of money (talents being a form of currency) with three servants. Two of them invested their money wisely and realized profitable returns. The other buried his talents and gained nothing thereby. The moral: we have an obligation to use our talents rather than bury them. http://www.nssa.us/nssajrnl/23_1/htm/07.htm; http://www.mccumc.org/docs/ncarchives/deceased.xls.

16. William Tyson Gaither (1826-1885) was a son-in-law and business partner of Wilfred Turner. He married Turner's eldest daughter, Mary Elizabeth "Betty" (1835-1929) in Iredell County on February 9, 1853. Gaither and Wilfred Turner operated a mill "about where Long Branch ran into Hunting Creek," which Turner and wife sold to Dr. John W. Ellis in 1872. Wilfred Turner paid $2,000 for Gaither's interest in the Eagle Mills Company further up Hunting Creek in 1869. The property included four hundred acres, mill houses, and machinery. Three years later, he presented his interest in the mill to his eldest daughter as a gift. "The factory" refers to the Turnersburg Cotton Mill. Keever, *Iredell Piedmont County*, 154; Iredell County Record of Deeds, 4:369, 936, 6:63.

17. Dr. Robert T. Campbell at Snow Creek was one of seventeen physicians listed in the 1860 Iredell County census. Keever, *Iredell Piedmont County*, 140.

18. Senator James R. Ellis of Hickory Tavern represented District 37 (Catawba and Lincoln counties), and H. P. Haynes of Pigeon River represented Haywood County.

19. Construction began on a hotel on Main Street in Salisbury in 1855, and the Boyden House opened in 1859. C. S. Brown was the proprietor in 1874. The hotel, which once featured a domed ballroom on the top floor, was later renamed the Empire Hotel. The hotel closed in 1963, but the building still stands. Statesville *Intelligencer*, January 17, 1874; *Branson & Farrar's Business Directory, 1866-'67, Containing Facts, Figures, Names and Locations* (Raleigh: Branson and Farrar, Publishers, [1866]), 9; *Salisbury Post*, March 4, 2001.

20. Samuel Wittkowsky (1835-1911) and Jacob Rintels (1836-1876) operated a wholesale and retail store in Charlotte during the 1870s. Previously, they ran a store in Statesville. In 1865, Wittkowsky drove Zebulon B. Vance to the train depot in Salisbury as the former governor departed for federal prison in Washington, D.C. *Dictionary of North Carolina Biography*, 6:253.

21. Built in 1840 as the Mansion House, the hotel was renamed the Central Hotel in 1873. Located at the southeast corner of Trade and Tryon streets, it was "for many years, considered the finest hotel between Richmond and Atlanta. Its spacious ballroom was the gathering place for Charlotte's elite. On one side of the lobby was the dining room, and the other the city's most elegant bar." The proprietor in January 1874 was H. C. Eccles. The hotel continued to operate until the late 1930s. LeGette Blythe and Charles Raven Brockmann, *Hornets' Nest: The Story of Charlotte and Mecklenburg County* (Charlotte: McNally of Charlotte, 1961), 295.

22. Former governor Zebulon B. Vance and his wife lived in Charlotte after the Civil War. The Reverend Mr. Davis is unidentified.

23. J. N. Bryson of Cashin's Valley represented Jackson County.

24. In the 1870 federal census of Raleigh Township, Lucy Evans, forty-nine, was listed as the head of household, "keeping house," with four "families" enumerated in the residence (the legislature was not in session when the census was taken in June). A directory of North Carolina businesses in 1866-1867 included among its listing of hotels, "Boarding House, Raleigh, Mrs. Lucy B. Evans, proprietor." The 1880 Raleigh city directory indicated that she was the widow of Henry L. Evans. The house faced McDowell Street, at the corner of Edenton Street. A Raleigh newspaper printed a legislative directory for the 1873-1874 session. Legislators whose residence was listed as "Mrs. Evans" included Senators J. M. Stafford and W. P. Welch, and Representatives Anderson of Clay, Blackwell, Dickey, Johns, Mitchell, and Turner. Ninth Census of the United States, 1870, Population Schedule: Wake County, N.C.; *Branson & Farrar's Business Directory, 1866-67*, 95; Charles Emerson and Company, *Raleigh Directory, 1880-'81* (Raleigh: Edwards, Broughton and Company, 1879), 68; (Raleigh) *Daily News*, January 29, 1874; J. H. Chataigne, comp., *Chataigne's Raleigh City Directory, 1875-'76* (Raleigh: J. H. Chataigne, 1875), 65.

25. Columbus's younger brother, Wilfred Dent Turner (1855-1933), was listed in his father's household in the 1870 census of Iredell County as fifteen years old, "at school." His older brother alternately referred to him in this diary as Will or Willie. Eugene B. Drake was editor of the *Iredell Express*, Statesville's first newspaper, established as a Whig Party organ in 1857. After Stoneman's cavalry burned the *Express* office in 1865, Drake and his son established the *Statesville American* as an organ of the Conservative Party. The paper switched political affiliation to the Republican Party in 1872. Ninth Census of the United States, 1870, Population Schedule: Iredell County, N.C.; Keever, *Iredell Piedmont County*, 292-293.

26. The statute authorized the Dan River Coalfield Railroad to purchase the Atlantic, Tennessee and Ohio Railroad in North Carolina. Rep. A. B. Johns of Rockingham County introduced the bill (HB 186) on December 5, and the House approved it the next day. The bill was ratified on December 18. *Laws and Resolutions 1873-'74*, Public Laws, c. 22, pp. 23-24; *House Journal 1873-'74*, 129, 140.

27. Joseph Gilmer of Guilford County introduced the bill in the House on December 4; it was approved by a vote of 69 to 31, Turner voting with the majority. The House concurred in senate amendments to the bill on January 28, and it was ratified the following day. *Laws and Resolutions 1873-'74*, Public Laws, c. 68, pp. 94-95; *House Journal 1873-'74*, 120, 279-281, 368.

28. Mary Jane Graves was the daughter of James Henry and Harriet Smith Graves of Culpeper County, Virginia. She was born June 16, 1841, and married Columbus L. Turner on January 16, 1867. She died of typhoid fever on September 11, 1873, and was buried in Hollywood Cemetery in Richmond. On April 23, 1874, and several times thereafter during a two-month sojourn in Richmond, Turner visited her grave. St. James Church, founded in 1831, was the third Episcopal Church in Richmond. http://www.gravesfa.org/gen836.htm; (Raleigh) *Daily Sentinel*, September 16, 1873; Columbus Lafayette Turner Diary, 1874.

29. Abbreviation for cassimere, now usually spelled cashmere or Kashmir.

30. Turner was a member of the joint standing committee on the insane asylum, of which Senator John W. Ellis was chairman. The committee's report noted that it was compiled "through the industry and careful examination of the expenditures of that institution" by Representative Turner and Senator Edward Ransom. A joint select committee was also raised during the session to investigate expenses at the asylum. Joint Committee Reports, General Assembly Session Records, 1873-1874.

31. Columbus's youngest sister, Emily Ella Turner (1853-1924), was educated at Davenport Female College in Lenoir. She married Marshall Knox Steele (1848-1912) in Iredell County on January 19, 1874. Wilfred Turner gave Steele power of attorney in 1884. In 1890, he presented Steele and his wife half-interest in the Turnersburg Mill and Cotton Factory, and the other half interest to L. T. Stimpson and his wife, Adaline Dorcas. They operated the mill under the name, Stimpson and Steele. Two years before his death, Wilfred sold eighty-five acres of the Turner homeplace to the two brothers-in-law. Iredell County Record of Deeds, 8:706, 14:405, 452-453, 23:57-58.

32. Senator Charles Sumner of Massachusetts introduced a supplementary civil rights bill in May 1870 and relentlessly pushed for its passage until his death on March 11, 1874. In its original form, the bill would prohibit racial discrimination in public schools, common carriers, inns, theaters, churches, cemeteries, and benevolent institutions. In his history of Reconstruction in North Carolina, J. G. de Roulhac Hamilton called the proposed bill "a menace that was apparent to all and it was not favored by a majority of the white Republicans. . . . This proposed legislation was . . . the chief connecting link between North Carolina and the new movement in national politics." More than any other factor, Sumner's measure "broke the last hold of the Republican party upon the State." The resolution (HR 99) in the General Assembly was introduced on January 17 by Rep. R. B. B. Houston of Catawba Station, representing Catawba County, "to protest against the passage of the civil rights bill by Congress." A motion to table the resolution was defeated 65 to 29, Turner voting with the majority. Edmund Jones of Caldwell County offered as an amendment, "that the General Assembly of North Carolina do most earnestly and respectfully petition the Congress of the United States not to pass the bill now pending in the House of Representatives, known as the Supplemental Civil Rights Bill, believing as we do that the immediate effects of such a law would be the suppression of our public schools, for both whites and colored, the closing of many of our houses of worship, the ruin of our landlords and hotel proprietors, as well as the thorough demoralization of our society, and the cause of bitter strife between the races. From a thorough knowledge of the situation, we are satisfied that the bill would operate disastrously to our best interests." The amended resolution was approved, 75 to 25. Turner voted for its passage; of the African American representatives, only Ellison voted in favor (Fletcher, King [sick], and W. P. Mabson did not vote). "A resolution protesting against the proposed civil rights bill passed both houses, a large number of Republicans voting for it," noted Hamilton. A watered-down version of Sumner's bill, which did not include integrated public schools, was ratified by Congress on March 1, 1875, but declared unconstitutional eight years later. Hamilton, *Reconstruction*, 598-599; *House Journal 1873-'74*, 293, 295-299.

33. African Americans in the 1873-1874 legislature included four in the senate—Henry Eppes of Halifax, George L. Mabson of New Hanover, James H. Harris of Wake, and John A. Hyman of Warren—and thirteen in the House—Israel B. Abbott and Edward R. Dudley of Craven, William P. Mabson and Willis Bunn of Edgecombe, John H. Williamson of Franklin, Hanson T. Hughes of Granville, John R. Bryant of Halifax, William H. McLaurin and Alfred Lloyd of New Hanover, Robert Fletcher of Richmond, Stewart Ellison of Wake, and George H. King and J. W. H. Paschall of Warren. Crow et al., *History of African Americans*, 233-235.

34. Squire Trivett of Jefferson represented Ashe County, James Blythe of Blue Ridge represented Henderson County, and Jacob Weaver Bowman (1831-1905) of Bakersville represented Mitchell County. Bowman studied law under Richmond Pearson. A former Whig, he served intermittently in the General Assembly from 1860 to 1882 and was appointed a superior court judge in 1898. For a sketch of Blythe, see n. 106 below. Stewart

Ellison (1832-1899) of Raleigh represented Wake County. Born a slave in Beaufort County, he was a building contractor, grocer, and commission merchant in Raleigh after the war. He served as vice-president of the North Carolina Freedmen's Convention in 1865. Four years later, he was one of the first three African Americans elected to the Raleigh Board of Commissioners. Ellison represented Wake County as a Republican in the General Assembly for six terms from 1870 to 1880 and served three terms as a director of the state penitentiary. During the 1890s, he worked as a janitor in the federal courthouse and post office in Raleigh and died in poverty in 1899. Edward Richard Dudley of New Bern represented Craven County. He was born in New Bern on June 10, 1840, the son of a free black who purchased the freedom of his wife, but both mother and child were sold back into slavery when Dudley was about three years old. He was finally freed upon the arrival of the Union army in New Bern in 1862. His mother taught him to read and write. A cooper by trade, Dudley was a member of the Common Council of New Bern in 1869 and later served as a city marshal. In the General Assembly, he introduced a civil rights bill. An active Methodist, he was a leader of the temperance movement in North Carolina in the 1870s and "innocently spent the most crucial years of Reconstruction storming the state for temperance." Israel B. Abbott of New Bern also represented Craven County. *Dictionary of North Carolina Biography*, 1:198-199, 2:152-153; Elizabeth Balanoff, "Negro Legislators in the North Carolina General Assembly, July 1868-February 1872," *North Carolina Historical Review* 49 (winter 1972), 29-30, 54; Elizabeth Reid Murray, *Wake: Capital County of North Carolina*, Vol. 1 (Raleigh: Capital County Publishing Company, 1983), 275-276.

35. Turner's resolution (HR 100) to raise a joint select committee on adjournment was introduced on January 17. The resolution asked that a committee of five (two from the senate, three from the House) be appointed "to take into consideration the amount of public business necessary to be transacted, and the time required, and report the earliest day practicable for this General Assembly to adjourn *sine die*." *House Journal 1873-'74*, 293; House Resolutions, General Assembly Session Records, 1873-1874.

36. Turner referred to an article on page 2 of the *Daily Sentinel* titled, "The Murder of Mrs. Surratt." The controversy involved former president Andrew Johnson and Joseph Holt (1807-1894) who, as judge advocate general of the army from 1862 to 1875, was the chief prosecutor in the military trial of the Lincoln conspirators. After the trial, Holt was accused of withholding evidence that might have helped some of the defendants. But the later controversy surrounding Holt and Johnson concerned the government's refusal to abide by the recommendation of the military court that the life of Mary E. Surratt, while guilty as charged and sentenced to death, be spared out of consideration for her age and gender. Five of the nine commissioners signed the plea for mercy, which was attached to the trial record and transmitted through Judge Holt to President Johnson. But on July 7, 1865, Mrs. Surratt was hanged for complicity in the assassination of Lincoln, the first woman to be executed by the United States. While Johnson was still in office, vague rumors circulated through the press that Holt had suppressed the document from the president's notice. In 1873, Johnson, eyeing a seat in Congress from Tennessee and hoping to assure voters of his innocence in the execution of Mrs. Surratt, joined the fray. He publicly accused Holt of withholding the plea for mercy, igniting a controversy that lasted for several years. Holt's response to Johnson was published in the *Washington Chronicle* and subsequently issued as a pamphlet titled, *Vindication of Judge Advocate General Holt from the Foul Slanders of Traitors, Confessed Perjurers and Suborners, Acting in the Interest of Jefferson Davis*. He contended that Johnson had read the recommendation of the court in his presence, but had insisted that Mrs. Surratt, who "kept the nest that hatched the egg," should die for her part in the conspiracy. In November 1873, Johnson published a formal reply to Holt's charges. Holt continued to serve as advocate

general until December 1, 1875, four months after the death of Johnson. (Raleigh) *Daily Sentinel*, January 18, 1874; Elizabeth D. Leonard, *Lincoln's Avengers: Justice, Revenge, and Reunion after the Civil War* (New York: W. W. Norton and Company, 2004), 297-301.

37. William Henry Dodd (1836-1904) and his wife, Roxanna Upchurch Dodd (1843-1925), were the "founders of the infant department in the First Baptist Church Sunday School and teachers for several decades." Dodd was mayor of Raleigh from 1882 to 1887. He lived in the Dodd-Hinsdale House on Hillsborough Street and is buried in Oakwood Cemetery. Grady Lee Ernest Carroll Sr., *They Lived in Raleigh: Some Leading Personalities from 1792 to 1892* (Raleigh: Southeastern Copy Center, 1977), 303-304.

38. Senator Andrew C. Cowles of Hamptonville represented District 33 (Surry and Yadkin counties), Senator Thomas A. Nicholson of Iredell County represented District 34, and Rep. Charles Anderson of Mocksville was the House member from Davie County.

39. Thomas J. Dula of Wilkes County introduced the road bill (HB 406) on January 16. After committee amendments were adopted, the bill was passed on January 19 and sent to the senate for concurrence. *House Journal 1873-'74*, 286, 305, 330.

40. This bill (HB 35) was introduced in the House on November 21 by Thomas A. McNeill of Robeson County. It was approved by the lower chamber on December 11 and sent to the senate for concurrence. The bill became law on January 27, 1874. *House Journal 1873-'74*, 53, 178-179, 193; *Laws and Resolutions 1873-'74*, Public Laws, c. 62, p. 89.

41. Haywood is in southeastern Chatham County on Deep River. The town was incorporated in 1796 as Lyons, but the name was changed to Haywoodsborough in 1797 and to Haywood in 1800. The town was named for John Haywood, state treasurer for forty years. Julia Louisa Turner (1838-1878), the third daughter of Wilfred and Dorcas Tomlinson Turner, married Robert Henry Wyche (1823-1904) on March 31, 1868, presumably in Turnersburg. They had met in Oxford in July 1867; he was the "bachelor uncle" of some of her friends. Together they had five children, only three of whom survived childhood. Wyche was the son of James and Pamela Evans Wyche of Brunswick County, Virginia, who moved to Granville County, N.C., the year after Robert Henry was born. James Wyche represented Granville County in the House of Commons during the 1833-1834 and 1834-1835 sessions, and in the state senate in 1835. Dr. Wyche is listed in the 1870 census of Cape Fear Township, Chatham County, as a 46-year-old physician. His wife Julia is 31, and four children are listed in the household: Hughes, Nancy, 12, "going to school": Della, 10, Mary, 4, and Martha, 1, at home. The relationship of the Hughes children to the Wyches is unclear. In the 1860 census, he is listed as Robert H. Wyche, 30, M.D., born in Virginia and unmarried. Powell, *North Carolina Gazetteer*, 219; Julia Wyche Cherry, notes on her grandmother; Eighth Census of the United States, 1860, Population Schedule: Chatham County, N.C.; Ninth Census of the United States, 1870, Population Schedule: Chatham County, N.C.; http://www.angelfire.com/ga/htpiii/w24gen.html.

42. Living nine households away from the Wyches in the 1870 census of Cape Fear Township was John W. Scott, 45, a farmer, and his wife, Cate L., 32. Scott was commissioned major of the Forty-ninth Regiment, Twelfth Brigade, North Carolina Militia, on November 21, 1861. Ninth Census of the United States, 1870, Population Schedule: Chatham County, N.C.; Adjutant General's Office, Roster of North Carolina Militia, 191.

43. The bill for a uniform interest rate is what Turner refers to as the "Usury bill." The bill (SB 261, HB 506) was introduced in the senate by Lott W. Humphrey of Goldsboro (representing District 10, Wayne and Duplin counties) on December 12 and approved by the upper chamber by a vote of 30 to 1 on January 24. In the House, it was first referred to the

Committee on Finance, then to the Committee on Banks and Currency; the latter recommended on February 11 the passage of a substitute bill. John Milton Worth (1811-1900) of Asheboro, brother of Gov. Jonathan Worth, represented District 25 (Randolph and Moore counties) in the senate from 1870 to 1874. A Whig and a Quaker, he was first elected to the senate in 1842. During the Civil War, Worth served as state salt commissioner and as colonel of the Sixty-seventh N.C. Regiment (Senior Reserves). As state treasurer from 1876 to 1885, he led the settlement of the state debt and the revision of the tax laws. The "Worth bill" was apparently SB 241 (an act to adjust the public debt), which the senator introduced on January 17. He was also the author of SB 260 (another act to adjust the public debt), which was introduced on December 10 but died in committee. *Journal of the Senate of the General Assembly of the State of North Carolina at its Session of 1873-'74* (Raleigh: Stowe and Uzzell, 1873 [*sic*]), 10, 145-146, 249-250, 271-274; *House Journal 1873-'74*, 368, 376, 491; *Dictionary of North Carolina Biography*, 6:271-272; Senate Bills, General Assembly Session Records, 1873-1874.

44. F. N. Luckey of China Grove represented Rowan County. On his motion, Turner was excused from attendance in the House on January 21, "on account of duties pertaining to a Joint Select Committee on the Insane Asylum." Edward Ransom (1833-1877) of Columbia represented District 2 (Tyrrell, Washington, Martin, Dare, Beaufort, and Hyde counties). A native of Virginia, he moved to Tyrrell County in the 1850s to farm and practice medicine. Ransom briefly served as assistant surgeon of the Thirty-second N.C. Regiment early in the war. He was elected as a Republican to the state senate in 1872, as an independent to the constitutional convention in 1875, and as a Democrat to the senate in 1876. At the constitutional convention, the Democrats nominated him for president of the body, as he was "one of the independents who had formerly been a Republican but had recently shown signs of inclining towards the Democratic party." Ransom declined the nomination but was ultimately elected anyway. *House Journal 1873-'74*, 309; *Dictionary of North Carolina Biography*, 5:175; Manarin, *North Carolina Troops*, 9:6; Hamilton, *Reconstruction*, 638.

45. Rep. Risden T. Bennett of Anson introduced a bill (HB 198) on December 6 to increase the amount of the homestead and personal property exemption. The measure passed its third reading on January 20 by a vote of 91 to 4, Turner voting with the majority. The bill was sent to the senate for concurrence on January 22. The bill would "increase" the personal property exemption to $500 and the homestead exemption to $1,000, but according to Battle's Revisal, those were the prevailing standards. *House Journal 1873-'74*, 136, 317, 330; House Bills, General Assembly Session Records, 1873-1874; William H. Battle, comp., *Battle's Revisal of the Public Statutes of North Carolina* (Raleigh: Edwards, Broughton and Co., 1873), c. 55, ss. 3, 8, 12, pp. 467-469.

46. Rep. J. R. Maxwell of Sampson County introduced a resolution (HR 108) on January 20 to raise a joint select committee to report on expenditures at the asylum. The resolution was adopted the same day and sent to the senate for concurrence. Senate amendments (SR 479) were received by the House and agreed to on January 23. House members of the committee were appointed on January 26: Maxwell, Kerr Craig of Rowan, Jacob W. Bowman of Mitchell, S. W. Reid of Mecklenburg, and F. M. Godfrey of Pasquotank. The senate appointed John W. Norwood of Orange, James H. Harris of Wake, and Woodville W. Flemming of McDowell. The resolution noted that it was apparent from the report of the joint standing committee on the asylum "that certain expenditures for provisions are unreasonable and extravagant," including $7,957.30 for "sundries." The joint select committee was instructed to "make a minute examination of the expenditures" to determine what extravagancies existed and what was included under the heading of "sundries." Turner's committee report noted that the asylum spent $67,408.27 during the year ending

November 1, 1873, including $20,714.85 for salaries and wages. Prices paid for specific goods included 41½ cents per pound of butter; $10.63 per bushel of flour; 12½ cents per pound of bacon; and 97 cents per gallon of syrup. *House Journal 1873-'74*, 312, 321, 326, 338, 349-350, 377; House Resolutions, General Assembly Session Records, 1873-1874.

47. Turner introduced a bill (HB 453) to regulate the fees of justices of the peace and constables, which was referred to the Committee on Salaries and Fees. On January 28, the committee recommended against its passage. The bill would have raised the fees allowed to justices of the peace and constables for performing various legal actions, such as issuing summons, subpoenas, and executions; taking affidavits; and preparing transcripts of judgment and attachment. *House Journal 1873-'74*, 322, 365; House Bills, General Assembly Session Records, 1873-1874; *Battle's Revisal*, c. 105, s. 26.

48. The bill (SB 306) was introduced in the senate on December 16 by C. Tate Murphy of Magnolia, representing District 14, Sampson County. On January 15, Senator Robert P. Waring of Charlotte (District 29, Mecklenburg County) offered an amendment to reduce the appropriation to $39,000, which was defeated. The bill passed a third reading the following day and was transmitted to the House. The lower chamber considered a House version of the bill (HB 428) section by section on January 22. Motions by J. W. Bean of Randolph and John M. Moring of Chatham to reduce the appropriation of $46,500 were rejected. The second section was amended by motion of M. V. B. Gilbert of Wake, and the bill was passed and returned to the senate for concurrence, which that body did on January 23. *Senate Journal 1873-'74*, 174, 228-229, 234, 247, 263; *House Journal 1873-'74*, 332-333; *Laws and Resolutions 1873-'74*, Public Laws, c. 59, pp. 85-86.

49. Josiah Turner Jr. (1821-1901) was "the most caustic and uncompromising enemy of congressional Reconstruction" in North Carolina. The son of a longtime sheriff and large landowner in Orange County, he was educated at Caldwell Institute in Greensboro and the University of North Carolina and was licensed to practice law about 1845. He served two terms in the state House of Commons and two in the senate before the war. Although opposed to secession, Turner raised a company of cavalry for Confederate service, but suffered a severe wound in April 1862 that curtailed his military career. Elected to the Confederate Congress as a peace candidate in 1863, he joined the opposition to the Davis administration. After the war, he was appointed a director of the North Carolina Railroad and in 1867 was elected president of the road. The following year, Turner bought the Raleigh *Sentinel* with funds borrowed from George W. Swepson, who was heavily implicated in the railroad bonds scandal. Turner quickly made the paper the leading Conservative organ, an antidote to the Raleigh *Standard* of his principal political rival, William W. Holden. The caustic Turner, the absolute "master of polemical journalism," contributed as much as anyone to the impeachment and removal of Governor Holden in 1870. J. G. deRoulhac Hamilton called Turner "a man of positive genius for political warfare, sparing not and caring little where he struck. Quick-witted, ingenious in putting an opponent on the defensive and keeping him there, and at the same time ignoring a counter attack, gifted with a keen sense of humor, he saw the ridiculous side of everything and employed it as a means to an end, realizing clearly that in politics a dangerous enemy is often rendered harmless by laughter and ridicule." Turner's erratic and destructive temperament eventually alienated his Conservative allies. In 1878, he was again elected to the state House but expelled for disorderly attacks upon his colleagues. *Dictionary of North Carolina Biography*, 6:67; Hamilton, *Reconstruction*, 388.

50. Judge Samuel W. Watts was a superior court judge (District 6) from Franklinton. Josiah Turner, who "had a diabolical genius for applying devastating nicknames to his enemies," reserved his "most withering" for Judge Watts, who was "known equally for his judicial

ineptitude and for his incredible dishevelment." Watts became "Greasy Sam," a nickname that "became synonymous with arrant incompetence" across the state. The ridicule Turner heaped upon Watts "prompted the North Carolina Bar Association to initiate the rotation of superior court judges. No county wanted 'Greasy Sam' longer than the mandatory two-week term." According to James A. Padgett, Watts was "mixed up in the railroad graft of the state, was ignorant and corrupt as a judge, and was allied with the carpetbaggers." Hamilton also described him as "ignorant and corrupt, being hand in glove with the corrupt carpetbaggers. . . . He was a bitter partisan and was very active in politics, taking the stump in every campaign, or rather making one of the bench." A committee was appointed by the General Assembly of 1870-1871 to investigate his conduct but chose not to impeach. Albion Winegar Tourgée (1838-1905) was "for many years the most thoroughly hated man in North Carolina." A native of Ohio, he served in the western theater during the Civil War, spending four months in Confederate prisons after being captured at the Battle of Perryville. After the war, he moved to North Carolina, leasing a nursery near Greensboro. Trained in journalism and the law, he soon became involved in radical Republican politics, organizing Loyal Reconstruction Leagues, publishing and editing two newspapers, and championing the rights of African Americans. Tourgée was elected to the state constitutional convention in 1868 and served as one of the three commissioners who rewrote the state's legal code. That same year, he was elected superior court judge in a district (Seventh) that became a hotbed of Ku Klux Klan atrocities. During his six years on the bench, Tourgée "provoked intense opposition with his outspoken, effective, and equalitarian Republicanism." But his knowledge and equal application of the law, as well as the obvious courage of his convictions, earned him the grudging respect of at least some of his political foes. Thad Stem Jr., "Absent with Leave, or How Musty Files Came Alive," *North Carolina Historical Review* 51 (spring 1974), 179; James A. Padgett, ed., "Reconstruction Letters from North Carolina, Part IX," *North Carolina Historical Review* 21 (January 1944), 59 n. 169; Hamilton, *Reconstruction*, 415, 561; *Dictionary of North Carolina Biography*, 6:47-48.

51. Josiah Turner's petition demanded the impeachment of Watts for "bribe taking, drunkness [*sic*], scandalous conduct in office, and of high crimes and misdemeanors." He accused Watts of "moral and judicial depravity" and charged that he "administers justice in a loose and disgraceful manner." Turner further alleged that Watts had accepted a bribe from John T. Deweese, of which Wake County sheriff Timothy F. Lee had sworn evidence. On January 24, Rep. Risden T. Bennett introduced Turner's petition to impeach Watts. Bennett then introduced another resolution (HR 116) for the same purpose, which was referred to the Committee on the Judiciary. The committee summoned Sheriff Lee, W. F. Askew, Alex McPheeters, Thomas P. Devereux, Gen. William R. Cox, and former Raleigh mayor William H. Harrison to appear on January 30. Among the evidence the committee reviewed was an interrogatory of Devereux that attested to the public drunkenness of Watts during a train excursion to Weldon. The judge succumbed to a mixture of whiskey and brandy, and offered a toast to the American eagle that concluded, "may she never fly so high as that the sun will scorch her Asse." On February 10, Rep. J. W. Bean of Randolph introduced a resolution (HR 142) asking that the committee make their report "at an early date," and that "if the Committee has not been furnished information Corroborating the said charges then the Committee be respectfully instructed to report a resolution condemning the memorialist." The resolution was not adopted. On the final day of the session, the Judiciary Committee reported: "in the investigation of the charges contained within, they have examined a number of witnesses, and that the testimony adduced does not sustain the charges. They further request that they were referred to a number of witnesses residing beyond the limits of the State, whose attendance it was impossible for the committee to

procure; they, therefore, ask to be discharged from its further consideration." The report was accepted and the committee discharged. Hamilton concluded that, "on account of the impossibility of conviction, because of the fact that so many important witnesses were outside the State, it was inexpedient to impeach." House Resolutions, General Assembly Session Records, 1873-1874; Petitions, General Assembly Session Records, 1873-1874; *House Journal 1873-'74,* 341, 343, 560; Hamilton, *Reconstruction*, 598.

52. The "election bill" (HB 193) was introduced by Rep. Kerr Craig of Rowan on December 6. On January 23, the bill was read a second time, upon which several amendments were inserted, and the measure passed. It was sent to the senate for concurrence the following day. Senate amendments were received on February 11, and the amended bill was ratified and returned to the senate on February 14. *House Journal 1873-'74*, 136, 339-340, 342, 496, 540.

53. A bill concerning the election of certain officers to replace the governor's appointees (SB 276, HB 571) was introduced in the senate by Charles Price of Mocksville (representing District 30, Rowan and Davie counties) on December 13. It was read a second time and amended on January 23. The House received the bill on February 5; the following day, the Committee on the Judiciary recommended against its passage. On February 10, the bill was considered a second time, with amendments proposed by the committee adopted. Originally the bill provided for election of the superintendent of public instruction (Republican James Reid had been elected in 1872, but died before assuming office); two N.C. Supreme Court justices to replace Thomas Settle and R. P. Dick, both of whom had resigned; and two superior court judges to replace E. W. Jones, who had resigned, and D. H. Starbuck, who declined the appointment. The House amendment removed the two judgeships from the bill. Discussion of the measure resumed the next day, and the bill passed by a vote of 54 to 42. Turner was late in returning for the evening session and missed the roll call. The bill passed a third reading on February 12 by a vote of 60 to 44, Turner voting in the affirmative. The senate concurred in the House amendment later that day. *Senate Journal 1873-'74*, 156, 268; *House Journal 1873-'74*, 436, 441, 500, 503, 513; Senate Bills, General Assembly Session Records, 1873-1874.

54. Risden Tyler Bennett (1840-1913) of Wadesboro represented Anson County. Before the war, he studied law under Richmond Pearson. He enlisted in the Anson Guards (Company C of the Fourteenth N.C. Regiment) at age twenty-one and was mustered in as a corporal. Bennett was promoted to sergeant on June 1, 1861, and appointed assistant commissary of subsistence with the rank of captain on September 28. He was elected lieutenant colonel of the regiment on April 27, 1862, and promoted to colonel, July 5, 1862, upon the death of Philetus W. Roberts. Bennett was wounded at Gettysburg, Spotsylvania Courthouse, and Cold Harbor. He was captured at Winchester, Virginia, on September 19, 1864, and confined at Fort Delaware until paroled on February 27, 1865. Bennett served in the General Assembly (1872-1874), the Constitutional Convention of 1875, Congress (1885-1887), and as a superior court judge. He donated one thousand books to start a public library at Wadesboro. *Dictionary of North Carolina Biography*, 1:138; Manarin, *North Carolina Troops*, 5:393-394, 415.

55. Turner's bill (HB 477) was referred to the Committee on Corporations, which recommended passage on January 27. The House passed the bill on February 6 and ordered it to be engrossed and sent to the senate. The measure was ratified on February 13. *Laws and Resolutions 1873-'74*, Private Laws, c. 99, pp. 422-423; *House Journal 1873-'74*, 343, 357, 445; House Bills, General Assembly Session Records, 1873-1874.

56. *Our Living and Our Dead* was published by Stephen Decatur Pool for the North Carolina Branch of the Southern Historical Society, first (1873-1874) in New Bern as a weekly in newspaper format, then (1874-1876) in Raleigh as a monthly magazine. "Its purpose was to present war reminiscences, registers of North Carolina troops, miscellaneous sketches, diaries, letters from correspondents, state news, and literary contributions." It was succeeded by the *Southern Historical Monthly*. Pool (1819-1901) was a native of Elizabeth City, where he was the principal of Elizabeth City Academy and editor of a Whig newspaper, *The Old North State*. He was commissioned captain of Company H, Tenth Regiment N.C. Troops in May 1861. He was captured at Fort Macon in April 1862 and subsequently exchanged. Pool was promoted to lieutenant colonel in October 1862 and to colonel in September 1863. After the war, he edited a New Bern newspaper (1866-1876) as well as *Our Living and Our Dead*. He served as clerk of the House of Representatives in 1873-1874 and as state superintendent of public instruction in 1875-1876. Pool was forced to resign from the latter position because of misappropriation of funds; he allegedly took money from the Peabody Fund to buy a house and lot in Raleigh. Afterwards he moved to New Orleans. Ray M. Atchison, "*Our Living and Our Dead*: A Post-bellum North Carolina Magazine of Literature and History," *North Carolina Historical Review* 40 (autumn 1963), 423-433; *Dictionary of North Carolina Biography*, 5:120-121; Hamilton, *Reconstruction*, 618.

Turner used the penname "Leroy" on at least three occasions. On April 13, 1874, he mailed an article to Pool that narrated the history of Company A of the Thirty-third Regiment at the Battle of New Bern, which was published in *Our Living and Our Dead* on April 22. On May 7, Turner submitted the first extract from his prison journal, which covered the period that the Confederate captives spent aboard the *Albany* in the Neuse River. This was published on May 20 under the heading, "Extracts From the Prison Journal of a Confederate." Both submissions were signed, "Leroy." Some time thereafter, he prepared a second extract. Titled "Extracts from my Prison Journal," the four-page narrative related the journey from Neuse River to Castle Williams and bore the same signature.

57. Burton Kimsey Dickey (1813-1885), a wealthy merchant from Murphy, represented Cherokee County. Turner and Dickey attended the First Baptist Church of Raleigh, at the corner of Salisbury and Edenton streets. The scripture verse was probably from Mark 2:13-17, which concludes, "And when the scribes and Pharisees saw him eat with publicans and sinners, they said unto his disciples, How is it that he eateth and drinketh with publicans and sinners? When Jesus heard it, he saith unto them, They that are whole have no need of the physician, but they that are sick: I came not to call the righteous, but sinners to repentance." *See also* Matthew 9:9-13 and Luke 5:27-32.

58. F. M. Jordan arrived at the First Baptist Church on January 15, 1874, to assist the pastor in conducting revival services and, according to the *Daily News*, was still there ten days later. Rev. F. M. Jordan has been called the "prince of itinerant missionaries." Over a period of sixty years, he "covered the greater part of all North Carolina and baptized between 5,000 to [*sic*] 7,000 Baptists and aided in establishing scores of churches." Beginning in 1871, he gathered the membership that would form the First Baptist Church of Winston-Salem, but resigned from that congregation in 1874. He was also a member of the board of trustees of Wake Forest College. The reference to the text in Haggai is from Chapter 1:1-12. First Baptist Church, Raleigh, N.C., Church Minutes, 1856-1874 (microfilm), North Carolina State Archives, Raleigh, entry for January 15, 1874; (Raleigh) *Daily News*, January 25, 1874; M. A. Huggins, *A History of North Carolina Baptists, 1727-1932* (Raleigh: General Board of the Baptist State Convention of North Carolina, 1967), 276; George Washington Paschal, *History of Wake Forest College*, 3 vols. (Wake Forest: Wake Forest College, 1935-1943), 2:74.

59. Thomas Henderson Pritchard (1832-1896) was pastor of the First Baptist Church of Raleigh from 1868 to 1878. A native of Charlotte and son of a Baptist minister, he graduated from Wake Forest College in 1854 and was ordained the following year. During the war, he served as chaplain to Gen. John B. Gordon's corps of the Army of Northern Virginia. Pritchard was a trustee of the University of North Carolina, Wake Forest College, and the Southern Baptist Theological Seminary. He served as chairman of the Board of Missions of the Baptist State Convention for seven years and as president of Wake Forest College from 1879 to 1882. The church minutes identify those baptized that evening as William Farriss, John W. Upchurch, James Williamson, Henry Allen, and John Enniss. *Dictionary of North Carolina Biography*, 5:149-150; First Baptist Church Minutes, January 25, 1874.

60. Senator Phineas T. Horton of Elkville represented District 34 (Iredell, Wilkes, and Alexander counties). During the war, he served two years in the Twenty-sixth N.C. Regiment, enlisting in Wilkes County on June 12, 1861, at the age of thirty-four. He was immediately elected second lieutenant of Company C but resigned on August 30. Horton was appointed regimental assistant commissary of subsistence with the rank of captain on October 14, 1861. He was present and accounted for until dropped from the rolls for unspecified reasons on August 26, 1863. Horton represented Wilkes County in the lower House in 1860, 1864, 1865, and 1866, and in the senate in 1872. Senator J. W. Todd of Jefferson represented District 35 (Alleghany, Ashe, and Watauga counties), John G. Marler of Yadkinville represented Yadkin County, and John M. Carson of Taylorsville represented Alexander County. Adelaide Boylan (1832-1909) was the "reputed daughter" of John H. Boylan (d. 1870), a son of William Boylan (1777-1861), who "at one time . . . owned most of southwest Raleigh." The younger Boylan inherited his father's Cape Fear Plantation in Chatham County and several lots in the town of Haywood. Adelaide, who managed her father's domestic affairs during the last eighteen or twenty years of his life, was probably acquainted with Turner's sister Julia, who lived in Haywood. Miss Thomas (elsewhere in the diary "Miss Thompson of Pittsboro") is unidentified. Manarin, *North Carolina Troops*, 7:464, 494; *Dictionary of North Carolina Biography*, 1:205; Will of John H. Boylan, 1870, Wake County Record of Wills (microfilm), 35:105-106, North Carolina State Archives, Raleigh; Will of William Boylan, 1861, Wake County Wills, North Carolina State Archives, Raleigh; Will of Adelaide Boylan, 1909, Wake County Wills; Carroll, *They Lived in Raleigh*, 14.

61. The Statesville *Intelligencer* was established by Charles R. Jones in 1872 as a Conservative newspaper when Eugene B. Drake's *Statesville American* switched its party affiliation to Republican. In January 1874, Jones bought the *Charlotte Observer* and left Statesville. "His move was no doubt accelerated by personal trouble in Statesville, trouble that ended with a physical attack on the editor." L. S. G. is unidentified. Keever, *Iredell Piedmont County*, 293.

62. Rep. William H. McLaurin, an African American legislator from New Hanover, introduced a bill (HB 412) on January 17 to incorporate St. John's Lodge, No. 12, Free and Accepted A. Y. Masons, in Greensboro. The measure barely passed by a vote of 36 to 34 on January 26, Turner voting in the affirmative. Two additional favorable votes were recorded the following day. The bill passed with an amendment in the senate on February 10, and the amended version (SB 551) was approved by the House the next day. Hezekiah Alexander Gudger (1849-1917) of Marshall represented Madison County. He later served a term as state senator from Buncombe County. Once an ardent Democrat, he switched to the Republican Party over the sound money issue. Gudger was head of the North Carolina Institution for the Deaf and Dumb and Blind from 1877 to 1883. He served two terms (1891-1892) as Grand Master of the Grand Lodge of Masons in North Carolina, as consul general to Panama (1897-1907), and as a justice on the Supreme Court of the Canal Zone (1907-1914). *House Journal*

1873-'74, 294, 346, 354, 356, 501, 523; House Bills, General Assembly Session Records, 1873-1874; *Dictionary of North Carolina Biography*, 2:382.

63. In the 1870 federal census of Raleigh Township, the inhabitants of "Mrs. Pullen's boarding house" were listed in household #318. The head of the household was James Pullen, 50, landlord. Also listed were Nancy Pullen, 42, keeping house, and two children, John, 17, and Lizzie, 16. The boardinghouse was on McDowell Street near Hargett. Ninth Census of the United States, 1870, Population Schedule: Wake County, N.C.; *Chataigne's Directory, 1875-'76*, 104.

64. On December 1, 1873, Rep. Hezekiah A. Gudger introduced a bill (HB 112) "to prohibit the sale of spirituous liquors in townships where the people so determine." Amendments proposed by the Committee on Propositions and Grievances were discussed and other amendments offered on December 13. The bill was then referred to the Committee on the Judiciary, which added further amendments and recommended passage. It passed a second reading as amended on February 7. During the third reading on February 10, further amendments were proposed and rejected, and the bill passed by a vote of 67 to 35, Turner voting with the majority. It was approved by the senate and became law on the last day of the session. *Laws and Resolutions 1873-'74*, Public Laws, c. 138, pp. 222-224; *House Journal 1873-'74*, 95, 198, 357, 458-459, 484-486, 493.

65. This bill (HB 439, SB 585), one of several considered during the session to amend the charter of the North Carolina Railroad Company (ratified December 20, 1873), was introduced by Rep. Risden T. Bennett on January 20. The Committee on Internal Improvements recommended its passage with amendment. The measure was recommitted to the committee on January 26 and further amended. The bill was approved by the House on January 28 and transmitted to the senate for concurrence. The senate Committee on Internal Improvements recommended against passage, preferring another version of the bill that originated in the upper chamber. *House Journal 1873-'74*, 314, 319-320, 337, 351, 361-363, 369, 375; House Bills, General Assembly Session Records, 1873-1874.

66. R. B. B. Houston of Catawba Station represented Catawba County, and J. G. H. Mitchell of Red Shoals represented Stokes County.

67. Dr. Eugene Grissom (1831-1902) was superintendent of the state asylum for the insane. A native of Granville County, he earned a degree in medicine from the University of Pennsylvania in 1858. On August 10, 1861, he was appointed captain of a company of infantry raised in Granville and Wake counties that was subsequently designated Company D of the Thirtieth N.C. Regiment. Grissom was wounded during a skirmish near Richmond on June 22, 1862. After brief service on the staff of Dr. Edward Warren, surgeon general of North Carolina, he resigned his commission to accept a seat in the North Carolina House of Commons. Grissom served as private secretary to W. W. Holden in the provisional government of 1865 and contributed to Holden's defense fund when the governor was impeached. In 1868, Grissom was appointed by Holden to head the asylum, replacing Dr. Edward C. Fisher. According to Hamilton, Grissom "had been active in politics since the war and had been a radical member of the convention of 1868. His politics constituted his sole title to the place." Yet he introduced new methods for treating mental illness and successfully urged the opening of branch hospitals in Morganton and Goldsboro. In 1889, he was acquitted but disgraced after a lurid trial for alleged abuse of patients and female staffers. Afterwards Grissom moved to Colorado. He committed suicide on the front porch of his son's home in Washington, D.C., in 1902. *Dictionary of North Carolina Biography*, 2:378; Manarin, *North Carolina Troops*, 8:352; Horace W. Raper, *William W. Holden: North*

Carolina's Political Enigma (Chapel Hill: University of North Carolina Press, 1985), 222, 276 n. 21; Hamilton, *Reconstruction*, 345.

68. J. S. Anderson of Hayesville represented Clay County. There were only two "Lines" listed in Clay County in the index to the federal census of 1870: Archibald C. Lyon, forty-six, and John A. Lyon, twenty-two, both of Hayesville Township.

69. Harrison M. Waugh of Dobson represented Surry County. He either harbored intense personal animosity toward Professor Kerr, or sincerely considered a geological survey and natural history museum inappropriate usages of state funds. On November 22, he introduced a resolution (HR 21) that would require Kerr to provide a detailed statement of expenditures for the geological survey for the years 1870-1873. The resolution was adopted by the House on December 2 and by the senate three days later. In the discussion in the House on January 26 of HB 228, a bill to prevent fraud in the sale of commercial manure, Waugh moved to strike the words "State Geologist" wherever they appeared, but his motion was rejected. On February 11, Waugh introduced another resolution (HR 147), asking for the appointment of a committee to investigate the expenditures of the state geologist and to examine his books. Another bill by Waugh (HB 404) to repeal c. 2, ss. 13-17 of the Revised Code, effectively abolishing the office of state geologist, was introduced on January 16. It was tabled on motion of Rep. John E. Brown of Mecklenburg on January 28 by a vote of 57 to 45 (Turner voted to table). A similar measure (SB 533) was offered in the senate that day by Senator W. H. Avera of Selma (representing District 17, Johnston County) and made the special order for discussion on January 30. Senate Bills, General Assembly Session Records, 1873-1874; House Resolutions, General Assembly Session Records, 1873-1874; *House Journal 1873-'74*, 285, 350, 371-372, 495; *Laws and Resolutions 1873-'74*, Public Laws, c. 69, pp. 96-97.

70. Washington Caruthers Kerr (1827-1885) was a native of Guilford County. Orphaned by the age of thirteen, he was educated by his pastor and mentor, Eli Washington Caruthers, and at the University of North Carolina, where he graduated with highest honors in 1850. After working for nearly five years in the office of the *National Almanac* in Cambridge, Mass., he served as professor of chemistry, mineralogy, and geology at Davidson College from 1857 to 1862. During the war, Kerr was chemist and superintendent of the Mecklenburg Salt Company near Charleston, S.C. He was appointed state geologist by Governor Vance in 1864, "but conditions in North Carolina during the final year of the Civil War precluded either systematic work or a salary." Gov. Jonathan Worth reappointed him to the position in 1866. Kerr's situation did not greatly improve after the war, as he was continually vexed by "the periodic meeting of the legislature and the inevitable confrontation between the state geologist, who favored plans for long-range economic development, and legislators, who expected immediate results of funds appropriated." The annual appropriation of $5,000 for the geological survey would not permit him to hire permanent assistants. Nevertheless, by 1870, Kerr had completed a statewide survey, but the legislature "placed so low a priority on the work" that his report was not published until 1875. Finally, beset by deteriorating health, he resigned in 1882 to join the U.S. Geological Survey. He died three years later and was buried in Oakwood Cemetery in Raleigh. *Dictionary of North Carolina Biography*, 3:357-358.

By joint resolution dated March 3, 1873, the General Assembly authorized Kerr to prepare exhibits for the World's Exposition at Vienna, in order to advertise the resources and products of North Carolina to potential immigrants and trade interests, " 'provided the expenses would be defrayed by the General Government.' " The exhibits included maps and samples of the state's natural resources and produce, including cotton, tobacco, grains, silk cocoons, minerals, and ninety-five specimens of wood. Kerr consulted with the U.S. chief commissioner, who told him that his funds were already exhausted. "There seemed nothing left to do but to abandon the enterprise, since the resolution . . . did not authorize any further expenditure out of the geological fund than was necessary to prepare the required exhibits. At this juncture several public-spirited citizens, appreciating the importance to North Carolina of having her resources & industries properly represented at this greatest of all world expositions, offered to advance the necessary funds." The resolution (SR 176, HR 96) to reimburse citizens who had advanced money to defray Kerr's expenses $1,277.65 apiece originated in the joint select committee assigned to consider Kerr's report on the exposition, which Governor Caldwell transmitted to the General Assembly on November 19. It was introduced in the senate on December 5 and in the House two weeks later. On January 21, the House Committee on Finance recommended against passage of the resolution. On January 29, Representative Bennett offered as an amendment that the reimbursement be taken from the "annual appropriations for geological purposes for the year 1874." Waugh moved to table the resolution, but his motion was voted down 62 to 44 (Turner voted against). Bennett's motion was eventually rejected, as was the resolution. *House Journal 1873-'74*, 245, 319, 377-378; Governor's Messages, General Assembly Session Records, 1873-1874; draft of report by W. C. Kerr to Gov. Tod R. Caldwell, November 7, 1873, Miscellaneous Reports, General Assembly Session Records, 1873-1874.

71. Howell C. Moss of Wilson represented Wilson County, John E. Brown of Charlotte represented Mecklenburg, and Montford McGehee (1822-1895) of Cunningham's Store represented Person County. A graduate of the University of North Carolina, McGehee attended law school at Harvard, read law under W. H. Battle, and opened a practice in Milton. He was a Whig before the war and a Democrat afterwards. He married a daughter of George E. Badger. McGehee was first elected to the assembly in 1864 from Caswell County and in 1872 from Person. He was a member of the board of trustees of the university from 1864 to 1868 and again from 1877 to 1893. Along with his brother-in-law, Richard C. Badger, a Republican, McGehee was credited with the 1871 ordinance transferring the appointment of university trustees from the Board of Education, as provided in the Constitution of 1868, back to the General Assembly, allowing the university to reopen in 1875. He served as commissioner of agriculture from 1880 to 1887. *Dictionary of North Carolina Biography*, 4:148.

72. The bill calling for a new county of Lillington (SB 185, HB 387) originated in the senate. On December 6, George L. Mabson, an African American senator from Wilmington, introduced legislation to create a new county to be called Jefferson. Senator C. Tate Murphy of Sampson County offered an amendment on January 13 to substitute "Lillington" for "Jefferson," which was overwhelmingly approved. The bill passed its third reading in the senate on January 14. It was announced in the House on January 28 and rejected the next day by a vote of 54 to 53 (Turner voted for). *Senate Journal 1873-'74*, 97, 219, 221-222, 229; *House Journal 1873-'74*, 371, 379-380.

73. The 1871 Badger–McGehee ordinance transferring election of university trustees to the General Assembly became part of the Constitution of 1873 after approval by the populace and was incorporated into the Constitution of 1876. Under the provisions of a statute ratified the previous day, the assembly convened in a special afternoon session on January 29 to elect by joint ballot sixty-four trustees, eight from each congressional district. The results returned only two members of the previous board, which had been selected by the Board of Education, while a number of prominent members of the pre-1868 board were returned to office. When the newly constituted board met in Raleigh on February 18, Governor Caldwell declined to preside, saying that the assembly had no power to elect trustees. He denied the validity of the constitutional amendment and refused to recognize the board. *Laws and Resolutions 1873-'74*, Public Laws, c. 64, pp. 90-91; Kemp P. Battle, *History of the*

University of North Carolina, 2 vols. (Spartanburg, S.C.: The Reprint Company, 1974), 2:50-51; Hamilton, *Reconstruction*, 629.

Rep. F. N. Luckey of Rowan submitted the nominations for the Seventh District, which included Turner's choice, E. Hayne Davis of Statesville. Davis enlisted in Surry County on October 7, 1861, as a private in what would become Company E of the Third Regiment N.C. Cavalry (Forty-first N.C. Regiment). He was appointed ordnance sergeant of the company on May 1, 1862, and captain of Company H of the Fifty-fifth N.C. Regiment on October 10, 1862. His resignation because of an unspecified illness was accepted on March 10, 1863. He subsequently served as drillmaster in the Confederate Conscription Bureau and as assistant enrolling officer in North Carolina. He was appointed assistant adjutant general in Brig. Gen. Robert D. Johnston's brigade in February 1865. He was the father of lawyer, author, and lecturer Hayne Davis (1868-1942). *House Journal 1873-'74*, 380, 385; Manarin, *North Carolina Troops*, 2:214-215, 13:506.

74. Bernice B. Culbreth was an 1858 graduate of Trinity College. He was assigned as pastor of the Cape Fear Circuit in 1869 and the Jonesboro Circuit in 1870. In 1873-1874, he served the Methodist Church as agent for Trinity College. On February 6, 1874, George W. Reid of Randolph introduced a bill (HB 583) to amend the charter of Trinity College, which might explain Culbreth's presence at the Capitol. He preached the evening service at Edenton Street Methodist Church on January 25. C. Franklin Grill, *Methodism in the Upper Cape Fear Valley* (Nashville: The Parthenon Press, 1966), 79, 80, 89; *House Journal 1873-'74*, 443; (Raleigh) *Daily News*, January 25, 1874.

75. The Wyches had a one-year-old daughter, listed as Martha in the 1870 federal census of Chatham County. Her name was actually Bertha, born July 16, 1870. Ninth Census of the United States, 1870, Population Schedule: Chatham County, N.C.

76. It was actually the Machinery Bill (HB 458) being discussed. The bill was read section by section, with many amendments and separate votes. The discussion continued the next day with further amendments, but the bill was finally passed and ordered to be engrossed. *House Journal 1873-'74*, 392-395, 399-402.

77. Household #303 in the 1870 federal census of Raleigh Township consisted of Thomas Fentress, 53, tailor; Margaret, 47, keeping house; Blanch, 25, teaching school; Thomas, 24, clerk in store; Maggie, 18, music teacher; Herbert, 13; Lula, 10; and Effie, 7. A directory of North Carolina businesses in 1866-1867 included in its list of hotels, etc. "Boarding House, Fayetteville street, Raleigh, Mrs. T. R. Fentress, proprietor." Ninth Census of the United States, 1870, Population Schedule: Wake County, N.C.; *Branson & Farrar's Business Directory, 1866-'67*, 96.

78. The Yarborough House on Fayetteville Street opposite the Wake County Courthouse was the most prestigious hotel in Raleigh. It was once called the third house of state government; from 1871 to 1891, the hotel served as the unofficial residence for several governors, as there was no executive mansion during that period. The hotel was built by architect Dabney Cosby and opened in 1850 under the original owner, Edward Yarbrough. It was purchased in the mid-sixties by J. M. Blair, who added the first "o" to the spelling (Yarborough). Proprietor George W. Blacknall remodeled and enlarged the building in the 1870s and adopted the spelling, "Yarboro." The hotel was destroyed by fire on July 3, 1928. Murray, *Wake*, 372, n. 179.

79. Turner's resolution (HR 100) to raise a joint select committee on adjournment was introduced and placed on the calendar on January 17, Brown's (HR 121) on January 28. Turner's resolution disappears from the record, but Brown's was read a second time,

amended, and adopted on January 31. Brown's version would raise a joint committee to determine whether remaining business would permit adjournment on February 9, but it was amended to read "the earliest day" upon which it could safely be done. *House Journal 1873-'74*, 293, 367, 402-403; House Resolutions, General Assembly Session Records, 1873-1874.

80. According to the *Daily News*, R. F. Simonton arrived at the Yarborough House on January 28. John McLeod Turner was engrossing clerk for the senate during the 1873-1874 session. During the war, he enlisted in what would become Company F of the Seventh Regiment N.C. State Troops. Born in Washington, D.C., he was a resident of Rowan County, a twenty-one-year-old engineer, upon enlistment. He was appointed captain of the company on May 16, 1861. Turner was wounded at New Bern, Second Manassas, and in the lungs at Fredericksburg. He was still absent wounded when promoted to major on May 3, 1863. Turner commanded his regiment at Gettysburg, where he was wounded in the abdomen while leading a charge and captured on July 3. He was confined at Fort McHenry and Fort Delaware until exchanged on September 18, 1864. Promoted to lieutenant colonel, November 28, 1864, Turner was paroled at Salisbury on May 1, 1865. According to one report, he was pierced by eleven bullets during the war and was partially paralyzed. He died in 1882. (Raleigh) *Daily News*, January 29, 1874; Manarin, *North Carolina Troops*, 4:405, 462, 744.

81. Robert W. Best was secretary of state from 1865 to 1868. Cheney gives his residence upon election (December 1, 1865) as Greene County, and notes: "Best may have been appointed earlier by Holden following the resignation of [Charles R.] Thomas since his name appears beneath that of Thomas in the Record Book; however, only the date 1865 is given. He was later elected by the General Assembly and served until the new constitution was put into effect in 1868." In the 1870 federal census of Raleigh Township, Robert Best, 37, was listed as a life insurance agent. Also in the household were Abselah, 45; Annie, 13; Sally, 9; Minnie, 7; and Roberta, 4. John L. Cheney Jr., *North Carolina Government, 1585-1979: A Narrative and Statistical History* (Raleigh: North Carolina Department of the Secretary of State, 1981), 194 n. 11; Ninth Census of the United States, 1870, Population Schedule: Wake County, N.C.

82. The Presbyterian Church was at the corner of Salisbury and Morgan streets. The *Daily Sentinel* (January 31, 1874) referred to Rev. Thomas Whaney of Virginia; the *Daily News* (February 1) correctly identified him as the Reverend Mr. Wharey. Thomas Wharey was an 1852 graduate of Hampden-Sydney College. He was "early recognized as an earnest and eloquent preacher and soon won the sobriquet, 'the Spurgeon of Virginia.' " Late in life, he had charge of a classical academy at Worsham, Virginia, and a pastorate at Briery Church in Prince Edward County. He died at Corsicana, Texas, where he had accepted a call. According to Richard McIlwaine, a college classmate, Wharey was "one of the loveliest of men, acknowledged on all hands as far ahead of any of his fellow-students as a preacher." If he had any fault as a speaker, "it was that he was too pathetic, while one of the most genial fellows in the world and full of fun. His voice, manner, and utterance were all plaintive. He exhibited pathos in everything he said and did." The murderer referred to in Wharey's sermon is Cain. The passage is from Genesis 5:20, in which God says to Cain: "What hast thou done? The voice of thy brother's blood cries unto me from the ground." (Raleigh) *Daily Sentinel*, January 31, 1874; (Raleigh) *Daily News*, February 1, 1874; Richard McIlwaine, *Memories of Three Score Years and Ten* (New York and Washington: The Neale Publishing Company, 1908), 61, 110-111.

83. The only Armstrong listed in the index to the minutes of the First Baptist Church for this period is a John Armstrong (in the minutes, all male members of the congregation are

referred by their surname only, with the title "bro.") The 1880 Raleigh city directory listed a John Armstrong as the proprietor of a bookbindery and blank book manufacturer in the Bagley Building. First Baptist Church Minutes; Emerson, *Raleigh Directory, 1880-'81*, 43.

84. The revenue bill (HB 459) was read in the House that day section by section, with numerous amendments offered. On February 3, it was read for the third time, again by sections. Turner offered an amendment to strike the words "for no other purpose" and insert "for other necessary purposes" in line 5, section 3, Class 1, but it was rejected. The bill passed 67 to 27, Turner voting with the majority, and was sent to the senate for concurrence on February 5. *House Journal 1873-'74*, 406-412, 417-421, 434.

85. Charles A. Carlton was a Statesville merchant and clerk to the town commissioners. The municipal records were reportedly burned in his store next to the Village Hotel in an 1854 fire. In 1874, he was county treasurer of Iredell County. He was also agent for the Statesville branch of the Bank of North Carolina. Keever, *Iredell Piedmont County*, 161, 163, 250; Wheeler, *Legislative Manual for 1874*, 257.

86. Turner's older sister, Sarah "Sallie" Elizabeth (1840-1910), married Newton A. Holman (ca. 1836-1901). Holman was a lumberman from Davie County who took his wife off to live in the woods of Tennessee and was often away on business. The Holmans lived near Moscow in Fayette County in southwestern Tennessee. After her husband's death, Sarah eventually went mad and died in the asylum at Morganton in 1916. Unidentified newspaper clippings, n.d., in Turner Family Papers, Burlington.

87. Turner introduced a petition from "citizens of Iredell, residing near Catawba church" on February 4, which was referred to the Committee on Propositions and Grievances. The African American petitioners stated that there was a house for the retail of liquor within two hundred yards of the church and asked that the sale of liquor be prohibited within one mile of the building. It was signed by twenty-three members of the congregation, as well as by six whites: R. A. Alexander, John F. Moore, J. R. McNeely, Isaac Harris, P. C. Carlton, and W. P. Turner. Isaac Harris was one of five town commissioners of Mooresville named in the 1873 act of incorporation, and he later served as mayor. He was a member of the board of county commissioners in 1874. He was also a large shareholder in the first cotton factory in Mooresville. *House Journal 1873-'74*, 422; Petitions, General Assembly Session Records, 1873-1874; Keever, *Iredell Piedmont County*, 275, 280, 353; Wheeler, *Legislative Manual for 1874*, 257.

88. The Raleigh and Gaston Railroad switching yard and machine shops were located at the north end of McDowell Street, three blocks from Mrs. Evans's boardinghouse.

89. Matthew Locke McCorkle (1817-1899) was born in Catawba County. He graduated from Davidson College and studied law under Chief Justice Richmond Pearson, opening a law practice in Newton in 1845. He was appointed interim clerk of superior court the following year and was subsequently elected to the office, serving until 1850. During the war, he organized a company, the Catawba Guards, which was mustered into service as Company F of the Twenty-third N.C. Regiment. Forty-three years old upon enlistment, McCorkle was elected captain of the company on June 6, 1861. He resigned because of ill health, ca. April 16, 1862, and subsequently served as major and commander of McCorkle's Battalion of the Senior Reserves. He served in the state senate, 1864-1867, and as a member of the Constitutional Convention of 1875. McCorkle was appointed judge of the Eleventh Judicial District by Gov. Daniel G. Fowle in June 1890. He was one of the first five city commissioners of Newton (1855) and president of the board of trustees of Catawba College. http://www.rootsweb.com/~nccatawb/McCorkle/d121.htm; Manarin, *North Carolina Troops*, 7:195.

90. On February 4, Turner introduced a resolution (HR 131) "to secure the attendance of certain non-residents, as witnesses concerning the impeachment of Judge Watts," which was placed on the calendar. The following day he moved for immediate consideration of the resolution, which was read and adopted. The resolution stated: "Whereas John T. Deweese and G. A. Mason non residents are said to be in the possession of facts which would establish the guilt of Judge Samuel W. Watts therefore"

"Resolved . . . that the Chairman of the Judiciary Committee of the House be authorized to telegraph them, or such other person or persons, as he may think proper, to the end of securing their attendance as witnesses."

John Thomas Deweese (1835-1906) was born in Arkansas and admitted to the bar in Kentucky in 1856. He entered the Union army on July 6, 1861, as a second lieutenant in the Twenty-fourth Indiana Volunteers, but resigned his commission in February 1862. On August 8, 1862, he was mustered in as a captain in the Fourth Indiana Cavalry and was eventually promoted to colonel. In the reorganization of the army after the war, Deweese was appointed second lieutenant in the Eighth U.S. Infantry, but he resigned his commission in August 1867 when elected to Congress from North Carolina. According to Hamilton, Deweese "had an extended career of disgrace in the army, [and] made a violent attack upon the President for which he was dismissed from the service." In April 1868, he was appointed judge of a probate court with jurisdiction over thirty-two counties and that same year was named register in bankruptcy for North Carolina. He served in Congress from July 1868 to February 28, 1870, when he resigned pending investigation. Deweese was censured by the House on March 1 for selling an appointment to the Naval Academy. He did not return to North Carolina but went to Ohio and resumed his legal practice. G. A. Mason is unidentified. *House Journal 1873-'74*, 425, 438; House Resolutions, General Assembly Session Records, 1873-1874; Hamilton, *Reconstruction*, 239, 247, 490-491; http://bioguide.congress.gov/scripts/biodisplay.pl?index=D000291.

91. Rep. John C. Gorman of Wake County, a member of the firm of Nichols, Gorman, and Neathery Printers of Raleigh, would have had a personal motive for criticizing the current holder of the state printing contract. His amendment, offered in the discussion of SB 512, HB 548 (one of several bills introduced that session to amend the charter of the North Carolina Railroad Company), read: "After the words 'grounds,' in section 11, line 13, insert 'or any one who has charged for the public printing by the letter 'M,' or who has been in any way connected, directly or indirectly, with any printing establishment which has 'overdrawn' from the State Treasury, and has been forced, by legislative action, to disgorge, refund, or make good the said 'overdraw.' " The amendment was rejected by a vote of 58 to 31, Turner voting with the majority. See n. 108 below for a biographical sketch of Gorman. *House Journal 1873-'74*, 431-432; Raper, *Holden*, 246.

92. "Mr. Falls" may refer to Samuel J. Fall, editor of the *Spirit of the Age*, a weekly newspaper published in Raleigh from 1850 to 1894. *Chataigne's Directory, 1875-'76*, 65.

93. The bill concerning North Carolina Railroad Company construction bonds was ratified on December 20, 1873. Worth's bill (SB 241) proposed the issuance of $800,000 of coupon bonds bearing 6 percent interest to pay off the North Carolina Railroad construction bonds, which represented a significant portion of the state debt. The bill was approved in the senate on February 5. In the House, a substitute measure was adopted, but the bill failed its second reading on February 13. *Laws and Resolutions 1873-'74*, Public Laws, c. 33, pp. 34-40; Senate Bills, General Assembly Session Records, 1873-1874.

94. Rep. Edmund Jones of Caldwell introduced the bill (HB 365) "in favor of" contractors on the Marion and Asheville Turnpike on January 13. It was read a second time on February 4, with several amendments offered. Discussion of the measure resumed the next day, and the bill passed 56 to 35, Turner voting in the affirmative. The bill instructed the public treasurer to pay "one half of the amount now due upon all warrants signed by the auditor and now outstanding which were issued to the contractors, officers, or appointees on the Marion and Asheville Turnpike." *House Journal 1873-'74*, 262, 430-431, 437-438, 541; House Bills, General Assembly Session Records, 1873-1874.

95. Robert Franklin Armfield (1829-1898) read law under John A. Gilmer. During the Civil War, he enlisted in Yadkin County at age thirty-one in Company B of the Thirty-eighth N.C. Regiment. He was elected first lieutenant of the company on October 16, 1861, and lieutenant colonel of the regiment, April 18, 1862. Armfield was wounded at Shepherdstown, West Virginia, on September 20, 1862, and resigned from the army in December to accept an appointment as solicitor of the Sixth Judicial District. After the war, he practiced law in Yadkinville, Wilkesboro (1865), and Statesville (1870), where he resided the rest of his life. He was elected to the state senate in 1874 and named president pro-tem after Lt. Gov. Curtis Brogden succeeded the late Governor Caldwell. Armfield was a superior court judge from 1889 to 1895. He won his reputation as a criminal lawyer, defending (with Zebulon B. Vance) Tom Dula. Turner's younger brother, Wilfred Dent Turner, read law under Armfield, and the two attorneys opened a practice in Statesville under the name of Armfield and Turner. After his death, his son, Charles H. Armfield, succeeded him in the practice. There were three Bryans in the 1873-1874 General Assembly: A. C. Bryan of Trap Hill represented Wilkes County; A. M. Bryan of Cherry Lane represented Alleghany County; and William H. Bryan of Newton Grove represented Sampson County. *Dictionary of North Carolina Biography*, 1:41-42; Manarin, *North Carolina Troops*, 10:8, 20; Statesville *Landmark*, August 29, 1899, in Black, *Newspaper Transcripts*, 3:200.

96. Probably William T. Alston, who had represented Warren County in the House of Commons in 1864-1865. The *Daily News* reported that W. T. Alston of Warren arrived at the Yarborough House on February 4. Alston "possessed an unusual degree of intelligence and good judgment. . . . He was very handsome in person, and his charming personality made him many friends and warm admirers." Cheney, *North Carolina Government*, 332; (Raleigh) *Daily News*, February 5, 1874; Lizzie Wilson Montgomery, *Sketches of Old Warrenton North Carolina* (Raleigh: Edwards and Broughton Printing Company, 1924), 360.

97. The railroad consolidation bill (SB 512, HB 548), "to amend the charter of the North Carolina Railroad Company, and for other purposes," was introduced in the senate on January 26 by Lott W. Humphrey of Goldsboro, representing District 10, Wayne and Duplin counties. On January 30, Senator J. W. Todd of Jefferson, representing District 35, Alleghany, Ashe, and Watauga counties, offered the amendment that would effectually bar William A. Smith from a leadership position with the railroad. The bill was received in the House on February 3 and referred to the Committee on Internal Improvements. It passed a second reading on February 5 and, after various amendments were debated, a third reading the next day by a vote of 60 to 38 (Turner voted with the majority). *Senate Journal 1873-'74*, 280, 319-321, 333; *House Journal 1873-'74*, 416, 439, 445-448.

William Alexander Smith (1828-1888) was a native of Warren County who, as a teenager, worked as a day laborer on the Raleigh and Gaston Railroad. He represented Johnston County as a Unionist at the state secession convention and was elected to the House of Commons in 1864. He joined the Republican Party after the war and was appointed head of the North Carolina Railroad by Governor Holden in 1868. Smith advocated expansion of the road by the merger of smaller lines, a strategy opposed by the General Assembly. He used the railroad to foil the Shipp Commission, spiriting George W. Swepson, a key witness, out of town on a special midnight train. Smith was elected to the state senate in 1870, but the election was contested. He purchased the Raleigh *Standard*, edited by Joseph W. Holden, son of the governor, in 1870 but sold the paper the following year. He was elected to the U.S. House of Representatives in 1872 and was the Republican nominee for lieutenant governor in 1876. Smith was appointed receiver of the Western North Carolina Railroad and later became president of the road. *Dictionary of North Carolina Biography*, 5:389.

The Shipp Fraud Commission was created by the 1870-1871 General Assembly to investigate allegations of corruption in the Holden administration. The members were Attorney General William M. Shipp, chairman; J. G. Martin; and J. B. Batchelor. The commission was unable to fix blame for misdeeds upon either Holden or the Republican Party, and its report aroused fear that the state would be forced to pay for its depreciated railroad bonds at face value. Raper, *Holden*, 142-143, 204.

98. On February 3, Rep. Thomas A. McNeill of Robeson introduced a petition from citizens of Robeson County asking that a new county be formed from portions of Robeson and Richmond. The memorial was referred to the Committee on Propositions and Grievances, which requested on February 5 "to be discharged from its further consideration," as its ten members were deadlocked. The bill (HB 481) was read a second time and rejected by the House the next day. Rep. Robert Fletcher of Richmond County offered an amendment proposing that the question be submitted to the voters of the two counties, which was adopted and the bill rejected. Judging from the volume and tenor of petitions from citizens of the two counties, the proposal was favored in Robeson but opposed in Richmond. *House Journal 1873-'74*, 413, 433, 449; House Bills, General Assembly Session Records, 1873-1874; Petitions, General Assembly Session Records, 1873-1874.

99. A forty-five-year-old farmer named J. M. Holmes appeared in the 1870 federal census of Turnersburg Township in Iredell County. Turner offered an amendment to his own bill in order to add Holmes to the trustees of Harmony Hill Camp Ground. Ninth Census of the United States, 1870, Population Schedule: Iredell County, N.C.; House Bills, General Assembly Session Records, 1873-1874.

100. Thomas Alexander Watts of Shiloh Township of Iredell County was commissioned third lieutenant in Company C (the "Town Company") of the Fifty-second Regiment of North Carolina Militia on August 30, 1862. He was promoted to major of the Seventy-ninth Regiment on July 1, 1863. Watts was a justice of the peace in Statesville in 1874 when he was elected sheriff, a position he held for ten years. Adjutant General's Office, Roster of North Carolina Militia, 214-217; Keever, *Iredell Piedmont County*, 300; Wheeler, *Legislative Manual for 1874*, 258.

101. Mr. McCoombs of Cherokee is unidentified.

102. Rep. Squire Trivett of Ashe County presented a protest, "signed by himself and others," against the adoption of an amendment to section 11 of the "Supplemental Consolidation" bill. After the protest was read, "the Speaker ruled the protest out of order, in that it impugned the motives of members, and was couched in terms discourteous to the House." The amendment was rejected on February 6 by a vote of 51 to 39, Turner voting with the majority. Turner probably referred to Rep. Edmund Jones of Patterson, representing Caldwell County, but there were three other members with that surname in the 1873-1874 House of Representatives: Simeon A. Jones of Shiloh (Camden County), Pride Jones of Hillsboro (Orange County), and B. Jones of Columbia (Tyrrell County). *House Journal 1873-'74*, 446-447, 453.

103. Turner introduced a resolution (HR 136, titled "Provides for sessions each night, except Sunday, till close of session") on February 7. It was read a second time on February 9, when the amendment of Edmund Jones of Caldwell was adopted and the amended resolution approved. Turner's resolution suggested that the House hold night sessions on Mondays, Wednesdays, and Fridays. Jones's substitute had it meet every night except Sundays. *House Journal 1873-'74*, 452, 471; House Resolutions, General Assembly Session Records, 1873-1874.

104. Senator William P. Welch of Waynesville represented District 41 (Haywood, Henderson, and Transylvania counties), Rep. David A. Blackwell represented Buncombe County, and Senator John M. Stafford of Salem represented District 32 (Stokes and Forsyth counties). All three resided at Mrs. Evans's boardinghouse. "There is a fountain filled with blood," a hymn by William Cowper (1731-1800), was often sung to "Cleansing Fountain," a nineteenth-century American camp meeting tune. The hymn, "We'll Storm the Skies," is unidentified. http://hymnsite.com/lyrics/umh622.sht.

105. James Madison Gudger Jr. (1855-1920) of Madison County was the son of a wealthy merchant from Buncombe County. The senior Gudger represented Buncombe County in the House in 1864-1865 and District 36 (from Yancey County) in the senate in the 1872-1874 session. He was one of the founding fathers of Waynesville in Haywood County. The younger Gudger attended Emory and Henry College in Virginia and read law under Chief Justice Richmond Pearson. In 1872, he was admitted to the bar and began practicing in Marshall. He was elected to the state senate in 1900 and served two terms in Congress, from 1903 to 1907 and from 1911 to 1915. He was a first cousin of Rep. Thomas Dillard Johnston. http://bioguide.congress.gov/scripts/biodisplay.pl?index=G000514.

106. James Blythe (1808-1897) was a Baptist minister, newspaper proprietor and editor, clerk of superior court, and state legislator. Born in the Crab Creek section of Buncombe County in 1808, he was baptized in 1835 and spent the next sixty-two years spreading the Gospel. Blythe was among the organizers of the Salem Baptist Association in Buncombe and Henderson counties. He was the first pastor of Green River Baptist Church (1837), Little River Baptist Church (1838), and the First Baptist Church of Hendersonville. He was one of the founders of the weekly *North Carolina Baptist* (1851) in Asheville, which was superseded two years later by Blythe's *The Carolina Baptist*, published in Hendersonville. The newspaper was absorbed by the *Biblical Recorder* in 1858. Blythe was described as "an able minister; a little in advance of most of his brethren in point of culture. . . . Few men ever had greater power over men; naturally impulsive, and being filled with the Holy Spirit, he preached as with the Holy Ghost sent down from God. In doctrine and spirit he impressed himself upon his people and his age." Blythe was first elected to the General Assembly in 1865, representing Henderson County in the House. He was reelected for the 1866-1867 session, to the senate in 1868-1869 and 1869-1870, and back to the House in 1872-1874, 1874-1875, and 1879-1880, representing Polk County in the latter session. He died on December 14, 1897, and is buried in Refuge Baptist Church Cemetery near Dana. Paschal, *History of North Carolina Baptists*, 2:444-445, 455; Henry S. Stroupe, "The Beginnings of Religious Journalism in North Carolina, 1823-1865," *North Carolina Historical Review* 30 (January 1953), 10-11, 17, 19; Cheney, *North Carolina Government*, 333, 335, 447, 449, 454, 456, 461; Pat Hicks Brigance, *Blythe*, vol. 1 (Maryville, Tenn.: P. H. Brigance, 1994), 247; Henderson County Genealogical and Historical Society, comp., *Henderson County, North Carolina Cemeteries* (Spartanburg, S.C.: The Reprint Company, Publishers, 1995), 220.

107. In the 1870 federal census of Raleigh Township, eighteen-year-old Betty Blake is listed in the household of Mary Blake, forty-eight, along with four older brothers. The 1880

Raleigh city directory indicated that Mary Blake, widow of Wesley S. Blake, lived at the corner of Davie and McDowell streets. Ninth Census of the United States, 1870, Population Schedule: Wake County, N.C.; Emerson, *Raleigh Directory, 1880-'81*, 49.

108. This truly was "Gorman's militia bill." On November 21, Rep. John C. Gorman of Wake County introduced the bill (HB 45) "to organize, equip and discipline the militia." According to a House message to the senate on November 24, the bill had been prepared by the adjutant general, who also happened to be John C. Gorman. (As George Stevenson Jr. noted, the proscription in the state constitution of 1776 that forbade multiple office holding was omitted in the Reconstruction constitution of 1868.) The measure was read for the second and third times on February 10-11, passed with amendments, and was ordered to be engrossed and sent to the senate for concurrence. In the reorganization of the state militia by the Holden administration in 1870, Gorman was appointed brigadier general of the Tenth Brigade. He was named adjutant general by Governor Caldwell on August 14, 1871, to succeed Abiel W. Fisher, who had resigned. Gorman served until 1877. A native of Alabama and a printer by trade, he represented Wake County in the House during the 1872-1874 session. Gorman also served as chief of the Raleigh Fire Department in 1871-1872 and as mayor in 1875. *House Journal 1873-'74*, 59, 487, 505, 508; House Messages, General Assembly Session Records, 1873-1874; Raper, *Holden*, 170, 315 n. 48; Cheney, *North Carolina Government*, 335, 430, 444 n. 2, 455.

109. The bill (SB 325, HB 534), which originally applied only to Burke and Rutherford counties, was introduced in the senate on December 17 by James Madison Gudger Sr. of Burnsville, representing District 36 (Caldwell, Burke, McDowell, Mitchell, and Yancey counties). On January 27, Senator Woodville W. Flemming of Marion, also representing District 36, proposed to add McDowell County, and Senator W. J. T. Miller of Shelby (District 38, Gaston and Cleveland counties) offered an amendment to include Cleveland County as well. The amended bill was passed by the senate the same day. The measure would allow the counties proceeds from sales of vacant lands within their boundaries, to be applied towards the counties' railroad bond debts. The bill was received in the House on February 2 and read a second time on February 10. Amendments suggested by the Committee on the Judiciary were adopted, and the bill was read a third time but rejected by a vote of 60 to 32 (Turner voted against). On motion of Jacob W. Bowman of Mitchell, the bill was reconsidered but again rejected, 47 to 37 (Turner voted for). *Senate Journal 1873-'74*, 182, 286; *House Journal 1873-'74*, 405, 487-489.

110. This bill was introduced in the senate on January 15 by John M. Stafford of Salem, representing District 32, Stokes and Forsyth counties. The proposal would make it a misdemeanor, subject to a $50 fine, to leave a burning campfire unattended in a campground. An amended version of the bill (SB 377, HB 646) was passed by the senate on February 11 and received in the House the following day. On February 14, it was read for the second and third times and then tabled. *Senate Journal 1873-'74*, 226, 417, 423; *House Journal 1873-'74*, 511, 557; Senate Bills, General Assembly Session Records, 1873-1874.

111. Representative Gorman of Wake introduced the resolution (HR 143) concerning immigration and the commemoration of the anniversary of the birth of St. Patrick. During the evening session on February 11, the memorial titled, "Resolution in favor of Immigration to the State of North Carolina," was adopted by the house. Father J. V. McNamara, the first resident pastor of the Catholic congregation in Raleigh, was among the memorialists who proposed a grand immigration convention in the city on March 17, 1874. The resolution requested the General Assembly to show support for the convention, and "to make the celebration of St. Patrick's day the occasion to assure, not only the sons of Ireland, but those of all other nations," that immigrants were welcome in the state and would be

treated equally under the law. McNamara also wrote to Governor Caldwell, the son of an Irish immigrant, urging him to attend and speak at the convention. The "ridiculous amendments" proposed in the senate included: "strike out St. Patrick's day & 13th [*sic*] day of March wherever it occurs & substitute 4th of July"; "Strike out the title and insert the following: 'Resolution to abolish the 4th of July and substitute St. Patrick's day March 17' "; and "Resolved further that we the Representatives and Senators do most solemnly declare that in our deliberate opinion that after passing the above and publishing the same to the world that we surely shall be entitled to the appellation of 'Solomons.' And we denounce all as Hardheaded fools, who do not cheerfully accord to us this title of distinction and wisdom." On the last day of the session, the senate approved a "Resolution in favor of Immigration" that was introduced by Senator Woodville W. Flemming of McDowell County. It noted that the executive committee in charge of the Immigration Convention, "in becoming deference to the opinion of the Senators of North Carolina have decided to change the time for the holding of the proposed convention" to March 8-9, 1874. The senate was then willing to support the convention. *House Journal 1873-'74*, 481, 487; Senate Resolutions, General Assembly Session Records, 1873-1874; Father J. V. McNamara to Gov. Tod R. Caldwell, February 5, 1874, Tod R. Caldwell, Governors Papers, North Carolina State Archives, Raleigh.

112. On February 5, Rep. Montford McGehee of Person County introduced a bill (HB 562) to sell vacant public lands in and around Raleigh, which was referred to the Committee on the Judiciary. McGehee proposed the sale of Nash Square, Moore Square, Burke Square, and "the Oak Grove in the North Eastern part of the City" to the City of Raleigh. The committee recommended passage of a substitute bill on February 11. Later that day, on motion of McGehee, the House rules were suspended, the bill was read a second time, and the amendments of the committee were adopted. Stewart Ellison, an African American representative from Wake County, offered an amendment asking that four acres "in the southwestern part of the City of Raleigh (commonly called Gallows Hill)" be "set apart and donated for educational purposes for the colored people." The amendment was rejected 65 to 35 (Turner voting against) and the bill passed, 57 to 47 (Turner voting for). On February 12, when the bill was read a third time, Rep. J. T. Brown of Davidson County offered an amendment directing that the proceeds of the sale be applied for the benefit of free public schools, rather than to the university, as the bill originally proposed. Brown's amendment was adopted by a vote of 56 to 45 (Turner voting against). A motion to table the bill was defeated, 55 to 50 (Turner voted to table). Later that day, Rep. Edmund Jones of Caldwell County moved to postpone further discussion of the matter, which was approved 58 to 43 (Turner voted for). *House Journal 1873-'74*, 435, 490, 497-500, 514-516, 517; House Bills, General Assembly Session Records, 1873-1874.

According to George Stevenson Jr., former private collections archivist at the North Carolina State Archives, Ellison's amendment places the postbellum site of public executions ("Gallows Hill") in the vicinity of Mount Hope Cemetery, a tract of land west of Raleigh and south of the governor's "palace" on Fayetteville Street extension (Old Fayetteville Road), which was acquired by the city ca. 1872 as a public cemetery for African Americans. Earlier in the nineteenth century, executions were conducted in the block south of the fairgrounds on the north side of the city: "Some years after the completion of the capitol, the quarry from which its building stone was taken became the execution site. The hundreds of spectators inevitably drawn to the spectacles stood around the rim of the excavation, within which the gallows stood." Murray, *Wake*, 404, 590.

113. Senator R. J. Powell of Pittsboro represented District 22 (Chatham County). Miss Thompson may be Adelaide Boylan's friend, "Miss Thomas," previously mentioned by Turner on January 25.

114. Kate McKimmon, twenty-one, appears in the 1870 census of Raleigh Township as a teacher at St. Mary's School. In 1880, Mrs. Mary Iredell and Miss Kate McKimmon were listed in the Raleigh city directory as teachers in residence at St. Mary's. Ninth Census of the United States, 1870, Population Schedule: Wake County, N.C.; Emerson, *Raleigh Directory, 1880-'81*, 89, 105.

115. James A. Heaton of Wilmington represented New Hanover County.

116. In the 1870 federal census of Raleigh Township, Sally Smith, thirty-three, and Emily Smith, thirty-nine, were listed in the household of Lucy Evans's boardinghouse. Ninth Census of the United States, 1870, Population Schedule: Wake County, N.C.

117. Tod Robinson Caldwell (1818-1874) was the son of an Irish immigrant who settled in western North Carolina and became a prominent Burke County merchant. The younger Caldwell prepared for college at the Bingham School in Hillsborough and in 1840 graduated with honors from the University of North Carolina, where he read law under Pres. David L. Swain. Caldwell returned home to practice law and was elected prosecuting attorney of Burke County, the first of a lifetime of successful political campaigns—he never lost an election. In 1842, at the age of twenty-four, he was elected to the state House and in 1850 to the state senate. During the Civil War, he maintained allegiance to the Union, refusing to take any part in the conflict, although his only son served in the Confederate army and was killed at Gettysburg. After the war, Caldwell served as president of the state-owned Western North Carolina Railroad and as private secretary to William W. Holden in the provisional government of 1865. He was one of the founders of the Republican Party in North Carolina and was rewarded with the post of lieutenant governor in the Holden administration. He succeeded to the governor's office when Holden was impeached and removed by the Conservative majority in the General Assembly. That same hostile majority refused to cooperate with Caldwell to resolve a number of critical issues; in particular, settling the state debt and adequately funding the public school system instituted by the Republicans. He was elected to a full term as governor in 1872 but died in office. See n. 53 above for a discussion of the election bill. *Dictionary of North Carolina Biography*, 1:305-306; Raper, *Holden*, 276 n. 21.

118. Tazewell Lee Hargrove (1830-1889) of Granville County was state attorney general from 1873 to 1877. A graduate of Randolph-Macon College, he studied law at the University of North Carolina and received his law license in 1850. He represented Granville County in the General Assembly from 1856 to 1859 and was a delegate to both the secession convention and the constitutional convention of 1861-1862. In February 1862, at age thirty-one, he enlisted in the Granville Regulators, which became Company A of the Forty-fourth N.C. Regiment. Hargrove was elected captain of the company on March 10, 1862, and major of the regiment, May 3, 1862. He was promoted to lieutenant colonel on July 28, 1862. Captured at South Anna Bridge, June 26, 1863, Hargrove was confined at various prisons, first at Fort Delaware and then at Johnson's Island, where he remained from July 20, 1863, to April 22, 1864, a fellow inmate of Columbus L. Turner. He also spent time at Point Lookout, Hilton Head, and Fort Pulaski. He was released at Fort Delaware on July 24, 1865. After the war, Hargrove became disenchanted with the Conservatives and switched to the Republican Party, which he represented in the General Assembly in 1870-1872 before being elected attorney general. Manarin, *North Carolina Troops*, 10:396, 399; http://docsouth.unc.edu/unc/browse/person.html#H.

119. Turner apparently refers to "The Home Over There," which was popular at the time. The words were written by DeWitt C. Huntington, ca. 1873, and the music by Tullius C. O'Kane. The second verse would have had special meaning for Turner:

"O think of the friends over there,
Who before us the journey have trod,
Of the songs that they breathe on the air,
In their home in the palace of God.
Over there, over there,
O think of the friends over there,
Over there, over there,
O think of the friends over there."

http://www.cyberhymnal.org/htm/h/o/homeover.htm

120. The North Carolina Institution for the Deaf and Dumb and Blind was located on Caswell Square, a block from Turner's boardinghouse. The building was completed in 1849. Among the blind students listed at the school in the 1870 federal census of Raleigh Township were Margaret Bromley, 18; Mary Shank, 16; and James Gay, 27. Narcissa Dupree, 21, blind, was listed as a teacher and Virginia Ayer, 29, as assistant matron. Miss Ballinger is unidentified. Ninth Census of the United States, 1870, Population Schedule: Wake County, N.C.

121. W. J. T. Miller of Shelby represented District 38 (Gaston and Cleveland counties).

122. The bill (HB 171) "to make the jurisdiction of justices of the peace final in certain criminal matters" was introduced by Rep. S. W. Reid of Mecklenburg on December 5. It was read a second time, as substituted by committee, on January 16, and amendments to the substitute bill were adopted. Senate amendments to the bill (SB 500) were read in the House and approved by a vote of 72 to 18 (Turner voted for) on February 14. The bill was ratified on the final day of the session. *House Journal 1873-'74*, 127, 289-290, 334, 556-557; *Laws and Resolutions 1873-'74*, Public Laws, c. 176, s. 13, p. 261.

123. Rep. John M. Moring of Morrisville, House member from Chatham County, introduced a bill on January 24 to adjust the public debt (HB 478) through the redemption of railroad bonds at depreciated value. After discussion was twice postponed, the proposal was referred to the Committee on State Debt and Liabilities. A similar bill from the senate (SB 241, HB 588) was announced in the House on February 13. During that evening's session, Rep. John E. Brown of Mecklenburg offered an amendment to the senate bill, which was adopted 50 to 36 (Turner voted for). Moring then offered his bill as a substitute for the amended senate bill, which was initially adopted but rejected on its second reading by a vote of 55 to 30 (Turner again voted against). Rep. Thomas Dillard Johnston of Buncombe offered HB 685 as a substitute but was ruled out of order. He then introduced the measure, which would appoint commissioners to ascertain the value of past bond issues and report to the next session of the assembly, as a new proposition. The next day a motion to table Johnston's bill was rejected. Moring's substitute bill was then reconsidered and, after a number of motions were rejected, passed by a vote of 53 to 43 (Turner voted against). Johnston's bill was then read a second time and also passed, 68 to 30 (Turner voted for). On February 16, the final day of the session, Johnston offered an amendment to his bill that would replace the original commissioners with Tod R. Caldwell, Joseph J. Davis of Franklin, and W. S. Battle of Edgecombe (the draft of the amendment also included D. W. Bain, but his name was dropped in the house journal). The amendment was adopted and the bill passed 68 to 21 (Turner voted for). Moring's bill was also read a third time that day and passed by a vote of 49 to 37 (Turner voted against). It was rushed to the senate "without engrossment,"

but the session closed before either bill reached the floor of the upper chamber. In the end, the General Assembly of 1872-1874 did nothing to address the state debt, perhaps the most pressing issue of the day. *House Journal 1873-'74*, 343-344, 465-466, 533, 535-538, 543-549, 569-570; House Bills, General Assembly Session Records, 1873-1874.

Thomas Dillard Johnston (1840-1902) of Asheville represented Buncombe County. On May 3, 1861, he enlisted at age twenty-one in Zebulon B. Vance's company, which was enrolled as Company F of the Fourteenth N.C. Regiment. Johnston mustered in as a sergeant but was appointed second lieutenant of the company. He was severely wounded at Malvern Hill, July 1, 1862. He was subsequently appointed assistant quartermaster with the rank of captain in Col. W. C. Walker's battalion of Thomas's Legion, but poor health forced him to resign. After the war, Johnston studied law under James H. Bailey and was admitted to the bar in 1867. He was elected mayor of Asheville in 1869 and to the General Assembly as a Democrat in 1870. He served on the judiciary and finance committees and as chairman of the Committee on Constitutional Reform. In 1879, he authored the bill that finally settled the state debt. Johnston represented North Carolina in Congress from 1884 to 1888. Manarin, *North Carolina Troops*, 5:445; *Dictionary of North Carolina Biography*, 3:308-309.

124. The bill titled "an act for the greater security [or "protection"] of human life" (SB 601, HB 646) was introduced in the senate on February 5 by W. H. Avera of Selma (representing District 17, Johnston County). It was passed by the upper chamber on February 13 and sent to the House the next day. The bill was read the second and third times during the evening session and passed by a vote of 46 to 24 (Turner voted for). It was speedily ratified and returned to the senate before the session ended. *Senate Journal 1873-'74*, 364, 455; *House Journal 1873-'74*, 542, 558-559, 562; *Laws and Resolutions 1873-'74*, Public Laws, c. 180, pp. 263-264.

125. In Chapter 35 of Genesis, Jacob purges his family of idols, goes as commanded to Bethel to build an altar, and has his name changed by God to Israel. The chapter also records the deaths of Jacob's wife, Rachel, and father, Isaac.

126. Jonathan McGee Heck (1831-1894), businessman, developer, and Baptist layman, was a native of western Virginia. He was commissioned colonel of the Thirty-first Regiment Virginia Volunteers, but was captured at the Battle of Rich Mountain and paroled. Afterwards he operated a bayonet factory in Raleigh, using mineral deposits along the Deep River in Chatham County. Heck promoted Northern immigration and investment in the South immediately after the war. He built the Heck House on North Blount Street in Raleigh, where he was a member of the First Baptist Church, a trustee of Wake Forest College (1865), and president of the Baptist State Convention. *Dictionary of North Carolina Biography*, 3:92-94.

127. Perhaps James Madison Leach (1815-1891) of Davidson County, then a representative from North Carolina in the Forty-third Congress. Turner's visitor may also have been M. T. Leach, a partner in Leach Brothers Wholesale Grocers and Commission Merchants on Wilmington Street. In 1875, Leach was a boarder at the Yarborough House. *Dictionary of North Carolina Biography*, 4:38-39; *Chataigne's Directory, 1875-'76*, 86-87.

128. Turner originally suggested in his resolution (HR 185) that the House change the hour of adjournment from noon to 10:00 P.M., but it was amended to 2:00 P.M., "Provided that no legislation be had after 12 O'clock." The resolution was introduced and adopted on February 16. House Resolutions, General Assembly Session Records, 1873-1874.

129. James Lowrie Robinson (1838-1887) of Franklin, Macon County. A merchant at the outbreak of the Civil War, Robinson enlisted at age twenty-two in Company H of the Sixteenth N.C. Regiment on May 14, 1861. A month later, he was promoted to

quartermaster sergeant of the regiment but returned to his company when elected captain, ca. April 26, 1862. He was wounded in the arm at Seven Pines, May 31, 1862, and resigned June 1, 1863, because of illness. Robinson was elected to the state House of Representatives in 1868, a staunch opponent of Republican Reconstruction. He served as Speaker of the House from 1872 to 1875. He was then elected to the senate, where he was twice president. In 1880, Robinson was elected lieutenant governor. He served on the board of trustees of the university from 1877 to 1886. A constant champion of western North Carolina, Robinson promoted construction of the Western North Carolina Railroad. He served on the commission with Gov. Curtis Brogden and Robert F. Armfield that bought the railroad for the state in 1875, and he was named director of the road in 1877. Rep. Edmund Jones (1848-1920) of Patterson, Caldwell County, was the younger brother of Col. John T. Jones, who was killed at the Wilderness. According to a recent biographical sketch, Jones enlisted at age sixteen in the Forty-first N.C. Regiment (Third Cavalry) in 1864 and served to the end of war, but he is not listed in that regiment, nor in any other of the fifteen published volumes of *North Carolina Troops*. He studied law at the University of Virginia under John B. Minor. He was elected to the General Assembly in 1870 at age twenty-two. Licensed to practice law in 1881, Jones opened an office in Lenoir. He raised a company for the Second N.C. Volunteers in 1898 and served as its captain. *Dictionary of North Carolina Biography*, 3:316-317, 5:236; Manarin, *North Carolina Troops*, 6:12, 74.

130. The following card appeared in the *Daily News* on February 17:

"To the public,

One EDWARD RANSOM, of Tyrrell county, in his place in the Senate at eleven o'clock on Saturday night, as I am credibly informed, made, unprovoked, a gross and malevolent attack on my personal as well as my official character, and HURRIEDLY LEFT FOR HIS HOME by the early train this Monday morning.

I am, therefore compelled, thus publicly, to brand the said EDWARD RANSOM as a MALICIOUS LIAR, a MALEVOLENT SCOUNDREL, a VICIOUS RASCAL, a DRUNKEN BLACKGUARD, a MISERABLE POLTROON and CRAVEN COWARD, unworthy alike the attention of gentlemen, or the notice of men of courage; and the people of his section were imposed upon when they placed this DIRTY FELLOW in a position forcing his association among men of character, standing and honor, in the Senate of North Carolina.

EUGENE GRISSOM"

Five days later, Grissom retracted his charge: "In deference to a public understanding that I was hasty and misinformed . . ., and in justice to Senator Ransom, as well as to myself and the public, I hereby withdraw the language of the card." (Raleigh) *Daily News*, February 17, February 22, 1874.

131. Eleanor H. White Swain was the widow of David Lowry Swain, former governor of North Carolina and president of the University of North Carolina, who died in 1868. She was the daughter of Secretary of State William White and the granddaughter of Gov. Richard Caswell. *Dictionary of North Carolina Biography*, 5:483.

132. According to the *Daily News*, the concert was "another of those charming soirees musicale, for which this institution has become noted." The performers were students at the school under the tutelage of musical director Albrecht Baumann, "assisted by the gentlemen of the Presbyterian Church choir." Baumann (1831-1892), a native of Saalfeld, Germany, was the head of the Music Department at Peace Institute and also served as organist at the Presbyterian Church. He is buried in Oakwood Cemetery. Peace Institute was established in 1857 when William Peace (1773-1865), a Raleigh merchant and elder at the First

Presbyterian Church, donated eight acres of land and $10,000 to begin a school for women. The school's opening was postponed because of the war. The nearly completed facility, now known as Main Building, served as a Confederate hospital and, after the war, as the Raleigh office of the Freedmen's Bureau. In 1872, Rev. Robert Burwell and his son leased the property and re-established Peace as an educational institution. That year, "a joint-stock company made up mainly of members of the Presbyterian Church funded a curriculum of 'three courses of instruction: Primary, Preparatory and Collegiate.' " (Raleigh) *Daily News,* February 19, 1874; http://www.peace.edu/content/page/id/174; http://www.cr.nps.gov/nR/travel/raleigh/pea.htm.

133. Timothy F. Lee was sheriff of Wake County. In the 1870 federal census of Raleigh Township, he is listed as thirty-five years old and a native of Ireland. Horace Raper referred to him as "the Wake County carpetbagger sheriff and leader of the local black Republican forces." When Lee was defeated for reelection in 1874, W. W. Holden remarked: " 'Tim Lee is beaten, and all honest men are rejoiced.' " Ninth Census of the United States, 1870, Population Schedule: Wake County, N.C.; Raper, *Holden*, 226, 234.

134. Presumably a gift to legislators from the directors of the Atlantic and North Carolina Railroad.

135. The *Sentinel*, acquired by Josiah Turner Jr. in 1868, led the editorial assault against the Holden machine. The *Daily News* was founded in 1872 by Jordan Stone and Samuel J. Williams and later merged with the *Observer*. The *Examiner* and *Herald* probably refer to Richmond, Virginia, newspapers.

136. A reported 235 Grangers attended the meeting at Tucker Hall in Raleigh on February 18. P. C. Carlton was the brother of Charles A. Carlton [see n. 85, above]. According to a listing of convention delegates in the *Daily News*, Carlton was Master of Grange No. 12. He later organized two fraternal orders in Statesville: the Royal Arcanum (1880) and the Knights of Honor (1887). He was also an original shareholder of the Statesville Cotton Mill (1893). *Our Living and Our Dead,* vol. 1, no. 5 (Jan. 1875), 447; (Raleigh) *Daily News*, February 18, February 19, 1874; Keever, *Iredell Piedmont County*, 250, 313-314, 353.

137. "Lone Rock by the Sea" was a ballad for piano with music by William Clifton and lyrics variously credited to Felicia Dorothea Hemans (1794-1835) and Charles Crozat Converse (1832-1918). "Pass under the Rod" was a sacred song for piano, music by Sue Ingersoll Scott and lyrics by Mary S. B. Dana. John Church and Company, Cincinnati, published sheet music for the song in 1862. http://www.csufresno.edu/folklore/ballads/R842.html; http://memory.loc.gov/cgi-bin/query/D?dukesmili.temp/~ammem_8F8m; http://www.lib.duke.edu/texis/smi/search/ more. htm?id= 37973ea081.

138. Six households down from Dr. Robert H. Wyche in the 1870 federal census of Cape Fear Township was Jonathan Farrar, merchant, thirty-seven, his wife Elisabeth, thirty-nine, and four children. Ninth Census of the United States, 1870, Population Schedule: Chatham County, N.C.

139. Cate L. Scott, thirty-two in 1870, was the wife of Maj. John W. Scott, who dwelt three doors down from Jonathan Farrar in Cape Fear Township [see n. 42, above]. Mrs. Pitman is unidentified. Ninth Census of the United States, 1870, Population Schedule: Chatham County, N.C.

140. Allen B. Wilson (born 1824) obtained a patent in 1850 for a sewing machine with a rotary hook and bobbin combination. In 1854, he patented the four-motion feed that is still used on sewing machines. He founded the Wheeler and Wilson Company at Watertown, N.Y., in 1851. Five years later, the company moved to Bridgeport, Conn., where it was

renamed the Wheeler and Wilson Manufacturing Company and began full-scale production. Makers of the most popular sewing machines in America in the 1850s and 1860s, Wheeler and Wilson began to lose ground to Singer toward the end of the latter decade. The company was bought out by Singer in 1905. http://www.geocities.com/Heartland/Plains/3081.

141. John Reilly of Cumberland County was state auditor from 1873 to 1877. Hamilton characterized him as a "carpetbagger." According to Kemp P. Battle, Reilly participated in the immortal cavalry charge at Balaclava. Hamilton, *Reconstruction*, 584; Battle, *History of the University of North Carolina*, 2:41-42.

142. Rev. John Lansing Burrows, D.D. (1814-1893), was pastor of the First Baptist Church in Richmond from 1854 to 1874. He published *The Christian Scholar and Soldier: Memoirs of Lewis Minor Coleman* in Raleigh in 1864. His sermon concerning the Battle of Shiloh was also published during the war. He was the father of Lansing Burrows, secretary (1881-1913) and president (1913-1915) of the Southern Baptist Convention and pastor of eight southern Baptist churches. http://www.rootsweb.com/~kygenweb/kybiog/daviess/burrows.jl.txt.

143. Richard Sharpe Mason (1795-1874), rector of Christ Church in Raleigh, was a native of Barbados. He graduated from the University of Pennsylvania at age seventeen and was ordained in 1817. He first served as rector of Christ Church in New Bern from 1818 to 1828, then was posted to churches in Pennsylvania, New York, and Delaware, and finally to Raleigh in 1840. *Dictionary of North Carolina Biography*, 4:234.

144. Tucker Hall was built by brothers W. H. and Rufus S. Tucker on one of their lots in Raleigh as the city's first hall for entertainment. The building was dedicated by former governor David L. Swain on August 24, 1867. The Tuckers "combined commerce with entertainment. The bustle of the first two floors of their establishment told all that the Tucker brothers' concern was the city's largest mercantile firm. But the third floor offered enchantment for all comers. The 1,200-seat Tucker Hall offered acts ranging from Col. W. F. 'Buffalo Bill' Cody to tenor Pasquale Brignoli, to Gov. Zebulon Vance's 1877 inaugural address." It was located at 23-25 Fayetteville Street, in the first block south of the Capitol. Rufus S. Tucker (1829-1894) inherited his father's mercantile store in 1851 and developed the business into the leading dry-goods house in the state. Tucker served as a director of the North Carolina Railroad Company, the Raleigh and Gaston Railroad, Seaboard Air Line Railway, Raleigh National Bank, and, for more than thirty years, the state Institution for the Deaf and Dumb and Blind. He was also a vestryman of Christ Church. He owned thousands of acres in and around Raleigh, including the land on which Meredith College stands. The Tucker building was partially razed in the early twentieth century and the remainder demolished in 1969. Murray, *Wake*, 268, n. 54, 581, 582, n. 86; *Dictionary of North Carolina Biography*, 6:58; *Cyclopedia of Eminent and Representative Men of the Carolinas of the Nineteenth Century*. Vol. 2, *North Carolina* (Madison, Wis.: Brant and Fuller, 1892), 2:510; http://www.raleigh-nc.org/portal/server.pt/gateway/PTARGS_0_2_306_203_0_43/http//%38pt03/DIG_Web_Content/category/Business/Strategic_Planning/Downtown_Planning/Fayetteville_Street_Renaissance/Cat-1C-2005307-081337-A_Glimpse_At_The_History.html.

Turner's reference to a "new congregation of Episcopalians" refers to the Church of the Good Shepherd, formed in 1874 as the first "free" Episcopal church in Raleigh; in the older Christ Church, all the pews were owned by various families of the congregation. The first service of the new congregation was conducted in Tucker Hall in February 1874. Services were also held in the House of Representatives chamber while the church was being built. The congregation was formally organized on February 25 and admitted to the diocese at its annual convention on May 21. Ground was broken for the new sanctuary at the corner of

Hillsborough and McDowell streets on September 24, 1874. http://www.cgs-raleigh.org/history.htm.

145. Rev. Edward R. Rich of St. Paul's Church, Clinton, was the first rector of the Church of the Good Shepherd, called in January 1874. He conducted the congregation's first service at Tucker Hall in February, assisted by the Right Reverend Theodore Lyman. The *Daily News* also referred to him as Mr. Rich of Maryland. The passage is from Matthew 16:21-23: "[21] From that time forth began Jesus to shew unto his disciples, how that he must go unto Jerusalem, and suffer many things of the elders and chief priests and scribes, and be killed, and be raised again the third day. [22] Then Peter took him, and began to rebuke him, saying, Be it far from thee, Lord: this shall not be unto thee. [23] But he turned, and said unto Peter, Get thee behind me, Satan: thou art an offence unto me: for thou savourest not the things that be of God, but those that be of men." (Raleigh) *Daily News*, February 17, 1874.

146. Theodore Benedict Lyman (1815-1893) was elected assistant bishop of North Carolina in 1873 and succeeded to the bishopric upon the death of Thomas Atkinson in 1881. He was a native of Massachusetts, ordained in 1840. Lyman served as rector of churches in Hagerstown, Pittsburgh, and San Francisco before he traveled around the world during the 1860s. After his election in 1873, he built a house in Raleigh and became a member of the Church of the Good Shepherd. *Dictionary of North Carolina Biography*, 4:110-111.

147. The school opened as Wake Forest Institute in 1834 and became Wake Forest College four years later. The college was closed from 1862 to 1865. Fritz Henry Ivey of Fayetteville graduated from Wake Forest in 1860 and received a master of arts degree there in 1866. He served as a chaplain in the Confederate army. In 1873, Ivey was appointed agent by the trustees of Wake Forest to visit churches and associations to solicit subscriptions in support of the school. He published a pamphlet concerning Wake Forest in 1879. Ivey served as pastor of Baptist churches in Georgia and North Carolina, including a posting at Goldsboro. He died May 5, 1893. According to the minutes of the First Baptist Church for February 22, Ivey preached in the morning and "bro." Walters made an address on behalf of the endowment of Wake Forest College. That evening after the sermon, Ivey also made an appeal on behalf of the school. The two communicants baptized that evening were George W. Vaughn and Miss Mary Loader. Paschal, *History of Wake Forest College*, 1:613, 2:24, 89, 94, 119, 171; First Baptist Church Minutes, February 22, 1874.

148. In the 1870 federal census of Raleigh Township, there were listed among the blind students at the Institution for the Deaf and Dumb and Blind: Jonas Costner, 20; Theresa Dettmiering, 16; Anna Honeycutt, 12; Mary Ryals, 12; Jackson Massey, 9; James Ryals, 15; and Alfred Page, 19. Misses Bromley (Brumley) and Shank, Mrs. Ayer, and Mr. Gay are identified in n. 120, above. Lilly McCarson is unidentified. Ninth Census of the United States, 1870, Population Schedule: Wake County, N.C.

149. Probably Aldert Smedes (1810-1877), founder and rector of St. Mary's School in Raleigh. A native of New York, he was ordained in 1834 and opened St. Mary's School in 1842. His brother, Rev. John E. C. Smedes, was president of St. Augustine's College from 1872 to 1884. His son, Bennett Smedes (1837-1899), succeeded him at St. Mary's. Thomas Atkinson (1807-1881) was the third Episcopal bishop of North Carolina. A native of Virginia, he graduated from Hampden-Sydney College and studied law before being ordained in 1836. After serving ministries in Norfolk, Lynchburg, and Baltimore, he was elected bishop of North Carolina in 1853, a post he held for twenty-eight "turbulent years." *Dictionary of North Carolina Biography*, 1:62-63, 5:367-369.

150. Woodward is unidentified.

151. It was Turner's thirty-second birthday.

152. The St. Charles Hotel was located on the east side of South Center Street in Statesville. According to local historian Homer M. Keever, "The old tavern of Robert Work, Whitfield Kerr, the Harbins, and A. M. Walker became the St. Charles Hotel." William Harbin bought the tavern in the mid-1830s. The hotel was torn down in the 1950s. Shields is unidentified. Keever, *Iredell Piedmont County*, 157, 318, 437.

153. Turner probably read an account of the crime in one of the Raleigh newspapers before he left the city. Nineteen-year-old Joseph D. Elliott was the son of H. C. Elliott, proprietor of the St. Charles Hotel. On the evening of February 19, Charles T. Neal of Richmond, Virginia, was killed in the lobby of the hotel by a single pistol shot to the chest. Neal was involved in the tobacco business and was an occasional long-term boarder at the St. Charles. He was indebted to the Elliotts for board and personal loans to the amount of $60 and had argued with both father and son earlier in the day. Joseph Elliott ordered him to pay his bill and leave the hotel. Several witnesses heard Neal make threatening remarks against the Elliotts. During the supper hour on February 19, Neal was sitting before the fire in the lobby when he was heard to make castigating remarks about some of the "damned mean people in Statesville," and to issue further threats against the Elliotts. H. C. Elliott walked into the room, placed his hand on Neal's shoulder, and told him to leave the hotel. Neal replied, "I reckon not," and grabbed Elliott's coat with both hands. The younger Elliott emerged from the dining room, borrowed a pistol from a stranger in the lobby, walked up behind his father, and shot Neal in the breastbone. As the elder Elliott ushered the wounded man towards the door to the street, Neal remarked that the shooting was a cowardly thing to do, then sank to the floor. He was left lying there for about ten minutes, bleeding from the mouth, before he was finally taken to a bed, where he soon expired. A coroner's jury viewed the body in the hotel, heard testimony of witnesses, and concluded that Neal came to his death at the hands of Joseph Elliott. From the county jail, Elliott applied for a writ of habeas corpus, which was issued by Judge Anderson Mitchell. The evidence was heard by two justices of the peace, who bound the case over for trial in superior court. At the spring 1874 term of Iredell County Superior Court, a grand jury returned a true bill against young Elliott for the murder of Neal. The defendant requested a change of venue because of prejudice against him in the county, caused in part by a sensational account of the homicide, with glowing accolades of the deceased, in a Statesville newspaper. On June 6, the case was transferred to Wilkes County. At the fall 1874 term of Wilkes County Superior Court, Elliott was found innocent of murder but guilty of "felonious slaying" and sentenced to five years in state prison. (Raleigh) *Daily News*, February 21, 1874; (Raleigh) *Daily Sentinel*, February 22, 1874; *State v. Elliott*, Iredell County Criminal Action Papers, 1874, North Carolina State Archives, Raleigh; Iredell County Superior Court Minute Docket, 1869-1875, 449-452, North Carolina State Archives, Raleigh; *State v. Elliott*, Wilkes County Criminal Action Papers, 1874, North Carolina State Archives, Raleigh; Wilkes County Superior Court Minute Docket, 1869-1874, 569, 571-576, North Carolina State Archives, Raleigh.

154. Turner's sister Virginia Ann "Jennie" Turner (1851-1925) would marry Rev. James Willson (1845-1922) on October 20, 1874. In the 1870 federal census of Turnersburg Township of Iredell County, sixteen-year-old Prissilla Ward is listed in the household of W. N. Ward, fifty-eight, a farmer and next-door neighbor of "Wiliford" Turner. Ward had ten children, including a son named Wilford. Ninth Census of the United States, 1870, Population Schedule: Iredell County, N.C.

AFTERWORD

1. Columbus Lafayette Turner Diary, March 19, April 7, April 13, 1874; *Our Living and Our Dead*, March 11, April 22, 1874.

2. Columbus Lafayette Turner Diary, March 12, April 10, 1874.

3. Columbus Lafayette Turner Diary, April-October 1874; *Our Living and Our Dead*, May 20, 1874.

4. Iredell County Record of Deeds, 7:492-494, 14:452-454; W. and D. Turner to James, Jinnie, and Mary Willson, April 8, 1881, in Turner Family Papers, Burlington; Statesville *Landmark*, May 1, 1890, November 25, 1893, in Black, *Newspaper Transcripts*, 2:153, 3:25.

5. W. and D. Turner to James, Jinnie, and Mary Willson, April 8, 1881, in Turner Family Papers, Burlington; Statesville *Landmark*, June 2, 1882 [extracted from (Hickory) *Piedmont Press*], in Black, *Newspaper Transcripts*, 1:99. The Monbo Cotton Mills, Invoice Book, 1908-1918, shows an indebtedness of $6,000 to Mrs. S. E. Holman and $800 to Mrs. M. E. Gaither on January 1, 1908. Monbo Cotton Mills, Invoice Book, 1908-1918, Rare Book, Manuscript, and Special Collections Library, Duke University, Durham.

6. Catawba County Record of Deeds, 1879-1918 (microfilm), North Carolina State Archives, Raleigh, 11:323-324, 13:176-178; Gary R. Freeze, *The Catawbans: Crafters of a North Carolina County, 1747-1900* (Newton, N.C.: Catawba County Historical Association, 1995), 127-128, 258-260.

7. In one of the actions at law (*P. C. Shuford and wife et al v. A. M. Powell et al*), the debtors involved were Tate, Powell and Company; Claywell, Powell and Company; Catawba Manufacturing Company; Powell and Shuford; and A. M. Powell. In another suit (*Joseph Turner v. A. M. Powell*), the court appointed a referee to sort out the liabilities of Powell, James A. Claywell, P. C. Shuford, J. C. Turner, W. W. Mott, L. A. Shuford, and S. D. Mc. Tate. *Charlotte Observer*, May 3, July 4, 1882; *Newton Enterprise*, June 10, 1882; Catawba County Record of Deeds, 20:250-252; Catawba County Superior Court Minute Docket, fall term 1883, 224.

8. Charles J. Preslar Jr., ed., *A History of Catawba County* (Salisbury, N.C.: Rowan Printing Company, 1954), 384; Reginald Turner memoir, chapter 6.

9. Letters to *Charlotte Observer*, n.d., and Statesville *Landmark*, July 24, 1882, quoted by James Turner in "Turner Family History."

10. The deed may have been drafted earlier. Both the grantee and grantor indexes give the date as 1882, and on the negative microfilm copy of the deed book, the "4" in 1884 is much bolder than the rest of the figures in the date. At the fall term 1883, the court ordered the receiver in the suit, *Joseph Turner v. A. M. Powell*, to have a survey made of the land "before making title to the real estate." Perhaps the original recordation was amended, or at least postdated, to conform to the survey. Monbo Cotton Mills, Invoice Book; *Manufacturer's Record*, February 17, 1887, quoted by James R. Turner in "Turner Family History"; Catawba County Record of Deeds, 20:250-252; Catawba County Superior Court Minute Docket, fall term 1883, 209.

11. Catawba County Record of Deeds, 24:157-158; letters to *Charlotte Observer*, n.d., and Statesville *Landmark*, July 24, 1882, in "Turner Family History"; Statesville *Landmark*, May 9, 1889, in Black, *Newspaper Transcripts*, 2:124.

12. James G. Blaine and Gen. John A. Logan were the Republican Party nominees for president and vice-president, respectively, in 1884. Reginald Turner memoir, chapter 6; *Newton Enterprise*, June 21, 1884.

13. Virginia E. Turner to Vincent Longinotti, December 15, 1886, quoted by James R. Turner in "Turner Family History"; Freeze, *The Catawbans: Crafters*, 240-244; *Catawba Cousins* 5 (April 1991), 168; Catawba County Genealogical Society, *Catawba County Cemeteries* (Hickory, N.C.: The Society, 1996), 8:26.

14. Monbo Manufacturing Company, Minute Book, 1887-1902, in possession of James R. Turner, Greensboro, N.C.; Catawba County Record of Corporations, 1883-1901 (microfilm), 26, North Carolina State Archives, Raleigh; Catawba County Record of Deeds, 32:268-272, 291-292, 35:139-140.

15. Statesville *Landmark*, July 5, 1888, in Black, *Newspaper Transcripts*, 2:98.

16. Reginald Turner memoir, chapter 7.

17. Monbo Manufacturing Company, Minute Book.

18. *The* (Statesville) *Mascot*, April 22, 1897; Monbo Manufacturing Company, Minute Book.

19. Gary R. Freeze, *The Catawbans: Pioneers in Progress* (Newton, N.C.: Catawba County Historical Association, 2002), 17; Cheney, *North Carolina Government*, 483; Reginald Turner memoir, chapter 2.

20. The *Newton Enterprise* reported in January 1911 that the Turner Mills Company's "big mill at East Monbo . . . is now practically complete and a portion of the machinery has already been set in motion, and within 30 or 40 days the entire plant will be in operation." Catawba County Record of Corporations, 1908-1925, 58; *Newton Enterprise*, January 12, 1911.

21. Freeze, *Catawbans: Pioneers*, 131-134; clipping from *Newton Observer*, n.d., in Turner Family Papers, Burlington.

22. Monbo Cotton Mills, Invoice Book; clipping from *Newton Observer*, n.d., in Turner Family Papers, Burlington.

23. *Statesville Landmark*, January 25, 1894, in Black, *Newspaper Transcripts*, 3:30-32; Freeze, *Catawbans: Pioneers*, 146; Iredell County Record of Deeds, D63:227-230.

24. Reginald Turner memoir, chapter 9.

25. Turner and his third wife had transferred their membership some years before from Rehoboth Church near Sherrill's Ford to Catawba Church near Monbo. In his later years, he reportedly joined the Disciples of Christ, or at least read their literature. Reginald Turner memoir, chapter 9.

APPENDIXES

APPENDIX A

1. Joseph H. Saunders, 21, enlisted in the six-months First North Carolina Regiment in Orange County on April 6, 1861. A month after being mustered out, he was appointed second lieutenant in Cowan's company of the Thirty-third. He was promoted to captain when Cowan was appointed major on April 25, 1862. Saunders was wounded at Second Manassas, August 29, 1862, and appointed major on May 13, 1863. Wounded and captured at Gettysburg, he reached Johnson's Island on August 31, 1863. He was promoted to lieutenant colonel while in confinement. He was paroled and exchanged in March 1865. It was Saunders who approved Turner's request to resign his commission in June 1863, with an unfavorable assessment of his subordinate's abilities as an officer. John M. Lazenby was an eighteen-year-old farmer in Iredell County when he enlisted on July 25, 1861. After being

wounded at New Bern, he did not return to duty until late 1862. He was promoted to corporal on November 1, 1863, but subsequently reduced to the ranks. He served to the end of the war, surrendering at Appomattox. John E. Murchison, another Iredell County farm boy, was nineteen when he enlisted on July 8, 1861. He was captured at New Bern and exchanged at Aiken's Landing on James River, August 5, 1862. He returned to his company, was wounded at Ox Hill on October 1, 1862, and killed at Chancellorsville, May 3, 1863. John T. Sherrill was a native of Catawba County who was farming in Iredell when he enlisted at age nineteen on June 10, 1861. Like Murchison, he was captured at New Bern, exchanged at Aiken's Landing, and killed at Chancellorsville. Jacob A. Halterman of Davie County was also across the county line farming in Iredell when he enlisted on June 12, 1861, aged twenty. He was captured at Fredericksburg on December 13, 1862, and exchanged a few days later. He was absent wounded in the summer of 1864 and on detached duty with the Pioneer Corps that autumn. Wounded in the leg on February 13, 1865, he was still in the hospital at Richmond when the building was surrendered on April 3. He left the hospital without permission three weeks later. A native of Lancashire, England, Samuel Whitaker, 22, was working as a mechanic in Iredell County when he enlisted on June 25, 1861. He was killed at New Bern. Manarin, *North Carolina Troops*, 1:24, 9:118, 123, 128-130, 132, 135.

2. William H. Stanley, a forty-year-old native of Philadelphia, was working as a surveyor in Cabarrus County when he enlisted on December 1, 1861. He mustered in as a sergeant. "Holliman" referred to Levi B. Hollins, who was born in Guilford County and enlisted in Cabarrus County on November 20, 1861, at the age of twenty-nine. Andrew J. Seaman, twenty-three, also enlisted in Cabarrus County on December 6, 1861. "Sheeler" was John M. Shuler, twenty-one. A native of Martinsburg, Virginia, he was working as a moulder in Orange County when he joined Company A on November 18, 1861. "Beaver" was James W. Beaser of Iredell County, who joined Cowan's company only sixteen days before the battle. He died of his wounds later in March. There was a Dennis Mahoney in the company, but he apparently survived the Battle of New Bern unscathed. Perhaps Turner was thinking of John Page, a twenty-year-old Iredell County farmer who enlisted on July 13, 1861, and was killed at New Bern. Turner can be forgiven for not remembering the names of the "two others" (in actuality, there were three) that were killed at New Bern: they were all Irishmen who had transferred to Cowan's company while Turner was absent sick. Hugh McCaffry and William Palmer, former laborers from Anson County, and John Ormsby, a bootmaker in Mecklenburg County, transferred from the Tenth Regiment North Carolina Troops (First Artillery) on February 1, 1862, and were killed at New Bern. Manarin, *North Carolina Troops*, 1:69-70, 712, 9:125, 129, 131-133.

3. David Ramseur Phifer, a private, was a twenty-two-year-old farmer in Cabarrus County when he enlisted in Company B of the Twentieth North Carolina (Tenth Regiment N.C. Volunteers) on April 18, 1861. He joined Company A of the Thirty-third on February 26, 1862, while it was stationed in Craven County. After being wounded at New Bern, he did not return to active duty, finally being released because of disability on March 3, 1863. Corp. David P. Kelly, twenty-one, was born in Lincoln County but was working as a mechanic in Iredell when he enlisted on July 10, 1861. He too did not return to duty after being wounded at New Bern and was discharged ca. March 8, 1864. Joseph H. Stamper, a nineteen-year-old Iredell County farmer who enlisted on June 10, 1861, was wounded in the arm and left lung at New Bern. He returned to duty in early 1863 but served as a hospital nurse in Richmond until October, when he rejoined his regiment. He was captured along the South Side Railroad a week before the surrender at Appomattox and remained in confinement in New York Harbor until released on June 19, 1865. An examination of the individual service records of the soldiers in Company A reveal only four others wounded at New Bern:

Reuben A. Deal, John N. Guy, Corp. James L. Henry, and David A. Rickert. Manarin, *North Carolina Troops*, 6:454, 754, 9:126-129, 131-133.

4. As noted earlier, Robert V. Cowan was a graduate of Olin High School who had attended the U.S. Military Academy at West Point until the outbreak of sectional hostilities compelled him to resign. At the age of twenty-three, he raised the company in Iredell County that would be mustered into state service as Company D of the Thirty-third North Carolina (re-designated Company A when transferred to Confederate service). He was appointed captain of the company ca. May 23, 1861. He was promoted to major of the regiment on April 25, 1862, and to lieutenant colonel on August 5, 1862. Cowan was wounded in the right arm at Chancellorsville and did not return to duty until early 1864. He was promoted to colonel of the Thirty-third on June 18, 1864. He served until the end of the war but refused to surrender the regiment at Appomattox, leaving that ignominious duty to Maj. James A. Weston. Manarin, *North Carolina Troops*, 9:118, 123.

5. Lewis Brock Tysor of Moore County enlisted in Company H of the Twenty-sixth North Carolina at the regimental camp near Fort Macon on September 7, 1861. He was wounded at New Bern and died on March 17, 1862. Manarin, *North Carolina Troops*, 7:571.

6. Clark Moulton Avery of Burke County was forty-one years old when he organized a company (the Burke Rifles) for Confederate service in the early days of the war. He was appointed captain of the company on April 25, 1861, when it arrived in Raleigh to be mustered in for six-months service as Company G of the First North Carolina Regiment. When the regiment was disbanded in November, Avery was appointed lieutenant colonel of the Thirty-third North Carolina. After Lawrence O'Bryan Branch was promoted to brigadier general on January 17, 1862, Avery succeeded him as colonel. He was captured in his first battle, at New Bern on March 14. He was confined at Fort Columbus, Johnson's Island, and Vicksburg before being exchanged at Aiken's Landing on November 10, 1862. He returned to duty and was wounded at Chancellorsville in May 1863 and in the Wilderness a year later. Avery died of his wounds at Orange Courthouse on June 18, 1864. Manarin, *North Carolina Troops*, 3:36, 9:118.

APPENDIX E

1. Reverend McFerrin is unidentified.

2. Henry Ward Beecher (1813-1887), son of the fiery abolitionist preacher Lyman Beecher and brother of Harriet Beecher Stowe, was perhaps the most renowned clergyman in the country in the mid-nineteenth century. From his pulpit in Plymouth Congregational Church in Brooklyn and in the pages of a succession of ecclesiastical journals that he edited, Beecher denounced slavery and secession and advocated women's suffrage, temperance, and the theory of evolution. Even a lurid civil trial for adultery with the wife of a friend could not dilute his influence upon American thought.

3. These are the first two lines of the first verse and the chorus of "The Old North State," written by Judge William Joseph Gaston (1778-1844) in 1835. Originally sung to a traditional melody, the now familiar music was arranged by Mrs. E. E. Randolph in 1926. The following year, it was adopted as the state song of North Carolina by the General Assembly.

4. Turner refers to Miles Osborne Sherrill (1841-1919) of Sherrill's Ford, who was clerk of superior court of Catawba County and represented the county in the state House (1883) and senate (1885, 1893). Three years after Turner's speech, Sherrill was appointed state librarian, a position he held until 1916. In the spring of 1861, he was a merchant or farmer in Catawba

County when he enlisted at age nineteen in what would become Company A of the Twelfth North Carolina. He mustered in as a corporal but was soon reduced to the ranks. Sherrill was promoted to sergeant in 1862 and to first sergeant on May 1, 1863. He was wounded in the right leg at Spotsylvania Courthouse on May 9, 1864, resulting in the amputation of the damaged limb. After several months in various Federal military hospitals, he was confined at Old Capitol Prison in Washington and at Elmira, New York. Sherrill was paroled and exchanged in February 1865. While serving as state librarian, he published an account of his wartime experiences titled, *A Soldier's Story: Prison Life and other Incidents in the War of 1861-'65. Dictionary of North Carolina Biography*, 5:333; Manarin, *North Carolina Troops*, 5:127.

5. J. M. Patterson, "the father" of Troutman, was postmaster at Troutman's Depot in 1872 and first mayor of the town when it incorporated in 1905. He died in 1913. Keever, *Iredell Piedmont County*, 280, 428.

6. Franklin H. Weaver enlisted in Iredell County at age twenty-one and was appointed second lieutenant of Company H of the Fourth North Carolina, to rank from May 16, 1861. He was killed "bearing the colors of the regiment" at Sharpsburg, where he was " 'greatly distinguished for courage.' " Clark also refers to him as Hal Weaver. Manarin, *North Carolina Troops*, 4:85, 746; Clark, *Histories of Regiments*, 1:231, 247, 272.

7. Twenty-four-year-old Boone T. Penry enlisted in Company F of the Thirteenth North Carolina in his native Davie County on August 6, 1861. He was hospitalized in June 1862 with a gunshot wound in his foot but returned to duty in September. Private Penry was promoted to sergeant on December 6, 1862, and to first sergeant on April 17, 1863. Two weeks later, he was killed at Chancellorsville. Andrew J. Anderson was a twenty-one-year-old merchant in Iredell County when he enlisted in Company C of the Fourth North Carolina on June 7, 1861. He was mustered as a corporal and promoted to sergeant on September 1, 1861. He was wounded in the hip at Seven Pines, May 31, 1862, and died in Davie County on June 19, 1862. John B. Turner of Iredell County enlisted at age twenty-one in Company H of the Fourth North Carolina on March 1, 1862. He died of consumption in a Richmond hospital on May 22, 1862. Manarin, *North Carolina Troops*, 4:36, 94, 690, 5:343.

8. George W. Weaver was born in Guilford County but was a resident of Iredell County when he enlisted at age twenty-six as a private in Company D of the Thirty-third North Carolina at the regimental camp near Raleigh on the first day of 1862. Within two months, Weaver was promoted to sergeant, then appointed third lieutenant on September 13, 1862. He was mortally wounded at Chancellorsville, May 3, 1863. Manarin, *North Carolina Troops*, 9:160.

9. Humphrey Summers was thirty-two and his brother Robert C. was twenty-eight when they enlisted in Company C of the Fourth North Carolina on August 10, 1862. They were both killed at Chancellorsville on May 3, 1863. Manarin, *North Carolina Troops*, 4:46.

10. Probably William F. Campbell, a resident of Iredell County who enlisted at age eighteen in Company A of the Seventh N.C. Regiment on September 4, 1861, when the regiment was in Craven County. He was killed at Fussell's Mill, Virginia, on August 17, 1864. Manarin, *North Carolina Troops*, 4:410.

11. John P. Tharpe resided in Iredell County when he enlisted in Company C of the Forty-eighth North Carolina on August 1, 1862. He was killed at Antietam on September 17, 1862. Manarin, *North Carolina Troops*, 11:406. Noah Ward is unidentified.

12. Turner probably refers to Amos S. Tomlin, a native of Iredell County who enlisted at age twenty-four in Company C of the Fourth North Carolina at its training camp near Garysburg on July 16, 1861. Tomlin died of unspecified causes at Richmond on July 29, 1862. Manarin, *North Carolina Troops*, 4:46. John A. Turner was Columbus Turner's younger brother, Gus.

13. For a biographical sketch of Cowan, see Appendix A, n. 4.

14. Abel Henry York was born in Guilford County and was a twenty-two-year-old farmer in Iredell County upon enlistment in Robert Cowan's company of the Thirty-third North Carolina on August 4, 1861. Mustered in as a private, York was promoted to musician prior to the Battle of New Bern, where he was captured with Turner. He was confined at Fort Columbus in New York Harbor until paroled and exchanged in the summer of 1862. He returned to his regiment and was wounded at Ox Hill on September 1, 1862. York again returned to duty in time to be taken prisoner at Fredericksburg on December 13 and exchanged four days later. Company muster rolls indicate that he was absent without leave after Gettysburg and listed as a deserter during the winter of 1864. But another contemporary source suggests that he was discharged in January 1865. Manarin, *North Carolina Troops*, 9:135.

15. See Appendix A, nn. 1, 2 for sketches of these soldiers in Company A of the Thirty-third North Carolina. "Speeler" probably refers to John M. Shuler.

16. See Appendix A, n. 1 for a biographical sketch of Saunders and identification of his brave volunteers.

17. From "The Lay of the Last Minstrel" (1805) by Sir Walter Scott (1771-1832).

18. Brothers David Washington and Robert William Shields of Mecklenburg County were working as mechanics in Iredell County in the summer of 1861. Nineteen-year-old Robert enlisted first, on June 25; David, twenty-two, followed him into the ranks of Cowan's company two weeks later. Both brothers mustered in as privates. David was promoted to sergeant in early 1862 and to first sergeant later that year. He was killed at Fredericksburg on December 13, 1862. Robert, who was promoted to sergeant when David was advanced to first sergeant, was captured on the day his brother was killed and exchanged on December 17. In the spring of 1863, he was promoted to first sergeant but was killed at Gettysburg on July 3. Manarin, *North Carolina Troops*, 9:132.

19. Eighteen-year-old Thomas A. Cowan enlisted as a private in his brother's company near New Bern on the first day of March 1862. He was wounded in the thigh at Ox Hill on September 1 but returned to duty before the Battle of Gettysburg. He succeeded David Shields as first sergeant on December 14, 1862, and was appointed first lieutenant on June 1, 1863. He was killed at Gettysburg on July 3. Manarin, *North Carolina Troops*, 9:123.

20. Henry Hyer Baker was a resident of Halifax County when he enlisted at age twenty-two in a company composed mainly of volunteers from the Piedmont. He was appointed second lieutenant of Company A on April 25, 1862, promoted to first lieutenant, October 6, 1862, and commissioned captain on May 13, 1863. He led the company in the final charge at Gettysburg on July 3 and was killed. Manarin, *North Carolina Troops*, 9:123.

21. James Albert Summers was a thirty-two-year-old mechanic in his native Iredell County when he volunteered on July 14, 1861. He was mustered into Cowan's company as a sergeant, promoted to first sergeant in the spring of 1862, and appointed second lieutenant on August 6, 1862. Summers was captured at Chancellorsville and briefly confined in the Old Capitol Prison. He was promoted to first lieutenant on June 1, 1863, and to captain after the death of Baker. He was again captured near Petersburg on April 2, 1865, and spent two

months at Johnson's Island before being released on June 20. Manarin, *North Carolina Troops*, 9:123.

22. Reuben Philander Campbell (1818-1862), a native of Iredell County, was a career soldier who graduated from the U.S. Military Academy in 1840. He fought against the Seminoles in Florida as a second lieutenant in the dragoons. Promoted to first lieutenant before the War with Mexico, he fought in three major battles in that conflict and earned a brevet for gallant and meritorious conduct at the Battle of Buena Vista. Campbell was promoted to captain in August 1851, but spent much of the following decade on sick leave of absence. At age forty-three, he resigned his commission on May 11, 1861, and was appointed colonel of the Seventh North Carolina five days later. He led a combined force of infantry and artillery at New Bern and was killed on June 27, 1862, leading a charge against enemy works at the Battle of Gaines Mill. http://www.library.ci.corpus-christi.tx.us/MexicanWar/campbellrp.htm; Robert K. Krick, *Lee's Colonels: A Biographical Register of the Field Officers of the Army of Northern Virginia*. 3d rev. ed. (Dayton: Morningside, 1991), 82; Manarin, *North Carolina Troops*, 4:395, 405.

23. E. Mansfield Campbell was practicing law in his native Iredell County when, at age thirty-nine, he enlisted as a private in Robert Cowan's company of the Thirty-third North Carolina on July 29, 1861. Campbell transferred to Company A of his older brother's regiment on January 10, 1862, with a second lieutenant's commission. He was promoted to first lieutenant on August 1, 1862, and was killed at Chancellorsville on May 3, 1863. Manarin, *North Carolina Troops*, 4:408, 698, 9:125.

24. When the war broke out, Junius Leroy Hill (1836-1862) was a twenty-five-year-old "student" in Iredell County, perhaps at the military academy in Statesville run by John and Clint Andrews. Hill raised a company of volunteers from Iredell and Alexander counties that was assigned to the Seventh North Carolina. His commission as captain ranked from May 16, 1861. He was appointed major in Col. Reuben Campbell's regiment on April 4, 1862, and lieutenant colonel after the death of Campbell on June 27. Hill was killed leading a charge against enemy breastworks at Chancellorsville. Manarin, *North Carolina Troops*, 4:405, 408; Krick, *Lee's Colonels*, 192; Keever, *Iredell Piedmont County*, 229.

25. Robert Clinton Hill was born in Iredell County in August 1833. He graduated from the U.S. Military Academy in the class of 1855 and served as a lieutenant in the U.S. Army, where he earned the nickname, "Crazy Hill," because of his excitable manner. He resigned his commission to accept an appointment as lieutenant of artillery in the Confederate States Army, to rank from March 16, 1861. He was appointed assistant adjutant general with the rank of major on the staff of Brig. Gen. Robert A. Toombs in August 1861. Hill was chosen for a similar position on the staff of Brig. Gen. Lawrence O'Bryan Branch in 1862. He was appointed colonel of the Forty-eighth North Carolina on April 9, 1862. Hill was absent sick during the summer of 1863 and died of neuralgia at his home in Iredell County on December 4, 1863. His successor as colonel, Samuel Hoey Walkup, accused Hill of cowardice in a postbellum memoir. Hugh Alex Hill was a thirty-year-old physician practicing in Iredell County when he enlisted in Cowan's company on July 14, 1861. He mustered in as first sergeant and was appointed third lieutenant ca. February 18, 1862. Promoted to first lieutenant on April 25, 1862, he was wounded at the Battle of Antietam on September 17 and died at Winchester, Virginia, on October 6. (The death of Hill resulted in Turner's promotion to third lieutenant.) Dr. M. W. "Mim" Hill opened a medical practice in Statesville in the late 1860s and also served as county physician. Krick, *Staff Officers in Gray*, 160; Krick, *Lee's Colonels*, 193; Manarin, *North Carolina Troops*, 9:123, 11:368; Keever, *Iredell Piedmont County*, 321, 404.

26. Twenty-six-year-old Absalom K. Simonton organized a company in Iredell County in April 1861 that was initially enlisted for twelve-months service as militia and sent to Fort Caswell. Simonton's commission as captain was dated May 16, 1861. In June, the company was designated Company A of the Fourth North Carolina. On May 1, 1862, Simonton was promoted to major of the regiment. He was killed at Seven Pines, May 31, 1862. Manarin, *North Carolina Troops*, 4:9, 13.

27. From another epic poem by Sir Walter Scott, *The Lady of the Lake* (1810), Canto 1, lines 624-627.

APPENDIX F

1. The "Catawba Marksmen" company was raised in Catawba County in March 1862, mustered into state service at Camp Mangum near Raleigh on April 16, and assigned to the Forty-ninth Regiment North Carolina Troops as Company I. Manarin, *North Carolina Troops*, 12:116.

2. Lt. Col. John A. Flemming of Buncombe County died instantly after being shot through the head at the Battle of the Crater, July 30, 1864. He may have commanded the regiment that day in the continued absence of Col. LeRoy M. McAfee, who was wounded at Drewry's Bluff on May 16, 1864, and returned to duty at an unspecified date. Manarin, *North Carolina Troops*, 12:26.

BIBLIOGRAPHY

PRIMARY SOURCES

Government and Official Records

Adjutant General's Office. Roster of the Militia of North Carolina, 1861-1862, 1864. North Carolina State Archives. Raleigh.

Tod R. Caldwell, Governors Papers, 1871-1874. North Carolina State Archives. Raleigh.

Catawba County Record of Corporations, 1883-1925 (microfilm). North Carolina State Archives. Raleigh.

Catawba County Record of Deeds, 1879-1918 (microfilm). North Carolina State Archives. Raleigh.

Catawba County Superior Court Minute Docket, 1881-1889. North Carolina State Archives. Raleigh.

Compiled Service Records of Confederate Soldiers, Seventh Confederate Cavalry (microfilm). North Carolina State Archives. Raleigh.

Compiled Service Records of Confederate Soldiers Who Served in Organizations from the State of North Carolina, 33rd Infantry (microfilm). North Carolina State Archives. Raleigh.

Davie County Record of Deeds, 1840-1860 (microfilm). North Carolina State Archives. Raleigh.

Eighth Census of the United States, 1860, Population Schedule: Chatham and Iredell Counties, North Carolina. North Carolina State Archives. Raleigh.

Eighth Census of the United States, 1860, Slave Schedule: Iredell County, North Carolina. North Carolina State Archives. Raleigh.

General Assembly Session Records, November 1872-March 1873. North Carolina State Archives. Raleigh.

General Assembly Session Records, November 1873-February 1874. North Carolina State Archives. Raleigh.

Iredell County Criminal Action Papers, 1874. North Carolina State Archives. Raleigh.

Iredell County Superior Court Minute Docket, 1869-1875. North Carolina State Archives. Raleigh.

Iredell County Record of Deeds, 1821-1919 (microfilm). North Carolina State Archives. Raleigh.

National Register of Historic Places Registration Form, Tabernacle Methodist Protestant Church and Cemetery, Greensboro, Guilford County. State Historic Preservation Office. Raleigh.

Ninth Census of the United States, 1870, Population Schedule: Chatham, Iredell, Randolph, and Wake Counties, North Carolina. North Carolina State Archives. Raleigh.

Randolph County Estates Records, 1781-1928. North Carolina State Archives. Raleigh.

Seventh Census of the United States, 1850, Slave Schedule: Iredell County, North Carolina. North Carolina State Archives, Raleigh.

Tenth Census of the United States, 1880, Population Schedule: Iredell County, North Carolina. North Carolina State Archives. Raleigh.

Wake County Record of Wills, 1868-1966 (microfilm). North Carolina State Archives. Raleigh.

Wake County Wills, 1771-1966. North Carolina State Archives. Raleigh.

Wilkes County Criminal Action Papers, 1874. North Carolina State Archives. Raleigh.

Wilkes County Superior Court Minute Docket, 1869-1874. North Carolina State Archives. Raleigh.

Manuscript Collections

First Baptist Church, Raleigh, N.C. Church Minutes, 1856-1874 (microfilm). North Carolina State Archives. Raleigh.

Joseph Mason Kern Papers, 1860-1865. Southern Historical Collection. Wilson Library. University of North Carolina at Chapel Hill.

Monbo Cotton Mills, Invoice Book, 1908-1918. Rare Book, Manuscript, and Special Collections Library. Duke University. Durham.

Monbo Manufacturing Company, Minute Book, 1887-1902. Original in possession of James R. Turner, Greensboro, N.C.

Olin High School Papers, 1859-1865. Rare Book, Manuscript, and Special Collections Library. Duke University. Durham.

Notley D. Tomlin Collection. Rare Book, Manuscript, and Special Collections Library. Duke University. Durham.

C. L. Turner to Wilfred Turner, January 1, 1862. In possession of James R. Turner, Greensboro, N.C.

Columbus Lafayette Turner Notebook, 1859-1861, 1865. In possession of James R. Turner, Greensboro, N.C.

Speech of Columbus Lafayette Turner to Confederate veterans at Catawba, N.C., April 1, 1897. In possession of James R. Turner, Greensboro, N.C.

Turner Family Papers. North Carolina State Archives. Raleigh.

Turner Family Papers. In possession of Nancy Jones, Burlington, N.C.

W[ilfred] Turner to C. L. Turner, September 3, 1863. In possession of Wilfred Turner, New Bern, N.C.

Newspapers

(Baltimore) *Manufacturer's Record*, February 17, 1887.

Catawba County News, April 27, 1904.

Charlotte Observer, May 3, July 4, 1882.

Newton Enterprise, June 10, 1882; June 21, 1884; January 12, 1911.

Our Living and Our Dead, March 11, April 22, May 20, 1874; January 1875.

(Raleigh) *Daily News*, January 25, January 29, February 1, February 5, February 17, February 18, February 19, February 21, February 22, 1874.

(Raleigh) *Daily Sentinel*, September 16, 1873; January 18, January 31, February 22, 1874.

(Salisbury) *Carolina Watchman*, March 4, 1867.

Salisbury Post, March 4, 2001.

Statesville *Intelligencer*, January 17, 1874.

Statesville *Landmark*, July 24, 1882; April 13, 1915.

The (Statesville) *Mascot*, April 22, 1897.

Printed Documentary Sources

Barbière, Joe. *Scraps from the Prison Table, at Camp Chase and Johnson's Island*. Doylestown, Pa.: W. W. H. Davis, Printer, 1868.

Barrett, John G., ed. *Yankee Rebel: The Civil War Journal of Edmund DeWitt Patterson* Chapel Hill: University of North Carolina Press, 1966.

Battle, William H., comp. *Battle's Revisal of the Public Statutes of North Carolina*. Raleigh: Edwards, Broughton and Co., 1873.

Black, Irene Clanton, comp. *Newspaper Transcripts from the* Landmark *Statesville North Carolina,* Volume I, *1874-1884*. Statesville, N.C.: privately printed, 1993.

_____. *Newspaper Transcripts from the* Landmark *Statesville North Carolina,* Volume II, *1885-1892*. Statesville, N.C.: privately printed, 1994.

_____. *Newspaper Transcripts from the* Landmark *Statesville North Carolina,* Volume III, *1893-1900*. Statesville, N.C.: privately printed, 1995.

Branson & Farrar's North Carolina Business Directory for 1866-'67, Containing Facts, Figures, Names and Locations. Raleigh: Branson and Farrar, Publishers, [1866].

Chataigne, J. H., comp. *Chataigne's Raleigh City Directory, 1875-'76*. Raleigh: J. H. Chataigne, 1875.

Cheney, John L., Jr., ed. *North Carolina Government, 1585-1979: A Narrative and Statistical History*. Raleigh: North Carolina Department of the Secretary of State, 1981.

Davis, George B., et al. *Atlas to Accompany the Official Records of the Union and Confederate Armies*. Washington: Government Printing Office, 1891-1895.

Emerson, Charles, and Company. *Raleigh Directory, 1880-'81*. Raleigh: Edwards, Broughton and Company, 1879.

Green, Wharton J. *Recollections and Reflections: An Auto of Half a Century and More*. Raleigh: Edwards and Broughton Printing Company, 1906.

Journal of the House of Representatives of the General Assembly of the State of North Carolina, at its Session of 1872-'73. Raleigh: Stowe and Uzzell, 1873.

Journal of the House of Representatives of the General Assembly of the State of North Carolina, at its Session of 1873-'74. Raleigh: Josiah Turner Jr., 1874.

Journal of the Senate of the General Assembly of the State of North Carolina at its Session of 1873-'74. Raleigh: Stowe and Uzzell, 1873 [*sic*].

Laws and Resolutions of the State of North Carolina Passed by the General Assembly at its Session 1872-'73. Raleigh: Stowe and Uzzell, 1873.

Laws and Resolutions of the State of North Carolina Passed by the General Assembly at its Session 1873-'74. Raleigh: Josiah Turner Jr., 1874.

McIlwaine, Richard. *Memories of Three Score Years and Ten*. New York and Washington: The Neale Publishing Company, 1908.

Shepherd, Henry E. *Narrative of Prison Life at Baltimore and Johnson's Island, Ohio*. Baltimore: Commercial Printing and Stationery Company, 1917.

Trinity College. *Catalogue of Trinity College, North Carolina, 1860-'61*. Greensboro, N.C.: Greensborough Times Office, 1861.

The War of the Rebellion: A Compilation of the Official Records of the Union and Confederate Armies. 150 vols. Washington: Government Printing Office, 1880-1901.

Wheeler, John H. *The Legislative Manual and Political Register of the State of North Carolina for the Year 1874*. Raleigh: Josiah Turner Jr., 1874.

SECONDARY SOURCES

Books and Articles

Atchison, Ray M. "*Our Living and Our Dead*: A Post-bellum North Carolina Magazine of Literature and History." *North Carolina Historical Review* 40 (autumn 1963): 423-433.

Balanoff, Elizabeth. "Negro Legislators in the North Carolina General Assembly, July 1868-February 1872." *North Carolina Historical Review* 49 (winter 1972): 22-55.

Barrett, John G. *The Civil War in North Carolina*. Chapel Hill: University of North Carolina Press, 1963.

Batchelor, John E. *The Guilford County Schools: A History*. Winston-Salem: John F. Blair, Publisher, 1991.

Battle, Kemp P. *History of the University of North Carolina*. 2 vols. Spartanburg, S.C: The Reprint Company, 1974.

Black, Russell C., Jr., and Irene Clanton Black, comps. *Iredell County North Carolina Cemeteries*, Vols. 2 and 5. Statesville, N.C.: privately printed, 1999.

Blythe, LeGette, and Charles Raven Brockmann. *Hornet's Nest: The Story of Charlotte and Mecklenburg County*. Charlotte: McNally of Charlotte, 1961.

Boatner, Mark Mayo, III. *The Civil War Dictionary*. New York: David McKay Company, Inc., 1959.

Brigance, Pat Hicks. *Blythe*, vol. 1. Maryville, Tenn.: P. H. Brigance, 1994.

Carroll, Grady Lee Ernest, Sr. *They Lived in Raleigh: Some Leading Personalities from 1792 to 1892*. Raleigh: Southeastern Copy Center, 1977.

Catawba County Genealogical Society. *Catawba County Cemeteries.* Vol. 8. Hickory, N.C.: The Society, 1996.

Catawba Cousins, vol. 5, no. 4 (April 1991).

Chaffin, Nora Campbell. *Trinity College, 1839-1892: The Beginnings of Duke University*. Durham: Duke University Press, 1950.

Clark, Walter, ed. *Histories of the Several Regiments and Battalions from North Carolina in the Great War 1861-'65.* 5 vols. Goldsboro, N.C.: Nash Brothers, 1901.

Crow, Jeffrey J., Paul D. Escott, and Flora J. Hatley. *A History of African Americans in North Carolina*. Rev. ed. Raleigh: Office of Archives and History, Department of Cultural Resources, 2002.

Cyclopedia of Eminent and Representative Men of the Carolinas of the Nineteenth Century. Vol. 2. *North Carolina*. Madison, Wis.: Brant and Fuller, 1892.

Freeze, Gary R. *The Catawbans: Crafters of a North Carolina County, 1747-1900.* Newton, N.C.: Catawba County Historical Association, 1995.

_____. *The Catawbans: Pioneers in Progress*. Newton, N.C.: Catawba County Historical Association, 2002.

Grill, C. Franklin. *Methodism in the Upper Cape Fear Valley*. Nashville: The Parthenon Press, 1966.

Hamilton, J. G. de Roulhac. *Reconstruction in North Carolina*. New York: Columbia University, 1914.

Henderson County Genealogical and Historical Society, comp. *Henderson County, North Carolina Cemeteries*. Spartanburg, S.C.: The Reprint Company, 1995.

The Heritage of Iredell County. Statesville, N.C.: Genealogical Society of Iredell County, 1980.

Huggins, M. A. *A History of North Carolina Baptists, 1727-1932.* Raleigh: General Board of the Baptist State Convention of North Carolina, 1967.

Iredell County American Revolution Bicentennial Commission. *Iredell County Landmarks: A Pictorial History of Iredell County*. Statesville, N.C.: Brady Printing Company, 1982 reprint.

Keever, Homer M. *Iredell Piedmont County*. Statesville, N.C.: Iredell County Bicentennial Commission, 1976.

Krick, Robert E. L. *Staff Officers in Gray: A Biographical Register of the Staff Officers in the Army of Northern Virginia*. Chapel Hill: University of North Carolina Press, 2003.

Krick, Robert K. *Lee's Colonels: A Biographical Register of the Field Officers of the Army of Northern Virginia.* 3d rev. ed. Dayton: Morningside, 1991.

Leonard, Elizabeth D. *Lincoln's Avengers: Justice, Revenge, and Reunion after the Civil War.* New York: W. W. Norton and Company, 2004.

Long, E. B. and Barbara Long. *The Civil War Day by Day: An Almanac, 1861-1865.* Garden City, N.Y.: Doubleday, 1971.

Manarin, Louis H., et al., comps. *North Carolina Troops, 1861-1865: A Roster.* 15 vols. to date Raleigh: Office of Archives and History, Department of Cultural Resources, 1966-.

Montgomery, Lizzie Wilson. *Sketches of Old Warrenton North Carolina.* Raleigh: Edwards and Broughton Printing Company, 1924.

Murray, Elizabeth Reid. *Wake: Capital County of North Carolina.* Vol. 1. Raleigh: Capital County Publishing Company, 1983.

Padgett, James A., ed. "Reconstruction Letters from North Carolina, Part IX." *North Carolina Historical Review* 21 (January 1944), 46-71.

Paschal, George Washington. *History of North Carolina Baptists.* 2 vols. Raleigh: North Carolina Baptist State Convention, 1930, 1955.

_____. *History of Wake Forest College.* 3 vols. Wake Forest: Wake Forest College, 1935-1943.

Poole, John Randolph. *Cracker Cavaliers: The 2nd Georgia Cavalry under Wheeler and Forrest.* Macon, Ga.: Mercer University Press, 2000.

Powell, William S. *The North Carolina Gazetteer.* Chapel Hill: University of North Carolina Press, 1968.

_____, ed. *Dictionary of North Carolina Biography.* 6 vols. Chapel Hill: University of North Carolina Press, 1979-1996.

Preslar, Charles J., Jr., ed. *A History of Catawba County.* Salisbury, N.C.: Rowan Printing Company, 1954.

Randolph County Historical Society. *Randolph County, 1779-1979.* Winston-Salem: Hunter Publishing Company, 1980.

Raper, Horace W. *William W. Holden: North Carolina's Political Enigma.* Chapel Hill: University of North Carolina Press, 1985.

Rumple, Jethro. *A History of Rowan County, North Carolina.* Baltimore: Regional Publishing Company, 1974 reprint.

Sanders, Charles W., Jr. *While in the Hands of the Enemy: Military Prisons of the Civil War.* Baton Rouge: Louisiana State University Press, 2005.

Stem, Thad, Jr. "Absent with Leave, or How Musty Files Came Alive." *North Carolina Historical Review* 51 (spring 1974): 170-182.

Stroupe, Henry S. "The Beginnings of Religious Journalism in North Carolina, 1823-1865." *North Carolina Historical Review* 30 (January 1953): 1-22.

Thomas, Emory M. *The Confederate Nation, 1861-1865*. New York: Harper and Row, 1979.

Wall, James W. *History of Davie County*. Mocksville, N.C.: Davie County Historical Publishing Association, 1969.

Unpublished

Cherry, Julia Wyche. Notes concerning her grandmother, Julia Louisa Turner, n.d. In possession of Pamela Cherry Lee, Sierra Vista, Ariz.

Clifford, Locke Turner. "Turners." Transcript of unpublished manuscript in possession of James R. Turner, Greensboro, N.C.

Harkins, Thomas F., associate university archivist, Duke University Archives, e-mail to Walter R. Turner, historian, North Carolina Transportation Museum, August 22, 2007.

Turner, James R. "Turner Family History." Unpublished manuscript, 1997.

Turner, Reginald. Untitled memoir, ca. 1970. Copy in Turner Family Papers. North Carolina State Archives. Raleigh.

Turner, Walter R. "Columbus Lafayette Turner and Turner Family Involvement with Olin High School." Unpublished research paper, enclosed in letter to editor, July 5, 2007.

_____. "Columbus Lafayette Turner's Years at Trinity College." Unpublished research paper, enclosed in letter to editor, September 1, 2007.

Web Sites

http://bioguide.congress.gov/scripts/biodisplay.

http://botanical.com/botanical/mgmh/g/ginger13.html.

http://docsouth.unc.edu/unc/browse/person.html#H.

http://etext.library.adelaide.edu.au/s/scott/walter/antiquary/chapter10.html.

http://gdl.cdlr.strath.ac.uk/mlemen/mlemen001.htm.

http://groups.msn.com/CaudillGenealogyGroup/general.

http://hymnsite.com/lyrics/umh622.sht.

http://memory.loc.gov./cgi-bin/query/D?dukesmili.temp/~ammem_8F8m.

http://www.angelfire.com/ga/htpiii/w24gen.html.

http://www.answers.com/topic/baptist.

http://www.archaeology.org/online/features/civil/words/inzer.html.

http://www.athelstane.co.uk.

http://www.bic-church.org/about/history.asp.

http://www.britannica.com/eb/article-9019856/Thomas-Campbell.

http://www.cgs-raleigh.org/history.htm.

http://www.civilwararchive.com/Unreghst.

http://www.civilwarhome.com/vallandighambio.htm.

http://www.cr.nps.gov/nR/travel/raleigh/pea.htm.

http://www.csufresno.edu/folklore/ballads/R842.html.

http://www.cwhistory.com/history/TeacherPack/Tppart3.html.

http://www.cyberhymnal.org/htm.

http://www.famousamericans.net/gooldbrown/.

http://www.geocities.com/Heartland/Plains/3081.

http://www.gravesfa.org/gen836.htm.

http://www.herbertasbury.com/asburycivilwar.asp.

http://www.johnsonisland.org/history/war.htm.

http://www.lib.duke.edu/texis/smi/search/more.htm?id=37973ea081.

http://www.library.ci.corpus-christi.tx.us/MexicanWar.

http://www.nccumc.org/docs/ncarchives/deceased.xls.

http://www.newadvent.org/cathen/02278a.htm.

http://www.norfolkhistorical.org/highlights/03.html.

http://www.nps.gov/history/history/online_books/founders/sitea22.htm.

http://www.nssa.us/nssajrnl/23_1/htm/07.htm.

http://www.ohiohistory.org/onlinedoc/ohgovernment/governors/brough.html.

http://www.peace.edu/content/page/id/174.

http://www.raleigh-nc.org/portal/server.pt/gateway.

http://www.rootsweb.com/~kygenweb/kybiog/daviess/burrows.jl.txt.

http://www.rootsweb.com/~nccatawb/McCorkle/d121.htm.

INDEX

A

B

C

D

E

F

G

H

I

J

N

O

P

T

U

V

W

Y